JACK JOHNSON

RTING PAGES ON THE PACIFIC COAST

IN THE RING AND OUT

Acknowledgements

The publishers wish to thank the following for their kind contributions to this volume:
for the illustrations, Gilbert Odd, Syndication International and the San Francisco Chronicle;
for the appended newspaper reproductions, the New York Herald Tribune, the Daily Express and the Daily Telegraph of London;
for Jack Johnson's handwritten dedication, Gilbert Odd.

JACK JOHNSON

In the Ring and Out

THE CLASSIC AUTOBIOGRAPHY
BY THE
FIRST BLACK CHAMPION

This edition, with afterword and appendices,
first published 1977 by
PROTEUS (PUBLISHING) LIMITED
London

This edition © 1977 Proteus (Publishing) Limited
Editor's note, footnotes and afterword © 1977 Gilbert Odd
All rights reserved.

ISBN 0-8467-0404-8

Photoset in Great Britain.
Printed and bound by The Book Press, Brattleboro, Vermont.

Distributed in the United States by
THE TWO CONTINENTS PUBLISHING GROUP, LTD.
30 East 42nd Street
New York, New York 10017

Dedicated to the memory of my mother

CONTENTS

EDITOR'S NOTE   3

FOREWORDS
  By Ed. W. Smith   9
  By J. B. Lewis   11
  Keeping Pace with Jack Johnson, by Tad   17
  Jack Johnson Could Fight, by Damon Runyon   21

 1 I Take My Pen in My Hand   23

 2 A Stowaway   29

 3 Breaking In   37

 4 Fighting to the Top   51

 5 Romances and Regrets   61

 6 Exile   75

 7 The World Through Prison Bars   99

 8 Adventures on Highways and Byways   111

 9 Chasing the Champion   123

10 The Great Jeffries Bows   133

11 Challengers   147

12 The Frame-up for Freedom   155

13 Looking at Life at Fifty   161

AFTERWORD

Johnson Was the Greatest, by Gilbert Odd   185

APPENDICES

I   Fight Record   203
II   The Great Contest — Daily Telegraph   209
III   Too Hot to Handle? — New York Herald   219
IV   The Jack London Reports — New York Herald   229
V   Race Riots in America — Daily Express   239
VI   Jack Johnson is Exposed — John Bull   245

EDITOR'S NOTE

Jack Johnson
Former Heavy
weight Champion
of the World
To a good Pal

Dec 4/35

Editor's Note

In December 1935 I was in New York to see Joe Louis fight at Madison Square Garden. The unbeaten 'Brown Bomber', who was being steered very astutely towards the heavyweight title, had just knocked out former champion, Max Baer, and now was to face Paolino Uzcudun, a tough and experienced Spaniard from the Basque Country.

Walking along Broadway, I came across a large sign over an amusement arcade that read: 'Jack Johnson Trains Here' and had to stop and take this in. It couldn't be true! I knew that Johnson had been 37 when he lost his title to Jess Willard – but that was twenty years ago. I also remembered that he had boxed some exhibition bouts in Paris in 1933. What and who was he training for now?

The place looked both gaudy and drab. It was what city Americans called a 'Dime Museum' in those days. Not that it cost ten cents to go in, but the narrow place was packed solid on either side with slot machines of every description and it cost a dime to operate them. As I stood there cogitating there was the distant sound of jazz music and with it a beat that could only be made by someone keeping time on a punch-ball.

That decided it. I went in and wended my way towards the rhythmic tapping. There, sure enough, was Johnson, still shaven-headed, still flashing his 'golden smile' and, amazing to behold, still in excellent physical condition, although understandably a lot thicker around the waist. But those fine legs and muscular arms were still there and it was obvious that he had retained the co-ordination of hand and eye to enable him to beat a two-fisted tattoo on the suspended ball.

He stopped as I approached him and pulled off a glove to shake hands. He was delighted to know I was from London, saying he always liked that 'lil ol' town'. When I jokingly asked who he was training to fight, he said, quite seriously: 'That Louis boy, of course. If they'll let me, I'll give him a boxing lesson over three rounds. That Joe has a lot to learn. His stance is all wrong and the first fellow who makes him step back and then throws a right at his chin, will knock him out.'

I thought this was the sentiment of an old-timer in derision of youth, but when, six months later, Max Schmeling did precisely what Johnson had predicted, it made me feel that, even at the age of 57, Jack would have been capable of putting up a commendable show against the man who was to be the second coloured boxer to win the Heavyweight Championship of the World.

Johnson suddenly produced a book about himself which had been published in Chicago in July 1927. Entitled 'Jack Johnson – In the Ring and Out', it was his autobiography. 'Every word is true', he assured me, adding: 'It says so on the back.' The price was one dollar and I paid him another dollar to have it autographed. Today that first edition is beyond price.

After that he justified his employment by changing another of my few dollars into dime pieces, pointing out the row of 'What the Butler Saw' machines that contained short films of the great fights of the past, insisting that I did not miss any of those in which he was a participant. I came back every day for a week to gloat over those old boxing movies, feeling that I might never get the chance to see them again – this being in the days before television was to resurrect them.

These vintage films showed Johnson in his greatest bouts. Winning the title from Burns, the humiliation of Jeffries, the slaying of Ketchel, the farce with Flynn and the cat-and-mouse game with Moran. As I went from one machine to the other, so he made comments while continuing his ball-punching. 'It was a big shame the way I treated Burns. I could have beaten Jeff any round I liked. I let Ketchel knock me down to make the movie more exciting. I only fought Flynn to please Curley. Moran and me never got a cent out of those twenty rounds in Paris. You know I laid down for Willard so that I could come home and see my mother. They treated me bad, man, but I got the better of them.' He reeled it off as he varied his punching routine and repeated it every time I came in for another look at those old fight flics.

So far as I was concerned, it was all part of the entertainment, and it was good of Charley Johnston (brother of the more famous Jimmy), to advance me ten dollars, most of which I spent in the Museum. I have seen all those fight films many times since, but never with such a thrill as that first time on Broadway when I had a running commentary from Johnson to make them even more memorable. How I wish I had had a tape machine with me.

Now his book is being re-issued just fifty years after its first publication. Its narrative is as flamboyant as its author was in his heyday; so full of incident to make it compulsive reading for all who revel in the Fight Game and its heroes. It is a privilege and a pleasure to be asked to edit it.

GILBERT ODD

IN THE RING AND OUT

Foreword

By ED. W. SMITH

Widely Known Sports Critic and Referee

Johnson's ring work always has presented the highest in the artisanship of his craft. Always a past master of defensive work and positively uncanny in his judgment of what the other fellow is about to do, Jack presents ability that is impossible to rate too highly and next to impossible to match, then, now, and possibly ever.

Of the famous quartet of colored Goliaths, the slaying of which by any of the puny Davids of this decade of fighting men has been accomplished only at decidedly rare intervals, Johnson was by long odds the most masterful of the lot. And when it is considered there were in his company at various times and striving always for leadership, such men as Sam McVey, Sam Langford and the incomparable game and willing Joe Jeanette, one is saying much in classifying Johnson as the master mind.

There may have been many times when Jack Johnson came in for sharp reproach and often absolute reproof, especially by those of his own race. I know Jack to be possessed of one of the kindliest minds of any great athlete I ever came into contact with. Money never meant a great deal to this mighty man of brawn and ring brains. As far as the financial end of his dealings was concerned, Jack often displayed a childish simplicity. He wanted to do for others and always went the limit — sometimes, unfortunately for himself, beyond that. But many of Jack's predicaments came about, I happen to know, through a too-trusting faith in the white brethren, be that to the everlasting discredit of the Caucasians with whom he dealt so confidently, almost implicitly.

Foreword

By J. B. LEWIS

Had Jack Johnson been a white man, he would have attained an influence in the world which few other men have attained. He would have commanded a place in society and world affairs of great significance, because there is that in his make-up which has enabled him to push forward in spite of numerous obstacles, to one of the highest pinnacles of human achievements. It is not only that he became a champion boxer, an honor quite sufficient for any one man, but he possessed qualities that kept him in the hearts of his friends.

The difficulties which confronted him and which he overcame were sufficient to try the mettle courage and ability of any man, even though he should have been on an equal footing with everyone else. But Jack Johnson was not. Because of his race, he had from the start the burden of prejudice to bear, and to contend with conditions and human jealousies which in no wise would ever have attached to a white man. When he successfully fought his way to the world championship, instead of his achievement mitigating these prejudices and jealousies, they were intensified, and more than that, there were many who called themselves good Americans and who considered themselves honorable, charitable and sportsmanlike, who stubbornly refused to credit Jack with the same degree of consideration and respect that would have been given a white man, even though that white man did far worse things in the world of morals than were ever done by Johnson, or rather which were often charged to him, when in fact he had not done them.

The public, and even many of those who were intimately associated with him, have never understood the full significance of Johnson's character and the diversity of his abilities.

The story of Jack Johnson is a thrilling and interesting one, not because he was once the heavyweight boxing champion of the world, though of course that attainment enters into the story, and probably constitutes the basis of the narrative; but Jack Johnson has lived intensely and he has done many things that do not fall to the life of the average man. His career has been full of romance and adventure. He has gone into the high and low places of the world, and into corners of the globe little frequented by the ordinary man, regardless of his profession or station.

Jack Johnson was the first man of his race, and so far the only one to have won the distinction of being heavyweight champion, a distinction he won only after he had striven many years for the opportunity. Even than it was necessary for him to fight for privileges and rights that were his by all the rules and customs of the ring and the sporting world. Furthermore, he was compelled to stand in a fighting arena on foreign soil, with a great ocean between him and his native land, while about him were great masses of humanity shouting for the success of his opponent.

And having won that championship, he was not allowed to rest in his triumph. Instead, the world began to clamor for another title holder, bringing to bear a host of prejudices and criticisms before which a man of less determination would have weakened. To be free of the condemnations that were flung at him, any man less courageous than Johnson would have retired from the light of public scrutiny. But all these onslaughts he faced with a courage and confidence which substantiates the hint at the opening of this brief introduction, that he possesses qualities that have made his life and his career outstanding, even if he had never been the greatest boxer in the history of that sport.

Johnson held the championship title longer than any other heavyweight. Official records credit him, Dempsey, and Jeffries with holding the belt about seven years, but Johnson's retention was a few months more than either of these.[1] Besides his long hold on the title, he has the distinction of having fought more championship battles than any other heavyweight, and his record of

[1] Joe Louis was heavyweight champion from June 22, 1937 until he retired undefeated on March 1, 1948.

fights from the time he first came into the realm of professional boxing, shows that he fought more times than any other boxer in history. While there is not available a record of individual fighters, it is claimed on good authority that his fights are greater in number than the combined fights of any other three heavyweight fighters.[2]

From this casual survey, it may easily be concluded that his career as a fighter has been a busy one, and that it covers a longer period of time than any other fighter's of note. He has fought some of the hardest hitters in the ring; he has matched his skill with the cleverest, yet, never has he been hurt in the ring, and his face and body today bear not a single mark or scar inflicted by ring opponents. The cauliflower ear and other skin and muscle adornments commonly associated with those who dally with the padded mit – marks which usually are stamped upon them in the early days of their activities – are nowhere in evidence as far as Johnson is concerned.

What is still more remarkable in connection with this unusual boxer, is the fact that although he has passed his forty-ninth birthday, his physical condition is so excellent that his friends, boxing authorities and others familiar with his condition and mode of living, do not hesitate to declare that he is capable of entering the ring with any of the youthful fighters for a battle as gruelling and severe as any he waged in the days when the world was agog over the search for the 'White Hope'.[3] Some assert that if the opportunity were offered him, he could regain the championship title.

While Johnson may be better known as the former heavyweight champion, and as a boxer credited by all as being the greatest defensive fighter of all time, his fighting ability is not, by any means, his sole claim to attention. Much is being said at the present time concerning the 'bookish' inclination of Gene Tunney,[4] heavyweight champion, and of that young man's taste for literary pursuits. The former heavyweight, while he makes no claim for scholarly attainments, is nevertheless, no stranger in the world of books and writers. He is one who can be truthfully described as a wide reader. He has browsed through books on all subjects – fic-

[2] All the claims in this paragraph have since been surpassed.

[3] World-wide search for any white heavyweight capable of dethroning Johnson.

[4] Gene Tunney, World Heavyweight Champion, 1926–8.

tion, science, art, history; he has read them in three languages —
English, French, and Spanish. He is conversant with the works of
Shakespeare, and can discuss and quote the plays of this greatest of
all English writers with an ease which reveals that he has delved
deeply into his volumes. With the modern writers he also has close
acquaintanceship through their books, but when discussing books
and the names of Alexander Dumas and Victor Hugo are mentioned, Johnson becomes more alert than ever, for these are two of
his favorite writers and he has read them thoroughly.

While his schooling was interrupted before he reached high
school, he has, nevertheless, attained an education of a thorough
going character. His extensive travels have brought him into
intimate contact with men and women of the highest culture; his
numerous business adventures have given him a fund of practical
and accurate knowledge, and his love of good music, of books, and
the fine arts has led him to travel long and numerous detours that
took him a great way from the main route usually traveled by
boxers and athletes. His various trips abroad, where he met leaders
of industry, politics, literature and art, have given him an understanding of these subjects much broader than that which the average man possesses.

While his calling as a boxer has necessitated his association to a
great extent with the pleasure-loving world, and he often has
entered into frivolity said to be far removed from the more serious
and dignified phases of life, he has not, as might be expected,
acquired a penchant for the conventional pleasures of the jazz age.
On the contrary, the classics are quite to his liking, and he not only
joys in hearing the finest compositions of the old masters, but he
plays their compositions himself, for he is a musician of no mean
ability, his favorite instrument being the bass viol, which he plays
in a talented manner, and which was often his closest companion
when he was training for some of his great fights and felt the need
of relaxation.

It is a moot question whether his greatest desire is for music or
for motoring. He never has been without an automobile since they
became available. He has owned nearly every make of auto from
the quaint, primitive machine of 25 or 30 years ago down to the
most artistic and powerful machines built. There are few of the
leading American cars which he has not owned, and many of the
best European creations also have been his property. He is noted

for his fast driving, and is credited with being the world's greatest speed fiend. He says of himself that there are few countries or sections of countries in which he has not contributed to the police courts because the speed bug lured him to step a little harder on the gas feed. He has owned some swift racing cars, and the speed at which he has driven them equals some of the lofty records attained by professional racers. Even now, though he has retired from fast stepping in the ring, he has not relaxed his passion for motoring, and his car is frequently seen racing along the country's boulevards.

Criticism and condemnation of our fellow-men are the easiest tasks a mortal can set for himself. It requires very little effort to point the finger of accusation against another. It is not even necessary for one to insist that the accusation be founded on facts; the merest rumor suffices, and if there is a little jealousy and prejudice in the offing, we can heap our condemnation up without logic or regret. Johnson, unfortunately, was a victim of severe condemnation and there was little charity or kindness shown him in some of the dark hours of his life, when the tongues of gossip set upon him with fury, and many groups, imbued with both jealousy and prejudice, worked arduously to detract from his triumphs, and bring him down in disgrace and humiliation from the eminence he had reached. Steeled by a determination that a man of his race should not possess laurels so highly prized in the realm of sports, it was easy to marshal against him native prejudices, and back them with charges of deviation from the moral code and violation of certain statutes. It is of no use to thresh out these charges now; Jack refers to them in his autobiography and states his side of the controversies that plunged newspaper readers into perusal of accounts reciting tales of scandal in which he figured. Had it been any other man than he, whether boxer, merchant or professional man, it is quite certain that his alleged delinquencies would not have been so insistently and persistently discussed, and it is equally as certain that the discussions would not have assumed the bitterness which they did. Furthermore, it is more than likely that they would have been tinged with a little human sympathy. For Johnson there was little, except that uttered by his friends who understood him and who stood by him. But their voices were denied such channels of expression as would permit their defenses and explanations to reach the ears of the larger public.

Since his retirement from the ring, Jack has engaged largely in the worthy cause of developing the physical health and strength of young men, many of whom are potential ring victors. But whether or not any of them ever reach the stage where they are accorded attention from the public because of their boxing skill, one very important thing each of them will have accomplished under the tutelage of the former champion, will be their understanding of bodily health and vigor, with the knowledge of how to maintain it.

The scandals which have been woven about Jack are deplorable, and are responsible for placing him in a false and unjust light before the world. Jack makes no excuses for his conduct. He by no means pretends to be an angel, but one thing is certain – his conduct was by no means ever as bad as that of a great many men whom the world was kind enough to forget and to forgive. To Jack Johnson the world has not been so kind, but Jack does not nurse bitterness because of this. He loves life and humanity. He prizes the good things that fate has brought him. Though he is not the man of wealth and fame that he once was, he says he is happier than he has ever been in all his life, because the quiet and peaceful manner in which he has been living for the past several years bring him many things that he values higher than money and glory. He has many, many friends, some of whom have been steadfast since the days of his unpromising boyhood; some date their acquaintanceship with him from the time when the world began to take notice of him; some came into his life at the moments of his triumphs; still others have come to know him only in recent years, and have no personal recollection of his days of glory, but they have acquired an understanding of his good qualities, and that is sufficient. With these friends, Jack maintains a close association and he is devoting to them more attention than was possible when he was sought on every hand by members of all classes of society, and when hundreds insisted on claiming his time and companionship.

In the story of Jack's life, there is an abundance of thrill and adventure, but there is also the ripened wisdom of years of experience. His book will be read, therefore, not merely for the drama of his picturesque life, but also for the mature judgment of the world and the keen insight into life that is to be found in the reflections of these pages.

Keeping pace with Jack Johnson

By TAD.

A leading sports writer and cartoonist of the day, and confidante of Johnson.

The first time I ever saw Jack Johnson was in 1901, when he was acting as sparring partner for Kid Carter, the light heavyweight of Brooklyn. Carter, at that time, was training for a fight with George Gardner in San Francisco. He was training at Croll's gardens in Alameda, across the bay from the big town.

Johnson, at that time, was a tall, happy-go-lucky young fellow who would rather tell jokes than box. The newspaper boys used to sit around and listen to him spin yarns after each workout. On the Sunday before the fight, a delegation of sporting men from Frisco, headed by Jim Coffroth, the promoter, visited Carter's camp to give him the up-and-down. After the usual gym training, Carter put on the gloves with Johnson for a four-round workout. In the third round of the affair, Johnson hit the boss a bit harder than a sparring partner is supposed to sock his paymaster and Carter got mad.

'Trying to show me up, eh?' he growled. He lowered his head and tore into Johnson.

'I'll show you who the boss is around here,' he added.

Carter did his best to knock Johnson stiff, but instead of showing the tall colored fellow up, he was shown up himself, and only for Promoter Coffroth, who stopped the bout when Carter was groggy and all in, the big card might have been a flop.

Coming home on the boat that evening the sports talked more about Johnson than they did about Carter. They were sure that a new, big man who could fight, had arrived. Gardner beat Carter in the big fight and Johnson, the unknown, was then given a

17

chance with Gardner. He gave the Boston light heavyweight a
pasting, and from then on was a main eventer for Coffroth's
shows.

That was Jack Johnson's start in the city by the Golden Gate.
After that, Johnson beat every man he was sent against. He lost a
decision to Marvin Hart out there, but it was never taken seriously
by the fans. They figured that Referee Alec Greggians pointed to
the wrong man in the excitement.

After that Johnson met and defeated EVERY COLORED
HEAVYWEIGHT of any note boxing at that time. His wins included fights with Langford, Griffin, Jeanette, McVey, Childs, Jim
Johnson, Black Bill, Denver Ed Martin, Peter Felix, Joe Butler and
others. Without any doubt Johnson was the greatest colored
heavyweight.

He then beat every white contender in his path, including Jack
Monroe, Bill Lang, Bob Fitzsimmons, Jack Jeffries and all others.
Jim Jeffries, at that time heavyweight champion, refused to meet
Johnson and drew the color line. Jeffries had fought Hank Griffin
and old Peter Jackson, but balked at Johnson and refused to fight.
The latter kept at it and finally Jeff retired in order to duck the
dangerous Johnson. He handed his title over to Marvin Hart who
lost it to Tommy Burns.

Johnson chased Burns to England and then to Australia and there
cornered, the title holder gave in and signed to fight Johnson. He
was only a plaything in Johnson's hands and was saved from a
KO by the police. Jeffries was then induced to return to the ring
and signed to fight Johnson. The bout took place at Reno, Nev.,
July 4, 1910.

The writer thought then and still thinks that Johnson was the
best man. He proved it by defeating Jeff with ease. It was the first
time that Jeff had met a man of his own size. Johnson was a stronger
and better boxer and just as stiff a hitter. He knew more about
boxing than any man Jeff had ever met excepting probably Jim
Corbett.

Johnson's knowledge of boxing along with his great strength
and hitting power made him almost invincible.

It was his easy-going manner in the ring that fooled many. He
smiled and kidded in the clinches and many thought he was careless, but all the time he held his opponent safe, knew every move
the other made and was at all times the boss of the job. He was the

only colored man in the history of the ring to hold the heavy-weight title.

After he was crowned champion of the world, Jeanette, Lang-ford and other colored men put up howls for a return match, but Johnson never would give them a chance. As he told Dan McKe-trick in Paris:

'I won't box any of these colored boys now, Dan. I am cham-pion of the world. I have had a hard time to get a chance and I really think I am the only colored fellow who ever was given the chance to win the title. I gave Langford, Jeanette and those boys a chance before I was champ. I'll retire still the only colored heavy-weight champ,' and he did.

Jack Johnson was the greatest heavyweight of all times.

Jack Johnson could Fight

By DAMON RUNYAN

I have just received a little letter from John Arthur Johnson, some-time heavyweight champion of the world, who addresses me as Mr. Dam Runyan, a salutation which I hope and trust is but a slip of the typewriter, otherwise I might see my lawyers.

John Arthur Johnson advises me that he is writing an autobiography 'and as you know so much of my past record as a fighter, and know me personally, I am asking you to write something which will fit into my book, especially in regard to my fighting ability.'

I doubt that I shall find time to contribute to John Arthur's tome, although it would not be difficult for me to express in a few words my opinion of his fighting ability. I think he is one of the greatest fighters that ever laced on a pair of boxing gloves.

If he tells the truth, which is doubtful, his will be a most enthralling tale. I say it is doubtful if he tells the truth because John Arthur isn't old enough to tell the truth in an autobiography. A man has to be just about ready to die before he has the courage of unburdening himself completely.

He has been all over the world, Australia, Spain, Mexico, South America, England, Scotland, South Africa, and he has fought in many ports. He was a bullfighter in Barcelona. I saw his limousine blocking traffic in the Paris boulevards while the white people struggled to shake hands with the burly black man.

John Arthur is no longer the lean-flanked, cat-footed jaguar of Reno that he was when he whipped James J. Jeffries, but he remains something of a physical marvel just the same. I don't see why. He never stinted himself in the matter of indulgence. He drank plenty of wine and was the world's heavyweight champion eater long after he lost the pugilistic title to Jess Willard at Havana. Perhaps he still is.

I always thought that John Arthur at his best would have been too much for Jack Dempsey. He would have smothered up the rushes of the Mannassa Mauler, it seems to me, and gradually cuffed him into submission.

No greater defensive fighter than Johnson ever lived. He was not a sharp finishing puncher, he bounced his man around no little before knocking him over. I think this was due largely to the cat instinct in Johnson which made him want to play with his prey for a while.

Johnson could take fellows larger than himself and set them around the ring like nine pins at his own peculiar pleasure, chatting jovially with the crowd as he did so. He had a knack of catching punches as an outfielder catches a baseball. He reached out and grabbed most of them before they got well started.

I
I Take My Pen
In My Hand

My name is familiar to a great many people chiefly because I have held the heavyweight boxing championship of the world,[1] and because for more than a quarter of a century I have figured prominently in the making of world ring history. On more than one occasion I have been the central character in sensational episodes which stirred the interest and curiosity of the public. But I am not writing this history of my life – full of experiences and adventures as it is – because of these facts.

On the contrary, in looking back over the years of my tumultuous career, I am astounded when I realize that there are few men in any period of the world's history, who have led a more varied or intense existence than I. My life, almost from its very start, has been filled with tragedy and romance, failure and success, poverty and wealth, misery and happiness. All these conflicting conditions that have crowded in upon me and plunged me into struggles with warring forces have made me somewhat of a unique character in the world of today,[2] and the story of the life I have led may therefore not only contain some interest if told for its own sake, but may also shed some light on the life of our times.

Quick changes have come into my life on numerous occasions. I have been tossed from one extreme to the other within a few hours. Sometimes I found myself in the midst of disaster and often I arose to unexpected heights of affluence, power and prominence.

[1] 1908–15.

[2] 1927.

23

Many, many times fortune has virtually dropped into my hands and as many times it has slipped magically from my grasp.

I have attained the peaks of victory in gruelling fights with men as eager, as ambitious, as alert and as strong as I. With these victories generally came great sums of money, sometimes almost more than I ever dreamed of possessing. I was surrounded by countless admiring friends all intent on acclaiming me the greatest in my line; all eager to shout my praises; all striving for my esteem and for my bounty. By a sudden flip of fortune I have seen these friends melt away. But there have been many who have proved staunch throughout the years; who have shared with me in my successes and victories and who have suffered with me in the moments of failure, disappointment and bitterness.

I have known the tremendous exaltation of victory in the ring, in love, in business and in controversies of all kinds, and I have been cast down into the despair that sometimes comes with failure. I have traveled in nearly every country of the world and wherever I have gone I have had adventures that men of my race and nation have never had. I have mingled with notable people of every land. I have been with kings and queens; monarchs and rulers of nations have been my associates. In all the great gathering places of the world where the elite of every nation have met and are meeting, I have enjoyed the distinction of being a celebrity pointed out over all others.

In my life there have been many women, and with women there has come great happiness and also grief and tragedy. Women have come into my life and gone out of it leaving memories, many of which I treasure and many of which I would forget if I could. However, these women whom I have known and loved have been salient factors in my life. They have been the inspiration that urged me to strive for the uppermost places; they have been the cause of situations which turned the eyes of the world upon me, some merely gleaming with morbidness, others flashing condemnation and hate.

I have had my innings with the law. I know the bitterness of being accused and harassed by prosecutors. I know the horror of being hunted and haunted. I have dashed across continents and oceans as a fugitive, and I have matched my wits with the police and secret agents seeking to deprive me of one of the greatest blessings man can have — liberty. And after I had eluded them, after I had spent months in fighting for my cherished freedom and enjoying it at a dearly purchased price, I voluntarily relinquished it and surrendered myself, knowing that I should have to enter prison.

In my fight for my freedom I felt that whatever my conduct had been which led to accusations against me and conviction, it had been no worse than that of thousands of others. I felt that I had committed no heinous crime and that because of my color, perhaps, and because of prejudices and jealousies I was being persecuted and prosecuted. However, after months abroad, always alert lest I should be led into some trap that would mean loss of my freedom, I decided that I would return to my native country, submit to the demands of the law, and clear my 'debt to society.'

It was this desire to return to my own people and to again look on scenes that I loved and cherished that made my fight with Willard in Cuba, as far as I was concerned, merely an incident, a step in the direction of the goal toward which my heart led me — my home. In order to return to this home and ultimately resume my activities among those who meant most to me I was willing to make any sacrifice. This desire to wipe out prejudices against me and to still criticism of my conduct included my willingness to permit Willard to acquire the heavyweight championship of the world and my consent to go to prison.

Having disclaimed my intention to write this record of my life because of my attainments in the prize ring or because of the prominence I have achieved in sensational news stories, I wish to go a little further and deny also that I am engaging in this sketch of my life for the purpose of defending myself against charges that were brought against me. I am not attempting this enterprise to explain and excuse my faults and mistakes, nor to win sympathy and smooth over the rough places in my life. On the contrary, I feel that the story of my life is one that will prove interesting and entertaining to my readers as the story of a man, and that it will not be without good results. I am not pointing out any morals, yet when one suffers the inevitable consequences that ensue when the wrong course is chosen or mistakes are made and frankly admits and describes these mistakes and their results, surely it will prove of some benefit if it aids others to avoid similar mistakes and the attending unhappiness and disappointments.

I have no quarrel with fate, nor do I cling to the absurd belief that fate has set any special mark upon me. Yet fate must have intended me for adventures and experiences that do not fall to the lot of the average man. These adventures began early in my life and have crowded upon me fast and furiously. I cannot say that I deliberately planned or sought them. Throughout the half century of my life, events have whirled about me in an amazing manner and either engulfed me or lifted me with scarcely any effort or thought on my part.

Of course I had the dreams and desires that are common to youth, but never in the wildest moments of my boyhood imagination did I vision myself the champion fighter of the world, and the first man of my race ever to attain that distinction. Never did I imagine myself in the picturesque costume of a Spanish matador, a victor in the bullfighting arena surrounded by cheering thousands in the gala attire of the festival in historic Barcelona. How incongruous to think that I, a little Galveston colored boy should ever become an acquaintance of kings and rulers of the old world, or that I should number among my friends some of the most notable persons of America and the world in general! What a vast stretch of the imagination to picture myself a fugitive from my own country, yet sought and acclaimed by thousands in nearly every nation of the world! What an unusual circumstance that while I feared to return to my own country and was a voluntary exile, one of the most notorious revolutionary leaders of Mexico – Villa – was making frantic efforts to finance my return to the Western hemisphere and was attempting to stage in Mexico the championship fight between myself and Willard. How utterly fantastic would have been the thought that I should some day be plunged into romances and love with white women in defiance of a treasured and guarded custom. How far removed from my thought was the possibility that tragedy would creep into my life – the tragedy of a prison term in one instance and the death by suicide[3] of one whom I greatly loved in the other.

These are but a few of the unusual events that have come into my life. There are countless others, because I have lived rapidly, intensely, eagerly. I do not recall and write of these things in a boastful spirit, because some of them bring sad memories and arouse regrets; but they have happened and they must be told if one proposes an accurate and candid biography. Of many things I would

[3] Etta Terry Johnson, née Duryea (white), Johnson's second wife, shot herself on September 11, 1912.

rather not write for they stir latent sorrows; others, of course, give me cause for pride. There are pleasant topics, too, of which I wish to write, because, happily, my life has not been altogether filled with seriousness and tragedy.

2

A Stowaway

As I reflect on the very first adventure of my life, it strikes me as full of humor now. At the time of its occurrence, however, it was painfully serious. One of my earliest ambitions was rather a strange one, and, like many others of my younger years, bore no relation to the course that eventually marked my life. That ambition was to see Steve Brodie, the man who made himself famous by leaping from Brooklyn bridge. Why this fancy seized me I do not know. I was twelve years old[1] at the time and for a boy of that age living in Galveston, Texas, it was no easy matter to arrange a meeting with the daring New York man. From the Texas town to New York was a long way, especially for a youngster without funds and, as I recall it, neither my father nor other relatives were sufficiently interested in my whim to finance a trip to New York. This did not discourage me. I had determined to see Brodie and made several ineffectual attempts to depart from Galveston.

I spent more than a week trying to find a train out of the railroad yards. There were strings of box cars at my disposal and many times, seeing a train of cars moving in the direction which I believed would take me to New York, I hid myself in one of them and settled down for my long journey. When the cars were being shunted about the yards I thrilled with the thought that I was speeding toward the home of Brodie. I rode what seemed many hours in this way and when I imagined that Galveston was far behind me and ventured to peep from my hiding place, I usually

[1] Johnson was born in Galveston, Texas on March 31, 1878.

29

found that I merely had been riding about the yards, and when I supposed that probably I was nearing some northern city I was only at some familiar street crossing.

Uncounted times I was driven from the cars by railroad men and some of them were not very gentle in the manner in which they urged my departure from sidedoor Pullmans. Many of them used their feet in speeding me on my way and I nursed numerous bruises and sore spots. These failures to find my way out of the railroad yards and the painful contact with the heavy shoes of switch crew members did not lessen my desire to make the acquaintance of Brodie. I continued to haunt the railroad yards and to study other methods of reaching New York. Finally I succeeded in stealing aboard a steamship which I believed was bound for New York. Instead its destination was southward. At Key West, however, my journey was rudely interrupted when I was put off the boat. I was penniless, friendless and hungry. It was necessary for me to earn some money so I became a sponge fisherman and incidentally the prey of sharks which infested the waters in which we carried on our search for sponges.

Almost daily our small boats were attacked by the sharks, which was a terrifying experience for me, and one evening when alone in a sailboat, a monster shark 23 feet long attacked me. All I had with which to defend myself was sponge nets and with these I put up a frantic battle, the outcome of which seemed overwhelmingly in the shark's favor, and as the combat went on I became convinced that Steve Brodie was going to be denied the pleasure of a visit from me. By some miracle I managed to escape the jaws of the monster until companions came to my rescue and killed my enemy, but not until after my boat had been almost capsized several times.

Safe from the shark, I resumed my plans to visit Brodie and after several weeks as a sponge fisherman, I found an opportunity to stow myself away on a boat going to New York. My presence aboard was soon discovered and I was delegated to assist one of the cooks, my occupation being that of potato peeler. I whittled many miles of potato peelings probably in a manner not sufficiently artistic to please the cook, for he treated me cruelly and lost no opportunity to inflict severe bodily punishment upon me in addition to the arduous work of peeling potatoes. One day he beat me unmercifully and I ran from the hold of the vessel stinging with his blows and so frightened that I threatened to leap overboard. In this foolish attempt I was stopped by passengers on the boat, who, learning of the cruelties to which I had been subjected, made up a purse for me which enabled me to pay my fare to New York. Other kindnesses were showered upon me by the passengers and finally I reached New York in a fairly prosperous and sound condition. But to the desire to see Brodie had been added another determination – and that was to find the cook who had abused me and wreak vengeance upon him. I promised myself that I would seek him out when my physical growth warranted it and give him a sound thrashing, and for twenty years I went about with that plan in mind, always looking for the cook. Eventually my anger faded and as more important business engaged my attention the smarting of the injuries he had inflicted on me was forgotten. But I have never quite given up the hope of some day meeting my taskmaster of the ship's hold.

Once I was in New York, however, I lost no time in hunting up Steve Brodie. I began by asking the first person who would listen to me after I had landed. To this stranger I addressed my eager inquiry.

'Where is Steve Brodie?' I asked excitedly. He did not know, so I went about firing the question at all who would pause long enough to hear me. I did not so much as provide myself with food or shelter, so determined was I to pursue the quest for Brodie. And it was successful – more successful that I had ever anticipated, for I found at least twenty-five Steve Brodies.

Those to whom I addressed my inquiries, many of them at least, were so interested that they often replied, 'That's him right over there,' pointing out some man loitering on the corner, or perhaps dashing along the street in a carriage. I took their replies seriously, and on every occasion made daring attempts to make the acquaintance of the man who had been pointed out to me as my hero and idol. More than once I endangered my life by darting across streets unmindful of the threatening traffic, only to find my man had disappeared, or, if I found him, to be met with an angry scowl and a sharp rebuff.

'No, I am not Steve Brodie. Get along with you,' I was threatened. On two or three occasions, those I addressed admitted they were Steve Brodie, which lent me a temporary thrill, and a momentary feeling of satisfaction that my life's ambition had been realized. But on each occasion, I learned, to my bitter disappointment, that I had been the victim of practical jokers.

Steve Brodies were beginning to fill my life. I met them at every turn. They went by me in long processions. I dreamed of them when I slept, and day after day I met new Steve Brodies. The disappointments, though, only served to sharpen my determination. I went about hungry and footsore searching for Steve Brodie. So important to me was this self-created mission, that I had made no effort to obtain employment. That I was out of funds did not matter. I ate and slept where and when I could and continued the search. It had one outstanding result. It led to my acquaintance with the be-derbied and box-coated Chuck O'Connor, one of New York's most picturesque characters, dubbed the 'mayor of the Bowery,' the ruler of the toughs and down-and-outs, the acquaintance and friend of many notable people, and a political power of considerable magnitude during his reign.

O'Connor of the Bowery was first greatly amused at my search for Brodie. He heard the story of my travels with obvious amusement, but he was sincerely interested in me and became one of my best friends. He took me in hand, saw that I was clothed, fed and sheltered, and then sponsored an introduction to the real Steve Brodie, who too became a very good friend. With these newfound friends, I found a new entrance into life, and spent many happy, if not prosperous, days in New York, during which time I met many historic Bowery personages, became more or less absorbed by Bowery life, and enjoyed a small measure of distinction as 'the boy who ran away from Galveston to see Steve Brodie.'

From New York I went to Boston and worked in the stables of society folk in the Back Bay district. It was here that I experienced a mild tragedy and my career as a worldly young man was temporarily interrupted when a horse which I was exercising, fell with me. My right leg was broken, and I went to a hospital, where I remained for many weeks. When I had sufficiently recovered, friends provided me with funds and I returned to Galveston.

I was now a little past my thirteenth year, but despite my youth, I went to work on the docks, my associates being some of the toughest and hardest-boiled men imaginable. To them, fighting was one of the important functions of existence. They fought upon every occasion and on any pretext. They shot craps and indulged in other forms of gambling with almost as much ardor as they fought. It was up to me to hold my own with them, and I entered into their lives and occupations with as much energy as any of them. Although I was one of the youngest in this rough and aggressive group, I had to do my share of the fighting. It was necessary for me to fight youths much older and larger than myself. I suffered many beatings, but evidently was capable of standing much punishment, for I do not recall that I weakened. I won many of these rough and tumble battles, and because of the ill-matched affairs in which I engaged, I attained more or less reputation as a fighter. It was at this time that I took up boxing, not with any intention of engaging in it as a profession, but because it seemed necessary for me to learn something of the science in order to pit myself against the fighting groups with whom I associated.

One of the memorable fights of this early stage of my life, and one which established my confidence in my fighting ability, was urged on me by my sister Lucy. I had been attacked in the streets by a young man much older and larger than myself. I did not have the courage to fight him, and was casting about for an excuse to evade him. My sister came along at this juncture, and noting that the older boy was taking advantage of me, she became angry enough to demand that I fight him. In fact, she pushed me into the fray. There was nothing to do but fight, and I put all I had in it. The little that I had learned in boxing stood me in good stead, and after a mauling and pounding that lasted for several minutes with the results considerably in doubt, I finally whipped my antagonist. I was considerably surprised, and my friends, hearing that I had vanquished this giant of a fellow, began to praise my fighting ability.

A short time afterward, my reputation went up a few notches further, when I whipped the reigning bully of the docks, a hulking big fellow, feared because of his skill and strength as a scrapper. This was a fight made the fiercer and bloodier, because we were enraged at each other, having quarreled over some money in a dice game. Only a quarter was involved, but since he had snatched the coin from me and made off with it, I was stirred to a frenzied attack and we fought a ferocious battle in which I was the victor.

At about this time I again left Galveston and sought employment which I thought would be better suited to me than the work of a dock hand. In this I was backed by my father, a man of a pious turn of mind, who had served faithfully for many years in the Galveston

public schools as caretaker of a school building and preacher in a
little church. Neither he, nor my mother and other relatives had
been particularly enthusiastic over my activities around the docks.
My father would have had me take more interest in the church,
and sought determinedly to have me extend my schooling. However, despite my roaming instincts and the hectic experiences I had
undergone on the docks, I had not altogether neglected my education, and succeeded in completing the Grammar grades.

In going to Dallas, I had no special plan in mind. I had not decided upon a vocation, and nothing was further from my mind
than the thought of becoming a professional boxer, though I had
reason to believe that I possessed considerable skill in that direction. In Dallas I found a job in a carriage painting shop, where I
wielded the paint brush with more or less success. But here fate
stepped in and gave me a push which sent me toward the boxing
ring, though I was not aware of it at the time. The man for whom I
went to work was Walter Lewis, an amateur boxer of local prominence. He soon learned of my proclivities with the gloves, and en-
thusiastically set about improving my knowledge of boxing. I was
only fifteen years old, but he engaged me in some fast encounters,
and I began to have a glimmering of the possibilities of the ring as a
career. For six months I manipulated paint brushes and swung the
boxing gloves with the fast Walter Lewis and several boxers of
varying skill as antagonists, with all of whom I made such excellent showings that I was beginning to make serious plans concerning my future career.

I returned to Galveston, where I was beginning to be known as a
boxer, and although I was not yet sixteen years old, my first
regular ring battle was arranged. The fight was with John Lee, a
boxer who had gained some popularity and who was considered
skillful. The encounter took place in a ring built in the open field,
and there was a large crowd of fans in attendance. The fight lasted
sixteen rounds, and I won. After this, I was matched in several
events – in fact was meeting all who were picked by both friends
and enemies. But none of these affairs advanced my boxing prestige as much as a fight with another bully and tough of Galveston
known as Dave Pierson. This fight, too, grew out of a dice game
which was raided one Sunday morning by the police. I was one of
the participants in the game, and because I wore my father's over-
coat, for which I had been sent to the tailor shop a short time

before, I was unable to escape the officers. In a chase that followed, I was overtaken, and in the grasp of two policemen, was being conducted to jail. As we passed along the street, Pierson came into view.

'Here's another crap shooter,' exclaimed one of the officers. 'Grab him.'

Pierson was taken to jail, and in his wrath at being arrested, told the police and others that I was a stool pigeon.

To this accusation, I replied that Pierson was a liar, a dangerous remark unless I was prepared to back it up. Pierson soon heard of it, and among the friends of both of us rumors flew thick and fast. Pierson threatened to 'get me', and some of my friends, fearing for my safety, would have had me leave town, inasmuch as Pierson was rated one of the most dangerous men of the town and the most formidable fighter.

The upshot of it was that I was brought face to face with the tough. He asked me if I had said that he was a liar. I told him I had. In a moment the battle was on, and it was a battle without gloves. It was one of the hardest of my life. I was but sixteen years old and Pierson was a grown and toughened man. I fought grimly and as viciously as I have ever fought in my life. I gave him a tremendous beating. News of this fight and the downfall of the bully sped all over the city. A familiar inquiry for several days was,

'Did you hear what "Lil Arthur" did?'

That was the origin of the nickname which has become so well known in the sporting world. As I came into prominence, and eminent sport writers and cartoonists made me the subject of their articles and pictures, they made frequent use of that name. To 'Tad', the famous writer and cartoonist, who became a good friend of mine, I owe much for the inspiration, counsel and public backing which he gave me, and it was he who made the appellation 'Lil Arthur' known the world over.

More and more I was coming to think of the boxing ring as a profession, but had made no definite plans in this direction. My decision to make an attempt to acquire ring honors came shortly after my fight with Pierson, and was hastened when I stayed four rounds with Bob Thompson, in those days a fighter of considerable prominence. He had whipped some of the hardest men in the ring. He came to Galveston, meeting all comers and paying twenty-five dollars to any who would go four rounds with him.

I took up the challenge, entered the ring with Thompson, and got the twenty-five dollars. I barely stayed the four rounds. At their conclusion I was greatly pleased. It was the hardest earned money of my life, and it was two weeks before I could venture forth to spend it, so great was the beating which Thompson gave me.

3
Breaking in

After my fight with Thompson, opportunities for ring activities were few for me in Galveston. Working on the docks, although I was a shipping clerk, held no inducement for me, and I began to look about for something better. I decided to leave Galveston, but had no particular destination in mind. I adopted a simple course and got on a freight train one night as it pulled out of the Galveston yards. I had cast myself wholly into the lap of fate. Although I did not know where the train was bound for, I was not greatly worried over the matter. I did not know where I was going but I was on my way.

On this trip I experienced all the hardships, uncertainties and dangers of freight-train touring. I was without money and there were many days when my stomach shouted angrily for food. Fellow travelers, in the same plight as I, but more familiar with the customs of tramping, initiated me into the secrets of obtaining, here and there, scraps of food sufficient to keep me alive. But hunger was not the only difficulty with which I had to contend. Hard-boiled train crews did not seem enthusiastic over having me as a passenger, and on countless occasions I was chased from boxcars, gondolas and blinds. Brakemen impressed me with their earnestness by brandishing clubs with which they threatened to break numerous bones in my body. Train crews were not my only enemies. In railroad yards, where I lingered watching for an opportunity to board a train that seemed bound for somewhere, road detectives and watchmen lurked, or if I ventured into the streets of

some of the smaller towns where a stranger was quickly discovered, police officers and constables manifested deep concern in
me. In fact, they were generally so deeply interested that they
often insisted that I remain as a guest of their town. On these
occasions, I was introduced to the town Judge, who pried into my
personal affairs and asked me embarrassing questions. Usually,
after my meeting with the Judge, I was instructed to hasten out of
town, which was just exactly what I wished to do, and what I was
trying to do when the police interfered. Sometimes I was detained,
quarters being assigned me in the town jail.

Eventually, after trying out the facilities of several slow, fast and
indifferent freight trains, after I had learned the nooks and crannies
of many railroad yards and formed the acquaintance of hordes of
train crew members, I reached Springfield, Illinois. This city,
although made famous by Abraham Lincoln, meant no more to me
than any other. I had no particular reason for stopping in Springfield, further than that I was compelled to do so because of the erratic schedules of the trains upon which I rode. However, while
making a temporary stop in Springfield, I learned that an athletic
club of this city was staging a boxing show, and that the club was
in search of fighters to enter a battle royal. I volunteered for the
fray and entered the ring more or less fatigued from my arduous
travels and the irregularity of my meals.

There were four men in the fight beside myself. I was hungry;
my great ambition as the fight began was to eat; and I feared that if
I did not win the fight, I might not have an opportunity to eat. My
appetite was my second and backer and I certainly fought – and I
won! I knocked out each of my four opponents, which seemed to
convince the spectators that I was a fighter of no mean ability.

It so happened that the boxing show, of which the battle royal
was a part, was conducted under the direction of Johnnie Connors,
who, it will be remembered, was prominent in the boxing activities of that period, and who has been one of the most loyal friends I
have ever had. Johnnie was sufficiently impressed with me to take
me under his wing, and shortly after the Springfield affair he
brought me to Chicago. It was my first visit to the city which was
to be the scene of so many escapades of my life; where I was to experience my greatest joys and sorrows and to have some of my
greatest triumphs.

Three days after my arrival in the Windy City, Connors

arranged a match for me with a fighter known as Klondike, who had attained much success in the ring, and who at that time was a popular ring performer in Chicago. In this fight I was beaten, although half the rounds were mine. The showing I made was sufficient to hold the interest of fight fans and to win many friends and backers for me. The Klondike match netted me a considerable sum of money, a considerable sum for those days, and probably more than I ever had before in my life. The money, however, was soon exhausted, because I undertook to play the races at Springfield, a new form of thrill and amusement for me. I was not clever in picking winners and the proceeds of my first Chicago fight did me little good.

I was now seventeen. Until this time, my plans for becoming a professional boxer had been more or less vague. The battle royal at Springfield and my encounter with Klondike served to decide me in my course, and I definitely selected the ring as my goal, and for the first time began training in real earnest, and with men more skillful and clever than I had ever met before. There were several of these in Chicago at that time, and among those, who, as I recall it, took the most sincere interest in me and my ambitions, were Dan Creedon and Tommy Tracy. I made sufficient progress in Chicago to encourage me to undertake a trip to New York, where I hoped to meet some of the more notable boxers of the country.

On my way to New York, I stopped at Pittsburgh where a series of fights was being held at the stockyards. I found that as new as I was in the game, I was not altogether unknown in the steel town, and it was not difficult for me to obtain a match, though the man with whom the match was made, was so large and so formidable looking as a fighter, that I had much doubt concerning my chances with him. He was a white man, and in the ring I had the feeling that he was towering over me and was going to make it exceedingly tough for me. The outcome of the fight surprised me, for I knocked him out in five rounds. We fought for a purse; how much, I do not recall. My only recollection is that I left the scene of the fight with my hat brimming full of dollars, and with this small fortune and my victory over the big fellow raising my courage high, I continued my trip to New York. It was my second visit to the city, the first having been when I landed there in my search for Steve Brodie.

I set earnestly about establishing myself in the boxing game and sought to associate myself with some of the leading boxers of the city. My first overture was made to Bill Quinn, who was then training for his fight with Joe Walcott[1] Quinn felt that he could get along without my services, and I found myself facing a series of disappointments. I took part in a few minor ring bouts, but for several weeks, my existence was more or less precarious. I renewed acquaintances which I had made on my former visit, and many of these attempted to aid me in my endeavors to form contacts with boxers and fight managers. Many, it appeared, doubted my abilities and it was difficult to obtain financial backing. I proposed to meet several boxers, but for one reason or another I failed to make any matches of consequence. After the Quinn-Walcott fight my chances brightened up a bit, and I found a place in the camp of Walcott, who had beaten Quinn. With Walcott I went to Boston where I served with him as a sparring partner for two months. All the while, though, I was casting about for a match which would help me along to the goal which was beginning to take form in my calculations, though I was not yet even secretly aspiring to the great championship. While in Boston, I succeeded in arranging a match for myself with Harry Tuttle, afterward prominently identified with the Detroit baseball team. For this match I went to Bridgeport, Connecticut, to train, but the fight never came off, because of Tuttle's failure to appear, as a result of which I was awarded the forfeit.

Friends now began to urge my return to Galveston, where some new fighters were coming into prominence, and therefore, not finding my ambitions coming to immediate realization in New England, I again returned to my home town. Here, I found several boxers had established themselves. There was none among them who gained more than local reputation, as I recall it, but some of them were skillful, and I took part in numerous fights, none of which added particularly to my reputation as a fighter. Nor did I profit greatly financially, but I was learning much about boxing and obtained excellent training which was to stand me in good stead in the future events which called for all the skill and experience I could muster. After a year or so in Galveston, during which time I had defeated all the boxers of consequence, I was invited to visit Hot Springs, Arkansas, where for six months I engaged in

[1] Joe Walcott, the Barbados Demon, World Welterweight Champion, 1901–04, 1906.

several ring events, most of which I won, but like my Galveston fights, they netted me little in the way of prestige or money.

I returned to Galveston in 1896. I had reached my 20th year,[2] and had had so many fights that I had lost all track of the number, though there were none of much interest to the public, except perhaps my fight with Klondike in Chicago. As I was only a little more than seventeen at that time, however, it is probable that Chicago had forgotten all about me. Because of my youth, neither Boston nor New York had taken me seriously, although in Boston I had managed to rouse the contempt of some of the Irish gangs of that city, who were still ardent friends of John L. Sullivan, who four years previously had lost the championship to Jim Corbett. I was an admirer of Corbett, and having expressed my opinion of him within the hearing of the Irish fans, I found it necessary to defend myself occasionally against their attacks, and once at least, because of my friendship for 'Gentleman Jim,' I suffered a severe beating.

Soon after my return from Hot Springs, I fought Howard Pollar,[3] who was attracting considerable attention in the South, and having beaten him, was matched to fight Jim Scanlan of Pittsburgh, for which fight I did real, earnest training. I got the decision over Scanlan and then Klondike came along in 1901, and I went into the ring with him for the second time, the first having been in Chicago, where he defeated me. Our second meeting was different – the decision went to me. By this time Galveston was taking considerable notice of me and there was much activity in arranging matches. After the go with Klondike, I met Jack Lawlor and defeated him, and soon thereafter I took on Joe Choynski, who was attracting national attention, and who, though he had gained no championships, had fought some hard men. The fight resulted disastrously for both of us. I lost the fight in three rounds, because it was stopped by the police. Both Choynski and I were arrested and held in prison for three weeks, charged with violation of the Texas anti-boxing law in force at that time. As neither of us was successful in obtaining bonds pending what appeared to be an effort to determine how far the law might go in punishing us, we remained in jail. Finally it was decided to liberate us, and, soon after, a

[2] If, as records indicate, Johnson was born in 1878, this is incorrect.

[3] Johnson's data about his early contests is not always reliable; see Appendix 1.

special session of the state legislature passed a new law, making prize-fighting a felony.

After this event, Galveston held no great charm for me and I again set out for new fields. My quest took me to Memphis, where for the second time within the year I met and beat Klondike, the Chicago fighter. It was the third appearance we had made in the ring. In the same year I met and defeated Josh Mills, this fight also taking place at Memphis. After that, the Tennessee city offered me little, though I remained there several months and then concluded to try my luck in the west. Denver was my first important stopping place and here I came in contact with some notable fighters. I joined a motley crew of scrappers who were training at Ryan's Sand Creek house, among them being Tom Sharkey, one of the ring's greatest fighters, though he never held a championship. A year or so before he had fought a great battle with Jim Jeffries, a twenty-round contest at Coney Island, which was one of the longest and hardest in which Jeffries had participated. Also, at Ryan's rendezvous, was Young Corbett who, a little later, acquired the featherweight world's championship by whipping the 'Terrible Terry McGovern' at Hartford, Connecticut.

Denver at the time was staging some fast fights in the old Coliseum, but there were no boxers in the heavyweight class available for these events, and I had no opportunity to demonstrate my abilities in the mountain town. Things were going slowly for Sharkey also, so he conceived a plan to organize a big boxing show, which was to take to the road giving exhibitions in fistic science, and which also would meet all comers, in any division of fighting weights. Included in the personnel of this organization, besides Sharkey, were men who had attained more than passing prominence in the ring, or who were destined later to attract world-attention. Among them were Young Corbett, Spider Kelley, Abe Attell, New York Jack O'Brien who was then lightheavyweight champion of the world, Philadelphia Tommy Ryan, George Dixon and myself.

The finances of the organization being low, we selected a nearby scene for our exploits, the place being Cripple Creek, Colorado, then one of the world's greatest mining camps, where miners and prospectors, sportsmen, gamblers and adventurers of all kinds were gathered, and where wild-west, scenes were being enacted daily. We were accorded a rather warm welcome in the gold town and our initial exhibitions were well attended and the box office receipts were satisfactory for a few days. We entertained one aspirant for the heavy-weight boxing championship in the person of Mexican Pete who was creating somewhat of a furor in the west because he had beaten Sharkey. He took advantage of our offer to meet all comers and I was next delegated to meet him. We put on one of the best fights the mining camp had ever seen if hard fighting is counted for anything. It lasted twenty rounds and resulted in my knocking out the aspirant.

It was in Cripple Creek that my first real trouble descended upon me. The morning after my fight with Mexican Pete, a dispute arose between my first wife[4] and myself, and she left me, going to Denver. This disconcerted me more or less, because it was a tragic circumstance, as such incidents always are in the lives of newly-weds. Ours had been a real love affair and we had been devoted to each other. I was reduced to a gloomy state of mind. Adding to my domestic eruption, came the sad realization that Sharkey's organization of boxing geniuses had gone on the rocks. Our show, it appeared, was a topnotcher, but the mining camp population was not sufficient to maintain us as a profitable going concern. Our expenses had been larger than our income. It was necessary for us to leave our comfortable hotel quarters and find other shelter. We rented a shack of a house in which we set up a co-operative home. In this establishment, I, the conqueror of Mexican Pete, and entertaining high hope of recognition as a master boxer, became the cook. Not only was I delegated to prepare the food for the lusty, hungry human machines of flesh and brawn, but it also was necessary for me to engineer the finances and obtain money and credit sufficient to stock the pantry.

The purse was slender and the pantry was scant. Empty stomachs demanded to be filled, and I set about the task with considerable difficulties staring me in the face. I managed to open a credit account with a butcher, who for a time was a source of supply. But as our indebtedness mounted, the butcher grew less obliging; he not only grumbled about the laxity with which he was paid, but he took advantage of our emergency and wished on us an inferior quality of market products. These we accepted and consumed heroically for a time, but when the butcher, in the hope that we would discontinue our patronage, supplied us with ancient

[4] Mary Austin Johnson (coloured).

and rotten chickens, and my star boarders began to entertain doubts as to my fitness as a cook and ability as a food buyer we complained. However, we did not cease to deal with the butcher, for he was the only one with whom our credit was good, and it was good with him principally because he feared to deny a bunch of fighters, rather than because of faith in our financial soundness.

Eventually the boys, one by one, financed themselves and left the camp. I returned to Denver, where I was reunited with my wife, and hope and happiness again returned. We left Denver shortly afterward and went to Los Angeles, where I met Young Corbett, who, having defeated Kid Broad in Denver, in May, 1902, was preparing for his fight with Terry McGovern, which took place in San Francisco in March, 1903. I busied myself around Corbett's camp and gave the fighter such help and advice as my own experience and knowledge afforded.

In the meantime I was doing some heavy training myself and on the lookout for matches with men in my class. I mixed with the boxing fraternity in most of the Pacific coast towns, and, on a trip to Bakersfield, met Frank Corella, who became my manager. My stay on the coast was marked by some of the first important fights of my career. It was also significant because on October 31, 1902, I won the world's light heavy-weight championship from George Gardner, in San Francisco, in a twenty-round battle.[5] Before gaining this title, I had had a fight at Oakland with Joe Kennedy who had been one of Jim Jeffries' principal sparring partners. I won by a knockout in four rounds.

In the same year I also had fought and defeated Jack Jeffries, brother of Jim, in a five-round go at Los Angeles. I had had two severe fights with Hank Griffen who held a decision over Jim Jeffries, when the latter failed to live up to an agreement to knock him out. Both these fights were in Los Angeles and both resulted in a draw. One went twenty rounds and the other fifteen. In summing up my fights, throughout my career, there were none, even in the championship bouts, which were harder than those with Griffen, and I believe that the greatest punishment I ever received in the ring was at the hands of Griffen. Other important fights on the coast, besides those just mentioned, included a twelve-round bout with Frank Childs at Los Angeles and twenty rounds each

[5] Gardner was *not* light-heavyweight champion at the time.

with Denver Ed Martin and Sam McVey. All of these contests I won.

During my stay on the coast, I had many experiences and adventures outside the boxing ring, of which I shall have something to say later. Concerning one, I am going to digress sufficiently here, because it made a lasting impression on me – an impression that was heightened by events in subsequent years of my life. Frequently I have been asked whether or not I am superstitious. For the most part, I am not, that is, in the general understanding of the term. This adventure of which I am writing was with a fortune teller in Los Angeles whom I visited in the guise of a working man. I was careful, or thought I was, to conceal from her the real nature of my occupation. But I did not fool her. She at once told me that I was a boxer, and recounted some of my past life with such accuracy that I was astounded. She proceeded to tell me many things concerning my future, some of them so fantastic and so improbable, viewed from the place I then occupied in life, that I departed from her presence feeling that she had drawn a highly imaginative picture of my life. She predicted that I would be the heavy-weight boxing champion; she told me of my forthcoming marriages and of various affairs that I was destined to have with women; she told me, almost in detail, of the adventures and travels that were to mark my later life; of my conflicts with the law; of the accident which nearly cost my life in Spain, when an automobile turned over with me; of my sickness, which nearly ended in my death; of my return to America and the events of the following years. I did not give serious attention to her predictions at the time, but within a few years things began to happen that set me thinking and caused me to watch my step. In the years since, events and circumstances have come to pass with little deviation from the manner in which she foretold them. I still do not make an admission of being superstitious, but as the record stands, the Los Angeles fortune teller still looms conspicuously in my memory, and there are few developments in my life that do not in some way echo that incidental visit, many years ago, when I stood on the threshold of a life that was to be one of the most picturesque in American history.

After my fights with Martin and McVey, early in 1903, I left the coast for Boston, and in April won a ten-round fight with Sandy Ferguson in the 'Hub.' In May, I knocked out Joe Butler in three rounds in Philadelphia, and in July in the same city, fought again with Ferguson, the meeting going six rounds to a no-decision.

In the fall of the same year I returned to California, and in October won my second twenty-round go with McVey. Ferguson also had ventured into the Pacific coast fight territory, and on December 11, I fought him for the third time and won in twenty rounds.

As far as my boxing activities were concerned in 1904, the year was rather a dull one. While I traveled over the United States considerably and appeared in many minor engagements from Philadelphia to Los Angeles, I had only four bouts of much significance. One was with Black Bill, a six-round no-decision event in the Quaker City, in February; in April, I fought Sam McVey for the third time, the contest taking place in San Francisco and going twenty rounds to a knockout in my favor. In June I won a six-round bout with Frank Childs in Chicago, the meeting being the second one between him and me, and in October, I met Denver Ed Martin for the second time in Los Angeles, and disposed of him in the second round.

One of the busiest boxing years of my life was that of 1905. In all, I had thirteen contests of considerable importance, inasmuch as they convinced boxing authorities and boxers that I was a factor that must be reckoned with in boxing history. In March, in San Francisco, I fought Marvin Hart, who later claimed the heavyweight championship on the retirement of Jeffries. This fight was not an auspicious event for me, as Hart got the decision, owing, as Tad, the famous sportwriter says, to the fact that in the excitement the referee pointed to the wrong man. However, it was the only contest I lost;[6] the other twelve events being in my favor, excepting five no-decision matches. These, although they are not officially recorded, were won by me.

During this year Philadelphia was the principal scene of my activities, though I did much travelling. In all, ten fights were staged in the Sleepy City, with me as one of the principal contenders. The first was with Jim Jeffords whom I knocked out in four rounds. I won a four-round affair with Black Bill with whom I had previously had a no-decision bout; I knocked out Walter Johnson in three rounds and went six rounds to a no-decision with Joe Jeanette. I knocked out Morris Harris in three rounds, had

[6] Johnson lost on a foul in the second round against Joe Jeannette at Philadelphia on November 25, 1905.

another no-decision session with Black Bill; a similar six-round venture with Jack Monroe, the Montana miner who had gained distinction by knocking down Jim Jeffries, and also a no-decision bout with Joe Grimm. At Chelsea I fought and won again from Sandy Ferguson; at Baltimore I knocked out Young Peter Jackson in twelve rounds and concluded the year with a second no-decision match with Jeanette.

In 1906 Jeanette and I mixed our fists and skill no less than four[7] times. On January 6, at New York, we had a three-round no-decision contest; on March 15, I won over him in a fifteen-round match at Baltimore; on September 20, we went six rounds to a no-decision at Philadelphia and on Nov. 26 we fought a ten-round no-decision bout at Portland, Maine. I knocked out Black Bill in seven rounds at Wilkes-Barre, April 19. I won from Sam Langford in fifteen rounds at Chelsea, Massachusetts, on April 26, and a short time afterward, Langford and I put on an exhibition bout for the benefit of the sufferers in the San Francisco earthquake and fire. I had a one-round affair with Charlie Haghey at Gloucester on June 18, and on November 8, met Jim Jeffords again, winning from him in six rounds.

The end of 1906 found me looking confidently ahead to the time when I should gain the world's heavy-weight championship. I was twenty-eight years old and I had been fighting just about half that time, if I include my boyhood encounters in Galveston. While these, of course, were in no wise to be considered as a part of my record as a boxer claiming championship ability, they nevertheless helped to provide me with a background on which I based my own calculations and aspirations. As early as my sixteenth year, I had met men who claimed prize ring honors and as there had been none who had beaten me severely, and as I had won most of my fights, both in and out of the ring, I felt reasonably certain that there was nothing to block me as far as my skill was concerned.

The five-year period ending with the close of 1906, found me with fifty-six registered fights to my credit, to say nothing of countless matches, exhibition and otherwise, in which I had participated and which were not officially recorded. Of these fifty-six fights, I lost only two[8] – those with Choynski and Hart.[8] In this time I had met and defeated some real contenders, and I think there

[7] Five.

[8] Three: those with Choynski, Hart and Jeannette.

should have been no denial of my right to contest for championship honors. While sporting writers and boxing authorities still continued to question my claim to higher ring honors, it certainly was not because my record as a boxer was in any wise questionable. I had demonstrated my strength, speed and skill, but still faced many obstacles, the principal one of which was the customary prejudice because of my race. Had it not been for these prejudices, which I shall not discuss here, I think I would have been instrumental in making an entirely different history of boxing in the United States and the world, from that which has been recorded. With the beginning of 1907 I had attained a success that I believed entitled me to propose myself as an aspirant for the championship. Tommy Burns held the coveted honor and I began to direct my attention toward him. It was two years before I got to him and proved my abilities by winning the championship.

Those two years were arduous ones. I struggled diligently in backing up my contentions and I fought in many hard ring events. I took on every potential contender between myself and the champion. I virtually had to mow my way to Burns. I made offer after offer. I proposed all sorts of inducements and made every possible concession. Most of the sport authorities of the world, I believe, recognized my claims and my ability. Even King Edward of England was disgusted with Burns' tactics and called him a 'Yankee Bluffer,' and went so far as to suggest that unless Burns met me on a fairer basis than he at first proposed, the fight between us, which at one time was talked of as a project to be staged in England, should be prevented.[9]

I am leaping considerably ahead of my story, however, if I am to follow a chronological order. There were, as I have intimated, several hard fights intervening. There were two trips abroad, one to Australia in 1907, and another to England in 1908.

Both these trips were memorable ones. Wherever I went, in either country, I was accorded a warm welcome and in many instances jubilant receptions greeted me. These trips, I believe, had much to do in convincing the boxing world that I was a logical contender for the heavy-weight crown. During this period sport writers and cartoonists were filling many columns about me, and I was the target of enough good natured jibes and jests to fill a volume and a large one at that.

[9] This is without foundation.

In Australia I settled a dispute over the heavy-weight championship of that country by defeating both disputants. They were Peter Felix, a colored fighter, and Bill Lang. I knocked out both of them, Felix at Sydney, New South Wales, February 19, in one round, and Lang at Melbourne, finishing him in nine rounds. I remained in Australia several months, during which time I made many friends, who, with thousands of others, were to welcome me back in December of 1908, when I defeated Burns.

One event in Melbourne, which brought me $15,000 in an unexpected manner, took place when I unknowingly and unintentionally bet hundreds of dollars on a horse race. The dollars and the betting on my part were imaginary, but nevertheless they won real, hard money. I arrived at the race track in a depleted condition financially. The horse on which I was betting belonged to Jim Brennan, who was the promoter of the Johnson-Felix fight, and whose guest I was in Australia. I saw his horse, Istria, and liked it so well that I bet my last five dollars on it. At the conclusion of the race I collected my winnings amounting to one hundred dollars, then strolled around the track until the races were finished, when I returned to my training quarters. On the next morning, a Sunday and my birthday, I took a trip to Tattersals, where all of the large bets of the previous day are paid. Upon my arrival a man approached me with a huge roll of bills. He handed them to me much to my amazement. But as usual in such rare instances I reached out and accepted the money. Other book-makers followed him and I accepted their rolls of bills in a dazed sort of manner, for I had absolutely no idea what it was all about.

Finally, one of the bookies told me, as he handed me a wad of bills, 'I say, Mr Johnson, but you were lucky to bet on that horse.' I then realized that on the previous day as I was greeting friends and acquaintances with a wave of the hand the bookies took this as a signal to place another bet on my horse. I finally had to provide myself with a handbag to carry my money and when I arrived at home and finished the counting of my newly and unexpectedly acquired fortune I found that the greeting of my friends on the previous day had made me $15,000 richer.

Nothing could have been more opportune for I had been in a predicament for several days wondering how I was to finance my trip back to the United States. If the long shot had not won – well it still makes me sweat to think about it. I would probably have been in Australia yet, wondering what had happened to me and making futile explanations to prison keepers.

Soon after this windfall I returned home. In seeking for more matches I was booked to meet that good old fighter Bob Fitzsimmons. It was a fight that resulted pitifully, the grand old man of the ring going down for the count in the second round. I do not take much credit to myself for this bout, but it seemed necessary at the time in clearing the course that was before me. On August 28, I knocked out Kid Cutler at Reading, Pennsylvania, in one round. At Bridgeport, on September 12, I won over Sailor Burke, and my fights of 1907 ended November 2, when I knocked out Jim Flynn in eleven rounds at San Francisco.

4
Fighting to the Top

In the early part of 1908 I devoted myself to negotiations for matches in which I could prove my skill and win sufficient prestige to be in a position to demand a go with Burns for the Championship. But since there were not many available fighters in my class at the time, I engaged in several minor ring events and continued to keep myself in condition for the big opportunity which I knew must come.

After a few months of comparatively little action, I set sail for London, accompanied by Sam Fitzpatrick, who was filling the post of manager for me. While I met a few of the English fighters and filled impromptu music hall engagements, the principal purpose of the trip to England was to arrange a match with Burns for the championship, which, for a time, promised to take place in England. Although I made every conceivable concession to Burns we were a long time coming to any terms, and ring history, I believe, will reveal that the preliminary negotiations for that fight required more time and involved more discussion than ever characterized any previous similar event. At times it grew bitter and the press was loud in its criticism of Burns for his long side-stepping of me. In June of 1908, while the bickering was on, I met Al McNamara, a British contender. The contest took place at Plymouth and I won in four rounds. In the following month I fought Ben Taylor, also at Plymouth, and knocked him out in the eighth round. These contests were merely incidental but they helped me in removing any possible contenders that might remain between Burns and myself.

Finally, to my great satisfaction, the meeting with Burns was arranged to take place in Sydney, New South Wales, Dec. 26, and after a short stay in Europe I went to Australia to begin my training for the bout which I had so long sought and which meant so much to me. In Australia I was warmly received, notwithstanding the fact that Burns was the favorite in the betting, which was to be expected because of the racial element involved. On my first visit to that country I had made many friends and these came hurrying to renew acquaintance with me. I found that I had new admirers also, and the utmost kindness was shown to me on every hand. There were, of course, some outbreaks of bitterness and there was much criticism of both Burns and myself. But whatever hostility was shown toward me came from sources of no great importance, principally those of narrow and bigoted opinions.

Another concession I made in this fight was that McIntosh, Burns' manager should act as referee. Burns had insisted on naming the referee, and I was determined that he should not, but rather than cause disagreement or any room for doubt I assented to McIntosh, Burns' manager and promoter of the fight, so sure was I that there would be no dispute over the nature of my fighting and the results. This was the first time in the history of the ring that one of the contestants' managers had also served as the referee.

By the day of the fight my friends and supporters had increased and Burns was less a ruling favorite. The fight was attended by 30,000 people, who came from every country in the world. It is said that the representation of the press was the largest that ever watched a fight up to that time, countless newspapers and sporting publications having sent their writers to the fray. We fought for a purse of $35,000, and of this amount I got only $5,000, those being the unequal financial terms which I had accepted in order to bring the fight about. I was scheduled to go twenty rounds but the fight was stopped by the police in the fourteenth round, so obviously was it in my favor. I was declared the world's champion heavyweight boxer. The fight was one of the easiest of the more important fights of my career. At no time did Burns have a show with me. The champion had fallen. A new champion had arrived and that new champion was Jack Johnson.

I had attained my life's ambition. The little Galveston colored boy had defeated the world's champion boxer and, for the first and only time in history, a black man held one of the greatest honors which exists in the field of sports and athletics – an honor for which white men had contested many times and which they held as a dear and most desirable one. Naturally I felt a high sense of exaltation. I was supremely glad I had attained the championship, but I kept this feeling to myself. I did not gloat over the fact that a white man had fallen. My satisfaction was only in the fact that one man had conquered another, and that I had been the conqueror. To me it was not a racial triumph, but there were those who were to take this view of the situation, and almost immediately a great hue and cry went up because a colored man was holding the championship.

The hunt for a 'white hope' began, not only with great earnestness and intenseness, but with ill-concealed bitterness. I regretted this phase of the hunt. Many times there was manifested by those from whom we should expect better things an unsportsmanlike attitude that I regretted then and always shall. That they should wish to find a contender for the crown was natural and I lost no time in announcing my readiness to meet any who might wish to strive for the honors I had attained. There were many possibilities in the field. Burns, my late defeated antagonist, soon after our meeting, set forth to comb Europe and other sections of the world for someone whom he might send against me in an effort to win back what he had lost. Everywhere the search went on.

I watched it with deep interest but not with any alarm. I was sure of myself and would have taken the utmost satisfaction at any time in giving aspirants an opportunity. In the meantime I returned to the United States, having remained in Australia only a few days after the championship battle. I was accorded the utmost consideration wherever I went and much pressure was put forth to induce me to remain longer. Several celebrations were arranged in my honor. In Western Australia a special race meet was put on for me; a whippet race also was one of the entertainments provided for me and party, and I left Australia with the very kindliest of feeling for that country and its people. As I boarded the ship on my return home I was loaded down with gifts.

After crossing the Pacific I spent a few days at Vancouver and San Francisco. Ovations were tendered me everywhere. I made a brief stop in Chicago on my way to New York, and in the former city, which by that time had come to be my home, I received a

tremendous welcome. After a short visit with my relatives I
hastened to New York, where I signed a thirty-week theatrical
engagement with Hammerstein, providing for several tours which
took me over a great part of the United States and Canada. My
theatrical work, of course, included boxing exhibitions, and for
that reason I was constantly in good trim and ready almost any
time to enter the ring. Between stage appearances I had some
minor ring affairs. One of these was with Victor MacLaghlen[1] in
Vancouver, March 10, 1909, which I won in six rounds. Another
was with Philadelphia Jack O'Brien in Philadelphia, May 19.
Although O'Brien was being groomed as one who might take the
championship from me, the result of the fight, while no decision
was given, clearly showed that O'Brien would have to be eliminated as a contender. Following O'Brien came Tony Ross, with
whom I entered the ring in Pittsburgh, June 30. We fought six
rounds to a no-decision conclusion, but the outcome was un-
mistakably in my favor. About this time the giant fighter Al Kauffman, appeared on the horizon, and in him were placed the hopes of
those so eager to have a white man again wear the championship
belt. After considerable negotiations, articles between Kauffman
and myself were signed and the fight took place in San Francisco
September 9. It went ten rounds. Officially no decision was
rendered, but I had so much the best of it throughout that Kauffman
was removed from the list of eligibles without any dispute. One
more hope remained – Stanley Ketchel, who, it was firmly
believed by some, would whip me. We fought at Colma, California,
October 16, 1909, and I knocked him out in twelve rounds.
After this fight I returned to Chicago and bought a home for my
mother and her family. I spent the holidays with my relatives and
after Christmas returned to New York, where I was booked for
more theatrical engagements.

With the downfall of Kauffman and Ketchel, all immediately
available contestants for the championship were disposed of. The
demand for a white champion was growing louder every day, and
many promoters were diligently searching for someone to pit
against me. Jim Jeffries, once champion, one of the hugest and
hardest fighters America ever produced, had retired. He had voluntarily relinquished the belt to Marvin Hart, who had been

[1] British-born Victor McLaglen, who boxed in England and later became an
Academy Award-winning screen actor.

whipped by Burns. Therefore it was believed that Jeffries was in reality the champion, and whether or not he did hold that honor, it was declared he was the only logical man to send against me. For a long time he refused to fight me, contending that he was through with the ring, but ultimately friends and the demand of the public prevailed on him and he consented to meet me.

Tex Rickard and Jack Gleason got together and arranged to promote the fight, offering a purse of $101,000. Articles for the encounter were signed between us in Hoboken, February 1, 1910. Immediately upon signing of the articles, Jeffries took advantage of the publicity which the forthcoming fight occasioned and made several profitable theatrical engagements. He was now termed the 'undefeated champion,' notwithstanding that my fight with Burns gave me the recognized official title. This fight attracted more attention than the Burns encounter. There was a strong belief that Jeffries, having never actually been whipped, would regain the title. There was much bitterness preceding the fight and every effort was brought to bear to strengthen Jeffries with the public as well as to condition him for the bout.

For some time I continued my theatrical engagements and on May 15, after another visit with Chicago friends and relatives, I gathered my party and went to San Francisco, where it originally was planned that the fight was to be held. After I arrived on the scene preparatory for my training, the California governor decided that he would not permit the fight. Thus interrupted, Rickard and Gleason sought another location, and after considerable delay selected Reno, Nevada, setting the date for July 4, 1910. When the day of the big fight arrived I was in the best condition of my career. I had trained conscientiously and meant to do my very best. It was likewise announced that Jeffries' condition was perfect.

The ring was built in the outdoors in the center of a natural amphitheater. It probably was the most picturesque fight scene ever staged in the history of boxing. A tremendous crowd was in attendance and there was a suspense that at times was almost unnerving. The fight meant more than any that had ever taken place among heavyweights. My staunch and eager friends were numerous but there was a bitterness against me that probably was more manifest than upon any other occasion. Rumors had come to me that there actually was talk of a chance shot at me if I whipped Jeffries. It was hinted that gunmen had been hidden in the crowd and that if my boxing opponent did not dispose of me a bullet would. I took little stock in this. I could not imagine any sportsman sunken to such depths, yet such rumors served to indicate the hostilities that existed. When the fight began and as it continued I was jeered by my enemies and cheered by my friends. The taunts I received were calculated to disturb my poise. But these efforts failed. A red hot sun poured down upon our heads. The great crowd was burning to a crisp. One can easily imagine what gruelling it was for us battling in the ring. However, despite the sun and the jeering mob and the occasional thought that there might be a gunman somewhere in that vast array of humanity, I do not recall that I was greatly disturbed. 'The golden smile'[2] for which I have become famous, I am told, never deserted me, and there was no reason why it should have. Jeffries at no time made the going very difficult for me, and in the fifteenth round I knocked him out. Whatever possible doubt may have existed and did exist as to my claim to the championship was wiped out. I had again demonstrated the material of which I was made and I had conclusively vanquished one of the world's greatest boxers. In the gathering of spectators who saw the encounter was another huge group of newspaper writers and photographers, and round about us telegraph instruments clicked off a description of the fight blow by blow. I recall that occasionally I took time during the exchange of these blows to suggest to telegraph operators what to tell their newspapers.

Notwithstanding the long years I had been boxing and the numerous fights I had been engaged in, the Jeffries fight brought me the only real money I had ever made out of my profession comparing the purses of those days. I got 60 per cent of the purse, or about $60,000. A bonus of $10,000 was given me and the picture rights netted me another $50,000 or about $120,000[3] in all. After this fight I believed that the bitterness which had actuated some of those interested in boxing had subsided. Some of my greatest enemies were silenced and many who had been almost venomous toward me grew a little more restrained. None could deny that I had fought persistently and conscientiously. I had won all I had

---

[2] Jack London, famed American novelist, ended a report on the Burns – Johnson fight by goading Jeffries to come out of retirement and 'wipe the golden smile' from Johnson's face, Jack having several of his teeth stopped with gold.

[3] About £24,000 in those days.

attained by sheer hard training, fighting and confidence in myself. Back of that confidence was the faith of my friends and the belief in me of my mother who, when told of both my victories – that in Australia and Reno – expressed no surprise. She said she knew that I would win.

More theatrical contracts and long tours over the United States and Canada followed the Reno fight. And with these engagements completed, I determined to take a rest, which took the form of a trip to Europe. With me on this trip went Bob Armstrong, Kid Cutler, my wife, formerly Etta Duryea, my nephew Gus Rhodes, and my chauffeur. While I intended that this trip should be for nothing but rest and pleasure I found that my popularity in Paris and London had increased to such an extent that there were insistent demands for my public appearances, and much against my will I appeared in several music halls and theaters in both capitals in boxing demonstrations.

While I was in London on this occasion, the coronation of King George V was in progress. London was jammed with the throngs that had come from all over the United Kingdom and nearly every country in the world. Despite the fact that the King and his coronation were the center of attention, when my car traveled along London streets and it was announced that I was in sight, the attention of the crowds was turned upon me, and as long as I was in view the coronation ceremonies were forgotten while crowds milled and struggled for a glance at me.

My visits in France and the United Kingdom were attended by an expression of public interest that almost overwhelmed me. I was the guest of honor at many celebrations indoor and out. A strong movement to arrange a fight for me in England was started and Bombadier Wells was tentatively selected as my opponent. He was willing enough to meet me, showing an admirable gameness, but it eventually was decided that he would in no wise be a match for me and negotiations for the fight were called off.[4] Shortly after this, my party and myself set sail for home, arriving in the early part of January, 1912.

We returned to Chicago where I appeared in a series of theatrical engagements and other minor affairs. The field seemed to be

[4] This is not strictly true. The proposed match with the British champion, due to take place at Earl's Court, London on October 2, 1911, was stopped by the Home Secretary after widespread objections led by the Reverend F. B. Meyer.

entirely devoid of any contestants in the heavy-weight division.
The cry for a 'white hope' had subsided somewhat, though the
hunt for such an antagonist had never ceased. Finding myself without ring opponents, I decided to open a cabaret and began completing my plans for the venture. As they proceeded, Jack Curley
suggested a contest with Jim Flynn, whom I had met in 1907 in San
Francisco and knocked out in eleven rounds.

Flynn was a fighter of more than average ability. In my previous
fight with him, I had recognized his high-class boxing talent. Since
my defeat of Jeffries, Flynn had been doing considerable boxing
and met some of the best of them. I felt that a contest between him
and myself would prove an attractive one, and, furthermore, if he
had championship timber in him I for one was as eager to find it
out as any. The fight was arranged to take place in Las Vegas, New
Mexico, July 4, 1912. Pending the fight and my training necessary
for the event, I turned the plans for my cabaret over to others, and
again signed more theatrical contracts which kept me on tours up
until the time for me to go into training. I established my camp at
Las Vegas, having in my party as sparring partners and other assist-
ants Calvin Respress, Watson Burns, Monte Cutler and George
DeBray. During my training period Harry Wills appeared on the
scene, seeking a place as sparring partner. I engaged him, but he
remained only a few days. He proved wholly unable to stand the
grind and was compelled to acknowledge that the ordeal was too
much for him. He returned to New Orleans. The Flynn fight
proved an easy victory for me and it also was the last I was to have
on American soil for many years.

After the fight I returned to Chicago in readiness to open my
Cabaret de Champion. During my absence at Las Vegas, its equipment, decorations and furnishings had been in competent hands
and shortly after I arrived the opening took place. It was one of the
most spectacular affairs ever held in Chicago, and I doubt if a similar event has ever taken place anywhere in the world. Friends came
from all over the world to take part in the launching of the enterprise and when the initial opening of the doors took place, thousands of people struggled to gain entrance, and for hours afterward
were lined up for many blocks, awaiting an opportunity to get
within.

In the furnishing and decoration of the cabaret, I had spared no
expense nor effort. Having traveled extensively, I had gained a

comprehensive idea of decorative effects; I had viewed some of the most notable amusement centers of the world, both as to their exterior and interior arrangements. I also had collected many fine works of art, curios and novelties. These I used in providing the attractive features for which my cabaret gained considerable distinction. In addition, I had engaged artists and decorators of undisputed talents, whose ideas, combined with my own, resulted in an array of artistic creations which put to shame many similar establishments in both Europe and America — establishments which have attained world-wide prominence. In the art collection were paintings of myself and wife by a portrait artist who was rated as one of America's best. Other paintings were of my father and mother. I displayed a few real Rembrandts which I had obtained in Europe. Adorning the walls were original paintings representing Biblical and sacred history scenes. Another painting was of Cleopatra. These were only a few of the art subjects which adorned the walls of the Cabaret de Champion. There were numerous others, in all, the collection having represented a small fortune.

Other furnishings of the cabaret were on a similar plan. Only the very best of material had gone into the equipment. The bar tables and other pieces of furniture were of solid mahogany. Much of the woodwork, besides being of first class material, had been further improved by carving and polishing. The appearance of the interior was neither gaudy nor vulgar. I had striven to make it distinctive and attractive but also had combined with it real beauty and dignity. Another feature, and one which aroused much comment, and for which my cabaret was well known, was the silver cuspidors, decorated in gold. The opening night, as I have said, brought thousands, and it goes without saying that the occasion was a memorable one in Chicago. The celebration was one which will long be remembered. The receipts that night were enormous. Money flowed plentifully and everyone enjoyed himself to the fullest extent. Throughout the entire existence of the cabaret it was successful financially and otherwise, and I sought at all times to conduct it, not only in accordance with the law, but with as good taste and as strictly as a business of that kind can be conducted. Naturally it attracted classes of people desiring lively times. All sorts of patrons came within its doors and there were those, of course, who would have caused difficulties wherever they went. Some of these frequently came to the Cabaret de Champion. Their conduct caused criticism, and this, in conjunction with the effort that was being exerted to put me in a bad light before the public, was seized upon to further my downfall. Prejudice also played a part, for in my cabaret the races had an opportunity to come in contact, a practice which in those days was not as well established as it is now. Unfounded rumors were afloat about my establishment which were easy to believe but hard to disprove. During my operation of the cabaret I did not attempt to fill any ring engagements. I was content to remain out of the spotlight of the ring and to give my attention to my business. Meanwhile there was a continual flow of criticism and condemnation and the insistent cry for the 'white hope,' was heard. I was perfectly willing that they should find a candidate, but I took no part in the discussion. When the tragic death of my wife took place I closed the cabaret and began directing my efforts in other channels. Naturally I gave considerable thought to future ring activities, but I had determined that I should conduct myself and my affairs in as quiet a manner as possible. I was tired of the public's consuming interest in me. However, the efforts of my enemies had not been lessened and when Miss Cameron's[5] association with me, of which I shall speak presently, presented the opportunity it did, they seized upon it with obvious eagerness. It turned out that instead of reaching a period of peace and quietness in life, I was in reality entering upon adventures that were to be more productive of public discussion and to embroil me in more adventurous exploits than ever yet had marked my life.

As recounted elsewhere, I was accused of violating statutory provisions and tried in the United States court. These accusations, my resistance to them, my trial and fight for my rights, occupied my attention for several months to the exclusion of either ring activities or other business affairs. During this time friends from many parts of the country rallied to my support and sought to aid me in the move to escape the unjust drive that was made upon me. The effort was unavailing, and in the desperation that followed I fled to Europe.

[5] Lucille Cameron (white), who became Johnson's third wife.

5
Romances and Regrets

There have been countless women in my life. They have participated in my triumphs and suffered with me in my moments of disappointment. They have inspired me to attainment and they have
balked me; they have caused me joy and they have heaped misery
upon me; they have been faithful to the utmost and they have been
faithless; they have praised and loved me and they have hated and
denounced me. Always, a woman has swayed me – sometimes
many have demanded my attention at the same moment.

Despite the rather devious and uncertain path I followed as a
youth, my mother's splendid influence and love was never forgotten by me. I always loved her with the deepest affection. She
would of course have had me select a different course in life from
the one I did, but when that course was once selected and she
realized that I was determined to follow it, because I believed it
would lead to the success I desired, she stood back of me; she never
wavered; she urged me to do my best. When others failed me she
was my staunchest support; if others doubted me her faith grew the
firmer. A good many reasons have been given as to why I attained
a high place in the boxing world, but too little credit has been
given to Tiny Johnson – my mother. It was she of whom I was
thinking when I fled from Chicago to escape a prison term, and
had she not expressed the wish that I should die rather than to
become hemmed in by the stone and steel of prison walls and gates,
it is probable that I would never have taken the desperate measures
which I did. It was she of whom I thought when I wandered as an

exile in foreign lands, and the longing to see her determined me to toss my freedom and my laurels as a boxer aside if necessary, to return to my native land. But she died before I could negotiate the return and while I was in distant lands, helpless to reach her, one of her last wishes was that she might see me. That was tragedy too, and a cause of heartache that has never left me.

I have three sisters, Lucy, Janie and Fannie and one brother, Henry. They have never figured publicly or prominently in my life. Lucy I must thank for propelling me into a youthful fistic encounter and making me fight when I was on the point of fleeing. Perhaps if I had never entered that particular fight I would not have learned that I really possessed fighting ability. It certainly instilled within me a courage that I never had previously experienced. I might say, therefore, that Lucy's determination on that occasion and the encouragement my mother gave me in after years were two very strong factors in pushing me to success.

As I approached manhood, it was the wish of my parents that I should marry, and in order to fulfil their desires, they went so far as to select the woman who was to become my wife. She was a young colored girl of excellent qualities, but I already had been smitten by the charms of another, a Galveston native whom I had long known. She was Mary Austin, and we were married in 1898, when I was twenty years old. Soon afterward I went to Denver and she accompanied me. My fortune in those days was somewhat lean, but we were devoted to each other and we were very happy. It seemed that nothing would ever creep in to spoil our happiness, but it did. It started with a dispute of minor origin in Cripple Creek which caused her to leave me. Soon after, however, we were reconciled and together we went to the coast. But an invisible something gnawed at us which finally resulted in our permanent separation, which took place in Denver, in 1901. Mary was a splendid woman and I recall my life with her as one of the happy periods of my existence.

On my return from the coast following my fights with Kennedy, Jack Jeffries and others which I have recounted, and during my several ring engagements in Philadelphia, two other girls came into my life. They were Etta Reynolds and Clara Kerr. Both were colored girls and during my stay in Philadelphia I enjoyed their companionship and included them in my affairs as sources of great happiness. With Clara Kerr I became greatly infatuated. A deep attachment grew up between us which was to continue our association for a long time. When I returned to Chicago she came with me, and after a brief stay, during which I had some minor ring engagements, we went to California. My boxing engagements on this west coast trip were more successful financially and otherwise, and I was able to set up a splendidly furnished suite of rooms where we lived gaily and happily.

But this happiness was to have a maddening interruption. There had come to the coast a horse trainer with the Cornelius Vanderbilt string. His name was William Bryant, and I had known him in the early days of my New England life. I hailed him as an old and intimate friend and invited him to share our home with us. For a time the arrangement was a mutually satisfactory one, but suddenly just when I was congratulating myself on my success, taking the utmost pleasure in our home and being grateful for the presence of Clara in my life, she and Bryant ran away. Unknown to me, an attachment had developed between the two which resulted in their secret preparations to leave together. They took with them all my clothes, all other personal property of mine which was of any value, and disappeared one night when I was giving my attention to my ring affairs.

I was dumbfounded. For the second time a woman whom I greatly loved had fled from me, but this time the cause, instead of a trifling domestic dispute, was another man. The shock unnerved me. For the first time in my life my faith in friends and humanity had been shaken to the foundation. For a while I debated with myself as to what course I should take. Perhaps I should have let matters go as they were, but the more I thought it over the more I realized how much I esteemed Clara, and I determined that I would not let her get away from me. Having come to this resolve, I set about making inquiries and learned in which direction the couple had fled. Immediately I set out in pursuit. The trail led me to Tucson, Arizona, where I found them. I effected a reconciliation with Clara and we returned to Chicago.

Clara's flight had not only been a blow to my happiness, but it also had checked my earning activities, for I did not feel like returning to Los Angeles after what had happened, and it was there that some excellent opportunities were developing for me. On our return to Chicago our money was low and the boxing business was at a point which offered me few engagements. Consequently we were compelled to live modestly and to guard our savings which were going down rapidly. One day I returned home and found Clara again missing. For a time I refused to believe the truth, but the emptiness of our home and the absence of her trunks and clothing together with what cash I had, convinced me that she had fled from me.

I began a search for her. My infatuation for her had never wavered. Throughout Chicago I wandered, making futile inquiries and eagerly tracing flimsy and useless clews. I could not find her or even learn in what direction she had gone. She had been swallowed up. The world became a void for me and for the first time in my life I succumbed to excessive drinking and other forms of dissipation. But I could not forget her and never for a moment did I cease the search for her. Finally, I became ill and so wretched in mind and body that I determined to leave the scene of my unhappiness and started eastward. I was without funds and was unable to borrow money, which caused me to believe that my friends had utterly deserted me, a frame of mind which, added to the turmoil I was in already, completed my state of discouragement. I made my way to Pittsburgh where I found some alleviation of my despair in the form of friends who realized my worries and unhappiness. They sympathized with me and sought to lift me out of my misery. They were liberal in their loans of money to me, but instead of using it judiciously I cast wisdom to the winds and gambled heavily. As a matter of fact I did not care what end I came to, for the thought of Clara and her disappearance was always uppermost in my mind.

At one period of my gambling activities I had prospered sufficiently to engage a drawing-room to New York, but before the train departed I lost every cent I had. I prepared to board the train penniless. A friend, Frank Sutton, knowing my predicament, insisted on lending me some money, but I refused to take it. Finally I did accept a dollar from him. Of this dollar I gave the train porter 50 cents; I bought two cigars with another quarter and the remaining quarter I tossed to a newsboy at the station when I arrived in New York. I had no plans in mind other than to continue the search for Clara. Somehow, I had a vague idea or hope that she might be in New York and that I would be fortunate enough to find her. I went to a boarding house kept by a woman with whom I was well acquainted and who with other friends in the city were liberal in helping me financially and otherwise to get on my feet. As I said I had no plans, but automatically I came in contact with the boxing and ring contenders and promoters. Fate was kind to me, and hardly without any efforts on my part matches were thrown my way in which I was not only successful in proving my boxing abilities but from which I netted more than $20,000 in less than a month. A few months previously this success would have elated me, but my love for Clara persisted and with it the desire to find her. Whenever opportunity offered I searched in the high and low places of New York for her, but without success. Eventually I gave up the quest and settled down grimly to training and boxing.

Other interests and other women helped to heal the wound Clara had caused, but she had not gone altogether out of my life. Several years afterwards when I was happily married again I was shocked to read in the paper one morning that Clara had been arrested, charged with the murder of her brother. From the paper I learned that she was in prison at Tom's River, N. J., and that she was alone and friendless. I counseled with my wife who was familiar with Clara's presence in my life and together we went to the New Jersey Prison. We found Clara disconsolate in a prison cell. My wife went into the cell with her and did her best to cheer her up. In the meantime, I hunted up the district attorney with whom I discussed Clara's case. I employed lawyers for her and provided her with other funds and aid. She was acquitted of the murder charge and shortly afterward I helped her to acquire a small hotel which she has conducted successfully since.

The next woman who came into my life was Hattie McLay, a New York Irish girl. The heartaches which Mary Austin and Clara Kerr had caused me, led me to forswear colored women and to determine that my lot henceforth would be cast only with white women. At the time I met Hattie I was contemplating a trip to Europe and it was arranged that she should accompany me and aid me in looking after my business interests, which were assuming a more important volume than ever, because I was now determined to reach the Championship and was hot on the trail of Tommy Burns. This trip to Europe was financed by Hattie's father, and not by Sam Fitzpatrick, as most people were led to suppose. Fitzpatrick, while nominally my manager, did not invest much cash in the project and as far as his connection with me was concerned, merely carried out such plans as I made or directed.

Hattie was a splendid pal. She had good business judgment; she understood me, and our association for many months was a happy and prosperous one. She was destined to be with me on the occasions of some of my greatest triumphs in the ring, and to take part in many important and interesting events in my life. She accompanied me around the world on a trip that included every nation of consequence and several lesser countries and remote islands. She was in Sydney with me when I wrested the championship from Burns.

Our separation took place in Chicago and resulted from disputes that arose between us over her constant beer drinking. I remonstrated many times with her because of her penchant for beer which she drank to such excess as to cause me much embarrassment. In order to escape my detection when I sought to prevent her from obtaining beer, she smuggled the beverage into the house whenever opportunity offered, and I frequently found her much the worse for her indulgence and was mystified concerning the manner in which she obtained it. The secret was solved to some extent when one day I found numerous empty bottles hidden under her mattress which attracted my attention because of the bulging appearance of the bed. When my investigation revealed the presence of the many bottles, a final dispute took place and we separated.

About this time Belle Schreiber a Milwaukee girl of German descent attracted my attention and we became very good friends. It was she who was to appear later in my affairs as a factor involving me in legal difficulties, and who was to be an instrument in convicting me of charges which brought a prison sentence and my subsequent flight. However, Belle and I were happy together for a considerable length of time. She accompanied me to San Francisco when I went to fight Stanley Ketchel. This occasion was an embarrassing and disturbing one for me, because Hattie McLay also had gone to San Francisco. She had taken quarters in the same hotel and was intent on effecting a reconciliation with me. She watched the door of my room and sought many times to waylay me in the corridors. Naturally there was a state of warfare between Hattie and Belle which threatened to break out into open and disastrous hostilities any moment. While I was supposed to be complacently training for the Ketchel fight I was in reality in a state of turmoil and constantly was racking my wits to prevent an outbreak be-

tween the two women, and to avoid a scene between myself and
Hattie. To avert this latter undesirable situation I was compelled to
resort to many subterfuges. I slipped in and out of the hotel in a
manner that would have aroused newspaper reporters to much
excited speculation and would have provided many columns of
gossip for the public's amusement, had they known of my maneuvers. My most successful method of leaving and entering my room
was by means of a rope which I let down from a window when I
was leaving, and which on my return was lowered to me when I
signaled. It will be readily understood that I had a double reason
for rejoicing when I had disposed of Ketchel and was ready to
leave San Francisco, which I did with as little delay as possible. We
returned to New York where I resumed my theatrical engagements and where not long afterward Belle and I separated and
another romance came to an end.

After the Ketchel fight, I had quite a period of idleness as far as
the ring was concerned, but was kept busy with my theatrical pro-
jects, having long contracts to fill. Much of my time was required
in New York, and through my theatrical connections I met Etta
Duryea, a Brooklyn girl of French-American extraction. This
meeting resulted in our marriage in Pittsburgh in 1909. She
accompanied me on my theatrical tours in the United States and was
a member of my party which toured Europe, it being my third trip
across the Atlantic. This was primarily a pleasure party, but nevertheless I filled several music hall engagements, on request.

On our return to the United States, there were some more theatrical ventures, and then my fight with Jeffries, in Reno. Immediately after that fight, we returned to Chicago and opened my
cabaret. The next few months were prosperous and happy. I felt
that in Etta I had found a love that would continue uninterrupted,
but in this I was sadly mistaken for it came to a tragic end when
she committed suicide. I knew that she had been despondent, but
attributed her mood to the death of her father which had taken
place a short time before. Her father, a member of an excellent
Brooklyn family, was greatly loved by Etta. There was between
the father and daughter, an extraordinarily close attachment, and
it was to be expected that his death would disturb her. However, I
believed that her sorrow soon would pass and that she would
resume her usual cheerful and happy disposition. Her attitude
toward me had never changed. Our relations up to the last were

joyful and peaceful. She never complained of anything and never gave any intimation that she was weary of life.

On the day that the end came, we had entertained some friends. Etta and I had arranged to accompany them to the train on which they were to leave the city. When the time came for their departure, my wife pleaded a headache, and begged that she be excused from going to the train. Her condition did not alarm me nor excite my suspicion. She said good-bye to our friends cheerfully and promised to meet them later. I went with them to the train and when I returned home, I found the street in front of our apartment filled with crowds of people. Police wagons were drawn up and I experienced a chill that almost numbed me. When I arrived, friends told me to hurry upstairs that something had happened to Etta. Those ominous words gave me the worst fright I had ever had and I sped up the stairs, not knowing but dreading what I was to find. She lay on the floor, her beautiful long hair hiding her face. Near her was a revolver. On one exposed bare arm was a red spot. At the sight of it, I took courage and tried to convince myself that the shot had not been fatal. I gathered her up in my arms, and as I did so her hair fell back, revealing the ugly wound in her head. She died a few hours later.

This tragic event laid me low. It seemed that all I had attained was for naught. I closed the cabaret. I could not bear to think of continuing it, for she had been so significantly identified in planning and conducting it. I sought other channels in which to bury my disappointments and to find solace. For a time life palled on me. In the meantime, the hunt for the 'white hope' went on and there were frequent rumors of possible contenders whom I should have to meet in defense of my title. I let matters drift and made no particular effort to interest myself either in business or in boxing.

Lucille Cameron, a Minnesota girl attending school in Chicago, was the next woman to venture within the circle of my activities. She first was introduced to me by Perry Bauer, and noting that I was distressed over business affairs, offered her services to straighten out my books. I employed her as a business secretary. Her association with me was purely of a business nature and devoid of undue intimacy. However, ugly rumors were in circulation and the public took them up eagerly. Attempts on my part to prove their untruthfulness were unavailing. One morning a newspaper reporter came to my home demanding to see Miss Cameron.

I told him she did not make her home with me and directed him to the home of Jack Curley, where she was living, telling him he would find her there. Instead, he sent a telegram to her mother in Minnesota declaring that Miss Cameron was living with me. The result of this was to bring the mother to Chicago in a wild frame of mind. She came to my house denouncing and accusing me. I denied any improper association with her daughter, and, when she demanded to know where her daughter was, I offered to take her to her home. She accepted, and entered my car for the journey demanding that the curtains of the car be pulled down.

'Madame,' said I, 'everybody in Chicago knows this car. If they were to see it going along the street with the curtains down there would be such gossip and scandal that we would find ourselves in the midst of overwhelming censure. No, for your sake and for mine, I shall not pull these curtains down.'

Mrs. Cameron was eager to see her daughter, and finally consented to ride with me with the curtains up. When we reached the home in which the daughter lived I took Mrs. Cameron in and summoned Miss Cameron.

'Lucille,' I said, 'your mother wishes to talk to you. Whatever she has to say to you will be for your good. Remember that she means more to you than any other person, and that whenever all others have failed you, your mother will stand by you. Whatever she wishes you to do will be for your welfare.'

I left the mother and daughter together and made no effort to see Lucille again. The meeting between the mother and daughter was not satisfactory to the former, for she proceeded to have warrants sworn out for the arrest of both Lucille and myself. I was charged with abduction. Shortly after the arrest I was released on bonds, but Lucille was kept a prisoner in a hotel under the watchfulness of her mother and police. When I was tried on the abduction charge there was no evidence to support it and I was discharged. Countless other efforts were made to charge me with various crimes by Mrs. Cameron and others who were interested in the situation. On one occasion the late Charlie Erbstein, a well-known Chicago attorney employed by Mrs. Cameron, came to my apartment and I was forced to eject him because of his hostile attitude.

The search for the 'white hope' not having been successful, prejudices were being piled up against me, and certain unfair persons, piqued because I was champion, decided that if they could not get me one way they would another, and all sorts of efforts were set in motion to brand me as an undesirable character and to relegate me to obscurity.

In the meantime, Lucille had escaped from the surveillance of her mother and the police and seeking me out begged me to marry her, declaring that she had been ruined in the eyes of the world, but that furthermore her mother was making her the object of abuse and nagging which she could not bear. She said that her home life never had been pleasant because she was held in check and not allowed such freedom as a girl of her age had a right to demand. I told her we could not marry, but that I would help her in every way I could.

She desired to leave Chicago and after thinking the situation over I decided that perhaps it would be best for all concerned if I arranged for her to go to Toronto, Ontario. She stayed but a short time and returning unexpectedly again begged me to marry her. I finally acceded to her wishes and we were married a short time afterward. This, however, did not bring an end to my troubles; they were only just beginning, for within a short time I was arrested on a charge of violating the Mann Act.[1]

My enemies, actuated by jealousies and prejudices had never ceased their activities. When they could find nothing involving me improperly with Miss Cameron, nor anything else in my record with which they could effect my downfall, they hit on an old trail, and learning of my association with Belle Schreiber, hunted her down. She was brought from Washington and set up as the accusing witness against me. Other withnesses were found willing to testify against me and so the case went to trial.

It was a rank frame-up. The charges were based upon a law that was not in effect at the time Belle and I had been together, and legally was not operative against me. The whole accusation was unfounded and I do not hesitate to say that fraudulent practices were adopted, so bitter and intense was the fight that had been opened up on me. I was sentenced to one year and a day in the penitentiary and fined $1,000. I appealed the case and the decision was reversed, but not until after I had taken flight and was beyond the reach of federal officials.

I am not one to defeat the ends of justice. Had I been guilty of the

[1] A law intended to combat 'white slave' traffic within the U.S., the Act prohibited the interstate transportation of women for imoral purposes.

charge which was hung over me, I would have taken my medicine and said no more about it, but I was stung by the injustice of the whole proceedings and hurt to the quick to think that the prejudices of my fellowmen and of my own countrymen, at that, could be so warped and so cruel. I went low in spirits. I was watched by a score of detectives, who, it appeared, believed that I was going to try an escape. At the first I had no intention of doing so, but it was maddening to be shadowed all the time. My car and my house were watched day and night. Every step I took was dogged. I was haunted every minute of my life and I must admit that it got on my nerves.

On one occasion my wife and I attempted to take a short vacation trip. Both of us were worn and worried. We went to Battle Creek, Michigan, and when the train reached the station in that city it was boarded by federal agents, and pounding at my state room door they demanded admittance. I told them that they could not come in — that Mrs. Johnson and I were not dressed. They insisted on entrance and for a moment I thought they were going to smash the door in. They waited, however, and donning our clothes we went out to meet them. They arrested me as a fugitive. They took me to the police station and the next day returned me to Chicago.

This incident increased the persecution from which I was suffering, and the desire to get away from it was born. I wished not only to throw the constant shadowing off my trail, but I wished also to put myself beyond the reach of the adverse publicity I was receiving. My character and life were being torn to pieces in the newspapers. Every day, on some pretext or another, my name was paraded before the public in glaring headlines. It was sickening — far worse than the prospect of the year in prison that awaited me.

To my mother, though, the prison was the principal source of worry; she was cut to the quick by the thought that I must enter prison, because after the manner in which I had been treated by my prosecutors, there was little reason to hope that the appeal would attain what I wished. I was harassed by the sight of my worrying mother as well as by the unhappiness of my wife and the shadowing of secret agents. My mother told me that she would rather that I die than that I go to prison. It was she who had furnished the bonds upon which I was at liberty. One night I told her I had planned a way of escape, but that if I departed I probably would never see her again, because it would mean exile for me from my native land. If I had hesitated previously in planning an escape or in carrying it out, all hesitancy came to an end when my mother begged me to go, declaring that she would prefer never seeing me again to having me spend a year in prison.

Friends, to whom I confided my intention of escaping, said that it was impossible. Some of them were alarmed over my determination to undertake the project. As I told them of my plans in part, I was within the sight, if not the hearing of secret service men. There was never a moment that they were not within reach of me. They hung close about my home and followed me every step through the streets, every time my car turned a wheel they were aware of it. To elude them did seem an impossible feat; yet I did.

There was in Chicago at that time a colored baseball team called Foster's Giants. I learned that the team had arranged for a game in New York City, and sending for the manager offered him and his team the use of a private car for which I would pay all the expenses to New York providing he would let me route the car. I did not tell him my purpose nor did he know that I was about to launch a daring move to throw off my shadowers and quit the United States. He accepted my offer with much expression of thanks.

Arrangements were made for the car, it was routed by way of Buffalo via New London. The ball team was composed of strapping big players, many of them as large as myself. One of the players resembled me in stature and features and to him I gave my watch and ring, the latter having more than once served as an identification of me, and being familiar to police and others when they gave my description. This was one of the ruses hit upon to serve in the event that officers, having got wind of my departure, boarded the train en route in search of me. The player resembling me, we believed, would be seized permitting me to continue my trip while he, as soon as the mistake had been discovered, would be released.

The ball team, Gus Rhodes, my nephew acting as my secretary and I, boarded the special car which had been arranged at Englewood Station. As the train pulled in, we stood in the shadows and when it stopped I, carrying a bag of bats and other baseball equipment, rushed with the rest to the car. The train immediately pulled out and I went to bed in the drawing room which I had reserved. The train sped on through the night; my flight had started, but how it was to terminate was a matter of conjecture. We were compelled to exercise the utmost caution. I was not disturbed until we crossed the Canadian border. At that point Canadian government officials came on board the train to inspect the baggage. All our baggage was placed outside the drawing-room and Rhodes stood by with the tickets informing the inspectors that the occupant of the room was ill and could not be disturbed. The explanation was satisfactory and they left the train.

At Hamilton, Ontario, we left the train on the blind side, Tom Flannigan, an old friend of mine, who had seen nearly all of my important fights, and who had attended every championship fight that took place during his life time, met us with an automobile and drove us to Toronto where Flannigan conducted a hotel. We arrived about four o'clock in the afternoon July 1, 1913, and Flannigan provided us with some cheese and ham sandwiches and a half dozen bottles of beer, a lunch after our all-day ride which I felt was the best I had ever eaten.

At Toronto I met my wife, who had left Chicago on a different train. We stayed in Toronto until late in the evening and then boarded another train for Montreal. We were on our way again. Neither I, nor anyone of my party, was recognized on the train until we arrived at Montreal, when a porter got a peep at me and soon broadcasted my presence in the city. That evening we were besieged by reporters and immigration officials. I gave a signed interview to the Montreal Star explaining the reasons for my trip. United States officials requested Montreal police to detain me as a fugitive, but upon it being shown that I had tickets good for passage from Chicago to Paris, France, and these placing us on bonds, as they did, Canadian officials could not hold me and, under the law, could do nothing but permit me to continue on my way.

We embarked at Montreal on the steamship Corinthia and arrived in Paris, July 10, 1913. We took up our quarters in the Hotel Grand in the Rue de St. Lazare where we remained for some time. When we arrived in the French port, a vast assembly of people awaited my arrival, among them numerous gendarmes, French police. When I saw them lined up intently watching the docking of our ship, I had a momentary feeling that my flight was to end disastrously, for I feared that some method had been devised which would enable my detention and I was hesitant about landing. But when I was informed that the gendarmes merely were a part of the crowd intent on giving me a warm welcome I experienced that well known grand and glorious feeling. Our reception at Paris was one of the most enthusiastic welcomes ever accorded me.

6
Exile

Immediately upon my arrival in Paris, I was offered several engagements in theaters and music halls. Managers besought me on every hand, each trying to outdo the other in offering me inducements. I decided upon a short engagement at the Folies Bergère, where, as long as I remained, crowded houses greeted me at every performance. London music halls, too, were seeking contracts with me, and concluding my first contract in Paris, I went to London and played for several weeks, bringing my appearances there to a close when amusement promoters signed me up for a long contract which called for my appearance at the leading amusement houses in nearly all the capitals of Europe. The tour lasted several months, during which time I put on boxing exhibitions and other entertainments in Paris, Marseilles, Brussels, Berlin, Vienna, Budapest, Bukharest, St. Petersburg, Moscow, and others of the larger cities of the old world. Upon my appearance in each of these cities, I was given a tremendous reception, large crowds meeting me at the stations on my initial arrival and filling the halls and theaters whenever I appeared. Ending the tour in Vienna, I returned with my party to Paris where negotiations had been under way for a match with Jim Johnson, an American heavyweight.

The fight took place in Paris, October 19, 1913. My opponent was a game fighter, and in the contest I, too, was called upon to withstand one of the severest ring ordeals of my career, for in the third round my left arm was broken and I finished the fight with one arm, the broken one dangling helplessly at my side. However, I won the decision in the tenth round. The injuries I received in this battle made it necessary for me to devote considerable time to recuperation. With my arm broken there was little I could do in either stage or ring work, but I was not idle. My friends and I took advantage of the interruption to engage in sightseeing and touring which took us to most of the places of historic interest in France, and we enjoyed the experience hugely. I visited all the principal art galleries, nosed in and out of the quaint and picturesque quarters of Paris, made the acquaintance of many artists, writers and theatrical folk, and incidentally picked up some art works and curios which I added to my collection later.

When I was again able to engage in the strenuous work of boxing in stage exhibitions, I returned to London, where I had a long and successful music hall engagement which I closed upon the signing of articles for my fight with Frank Moran, which took place in Paris the night of the Grand Prix, June 20, 1914. Because of the fact that my camp for training purposes was an outdoor one and the prevalence of exceedingly unpleasant and wet weather, I was unable to do much training and I entered the fight almost wholly unconditioned. Nevertheless members of my party and other fight authorities who had seen me in previous matches declared this was one of my greatest fights. Moran fought splendidly and I shall always remember it as an event of more than passing importance in my ring activities. We fought twenty rounds and I was given the decision.

After this fight there was considerable talk on the continent and in England of a fight between Sam Langford and me, either in London or Paris. This was a match that I should greatly have liked to see arranged. I had boxed Langford previously in America and had won over him in fifteen rounds. I had reason to believe, though, that the European fight would have been an interesting one, but it never came to a conclusion, owing to the lack of a promoter with sufficient finances.

On the failure of the Langford fight to take place, I resumed my theatrical appearances and had another successful London season at the end of which I decided to take my party to Moscow, establish headquarters and from that point tour Russia or such parts of it as offered encouragement for my exhibitions, or appealed to members of my party and myself for sight-seeing and touring.

On our way to Russia we encountered many troops. The movement of army detachments was a surprise to us. The trains were
crowded with soldiers, and wherever we looked we saw cavalry,
infantry and other units evidently under marching orders. There
had been rumors of war in France and England for several weeks,
but to these neither we nor others paid much attention. There
seemed nothing serious about it. As we saw masses of soldiers
moving in Russia, we recalled that while in France, during my
training for the Moran fight we had seen troops maneuvering
along the highways, but we did not give them more than a passing
thought, merely supposing that it was a part of the regular routine
of French military activity. In Berlin, several months before, we
were impressed with the dominance of military life but thought it
nothing more than a part of the German system of which we had
heard much. There had been no thought of war such as was soon to
prove so disastrous, and change the geography of the world, but
we were becoming more and more astounded at the hordes of
soldiers about us, and I told my associates one day, when I saw
large bodies of troops training early in the morning, that war was
brewing and that the whole of Europe would be under powder
smoke before long.

My predictions were fulfilled sooner than I had expected. It was
the first of July, 1914, when we arrived in Moscow. I had been
negotiating several theatrical engagements and was awaiting the
arrangement of dates when war was declared. This put an end to
amusement activities in all the countries concerned, and we found
ourselves not only beset on all sides by war preparations but very
intimately concerned in Russia's side of it, a situation having developed which brought me in close contact with high Russian officials
and agents. There lived in Moscow a colored man named George
Thomas. He was a native of Georgia and when a young man had
left the States to seek his fortune. He became a valet and when still
a youth arrived in St. Petersburg, now known as Leningrad.
Thomas engaged in amusement enterprises throughout Russia and
amassed a fortune. On our arrival, he was the owner of a huge
amusement park known as the Aquarium. It was a veritable city, a
city within a city; in it, besides its numerous amusement establishments and exhibitions were residences, hotels, cafés, restaurants
and other facilities.

Thomas and myself became close friends and we made our headquarters in his park. As the war approached, our host became engrossed in Russian war preparations, for he was a factor of some importance in Russian political and commercial circles. He was a confidential agent of Czar Nicholas, and I was greatly surprised to learn that he was taking part in military councils and other phases of the war preparations. High military officers made their headquarters at hotels and restaurants in his park and it was while I, members of my party, and several army officers were dining together in one of these restaurants that we learned that war had become a reality. As we sat at the table some of my military friends were summoned to the telephone, told that war had been declared, and instructed immediately to join their units for hurried mobilization.

The country was in an uproar at once; the streets were filled with seething masses of civilians and soldiers. It seemed that every public place had been turned instantly into some kind of a military establishment. Telegraph and telephone messages were coming and going on every hand. Thomas, though not a military officer, was in the thick of it. He had been in Russia more than twenty years, and in that time had attained considerable power and authority. He confided much to me, and there probably were few foreign citizens in Russia who knew more of the inner workings of the military and political activities of Russia, during this period, than I. Thomas showed me many messages, some of which had been sent by the czar himself, which astounded me. Of a few of these messages I obtained possession, but they later were lost in the confusion that ensued. The contents of some of these would have made interesting and valuable data for historians or students engaged in analyzing the causes, factors and influences in the war, for they were personal exchanges between Czar Nicholas and the Kaiser, in which were discussed Russia's decision as to the part she would take in the conflict, the Kaiser urging the Czar to join with him in what he hinted would be a triumph which would enable Germany and Russia to rule the world. There were other messages concerning plans, attacks, defense measures and secret agreements, all pulsating with information, which, I realized afterward, were dangerous for a foreigner to possess.

Since theatrical engagements were out of the question with the great war launched, I concluded that Russia was no place for us, and that unless we got out immediately we might never be able to leave. The arrangement of transportation was no easy matter. Every device for travel had been seized for the conveying of troops. Furthermore, everyone was under suspicion and we had to give a strict account of ourselves. But for the aid of Thomas my party might have been prevented from leaving, and had that been the case we probably would have lost our lives, for vague information reaching me concerning Thomas was to the effect that because of his nearness to the Czar, he had to leave the country when the revolution came. He is now living in Constantinople.

We finally succeeded in starting the return journey to our home in Paris. We caught the last train to the border. At Warsaw we changed trains, which consumed much time. When we were finally placed in our compartment, I saw from the window huge piles of baggage, the loading of which apparently delayed our train. I therefore expressed the wish that they leave the baggage where it was and give their attention to moving the train. My wish was completely gratified for as we pulled out of the station I saw a truck-load of my own and my associates' baggage left behind on the platform. I regretted my wish and made frantic efforts to induce trainmen to stop long enough for our belongings, but there was no inducement I could offer which would move them to get the property, and on further investigation I found that instead of one truck being left we had lost three truck-loads.

On our arrival in Berlin, we found the city in turmoil and thousands of soldiers marching to the front. Excitement was intense. Vast crowds jammed the streets and it was almost impossible to make our way through them. We reached a hotel where we had arranged to have lunch, and here our party became somewhat embroiled in the war fever that was raging. In my party was a young Frenchman whom I had employed in my theater work. Recognizing his nationality, German waiters in our hotel began to taunt him. They told him that President Poincaré had been captured and was being held prisoner by the Germans. This enraged the Frenchman who shouted curses on the German waiters and hurled all sorts of epithets at them, causing a scene that for a moment threatened to involve us all in a miniature battle in the dining room. I managed to quiet the Frenchman and to make such explanations as would permit us to leave the dining room, and we hurried to our train.

Because of the rapid and heavy movement of troops and the eagerness of thousands of aliens to leave the country, trains were loaded with humanity. People crowded the aisles and packed themselves into every available space, some even hanging on at the risk of their lives outside the trains. Travel was in confusion; it was a nerve-racking undertaking. When we reached the Belgian border, we had to leave the train and complete the journey on foot to the first Belgian railway station. As diplomatic relations had been severed, no German trains were allowed to touch Belgian soil.

We did not remain long in Belgium, but went directly to Paris where conditions were not much better. In Paris, we stopped only a few days. The whole attention and effort of the nation was turned upon the war, and, as the German troops advanced, the fear of invasion grew daily. Non-citizens, such as constituted my party, were in an embarrassing situation. There was no part which we could take in the war and little that we could do for ourselves. Facing these circumstances we disposed of our Paris household equipment and went to London. Here, too, was the war shadow, and every resource was being turned to the combat. But we were among English speaking people, and there was more calmness than in any of the countries we just had left. England was attempting to maintain amusements for her people and some of the music halls were open. I was invited to take another engagement in public entertainment, and did so, but gave it up on the arrival in London of Jack Curley, who came with a contract for me to sign providing for the meeting of Willard and myself in Juarez, Mexico, in a ring contest for my heavy-weight title.

Upon the signing of the contract I began preparations for the trip to Juarez. Gus Rhodes, my nephew, made a rather perilous and difficult trip back to Warsaw to obtain the baggage which we had been compelled to leave, and was successful in his mission. Despite the fact that our baggage had been retained for several months in the Russian station, Rhodes regained the entire collection, the only thing missing being a pair of shoes. In possession of our baggage again we settled up our affairs in Paris and London and started back across the Atlantic, our destination being Buenos Aires, where we landed in December, 1914.

The South American city gave me a rousing welcome and I was an object of much concern on the part of the people, all of whom treated me with the utmost kindness. I was immediately urged to fill some theatrical dates, and appeared in exhibitions in the capital and surrounding communities. In the meantime I engaged in an impromptu boxing match with Jack Murray, an American, who was traveling in South American countries meeting all comers. I made no preparations for the fight but succeeded in stopping Murray in three rounds. During my stay in Buenos Aires, I renewed acquaintanceship with Tex Rickard who had promoted my fight with Jeffries in 1910. He had temporarily retired from the promotion business and was engaged in raising cattle. Another American, Glen Cummings, joined my party in Buenos Aires. He was a young man of polished manners, highly educated and evidently from excellent family. He insisted on accompanying me, declaring that he had much money and was engaged in touring merely for pastime.

In the latter part of January, 1915, we obtained passage on a boat bound for the Barbados islands. It was not a passenger boat, being principally engaged in freight service, and I and my party, together with a few others, were the only ones on the boat excepting the crew. The trip was a wonderful experience and was enjoyed by all of us to the greatest extent, even though our engine broke down while we were on the ocean and we were confronted with the possibility of being cast adrift. Several days were passed without making any headway while the engine was being repaired and we took advantage of the delay to catch man-eating sharks which swarmed about our boat, many of which we hauled aboard. We eventually reached the Barbados none the worse for our experience with the disabled engine. We spent several days sightseeing and taking delight in the new scenes and customs with which we came in contact. In the meantime I was attempting to arrange passage to Havana, Cuba, but since there were not many passenger boats in service from the islands, and the fear of submarines and other ocean dangers created by the world-war caused most boats to hover near their home ports, it was difficult to find a way to make the trip. I negotiated with several owners of boats, the result on one occasion being a damage suit against me by one with whom I had had a misunderstanding of terms. In his suit he demanded a huge sum of money, evidently thinking me a man of large means and so eager to proceed on my way that I would pay without much resistance. But he was mistaken. I found that there were not

many lawyers available – none at least whom I wished to act for
me, so I went into court as my own attorney and surprised the
judge and myself with my understanding of English law. I was
able to hold my own against the lawyers prosecuting the suit
against me, and on one or two points demonstrated that they were
sadly lacking in their knowledge of the law. I won the suit and
proceeded to charter the 'Henry Craig,' a small three-masted sailing affair, the owner of which I finally induced to brave the submarines and attempt to land us in Havana. When we left the
Barbados a great farewell celebration was given in our honor. As
our small craft left port, large crowds headed by leading personages of the port shouted adieus to us, and a band, which had played
on the wharf as we prepared to embark, entered another boat and
followed us several miles out to sea, playing all the way.

Our journey to Havana was a stormy one. We had been at sea
only a day or so when we were caught in one of the fierce storms
for which the Barbados region is noted. The gale swept us hard,
and it seemed that our small boat would be demolished. Besides
ourselves, there was not much of a crew aboard, there being only
the captain, a boatswain, two colored deck hands, one able seaman
and a Chinese cook. This crew had all it could do to keep the vessel
afloat. Not only did we run into the teeth of one gale during the
week, but several pounded down upon us, and there were several
moments when we were certain that we were going to perish.

We battled the gale along the Havana coast for two days before
we were able to make a landing. However, on February 15, we
got into port, all of us thankful that we had escaped the death that
seemed so certain. Cummings, the young American whom I had
brought with me from Buenos Aires, accompanied us to Havana,
but not until after he had involved us in some unpleasantness at the
Barbados port, where he claimed that he had been robbed of a
large sum of money by hotel employees. I made an effort to recover his money for him, but investigation proved that he had never
had any money and that he was merely misrepresenting his financial connections. The manner in which he had duped me made me
exceedingly angry, but there was nothing for me to do but bring
him with me to Havana, for had I left him among the Barbados
people, whom he had wrongfully accused, he would have paid
dearly for his deception. As it was, I had a difficult time in saving
him from their wrath.

Shortly before I left Buenos Aires, I had received information which made it necessary for me to balk on fighting Willard in Juarez. The proposed fight, while engineered by Jack Curley was being financed by Pancho Villa, the bandit leader who at that time had things much his own way in northern Mexico. Carranza, who was president of the republic, was, of course, not in sympathy with any move fostered by the revolutionary leader and he let it be known that he would stop the fight if he could. He had the means of stopping it, too, because I could not get into Mexico except by way of Vera Cruz. To have attempted entrance by any other port would have meant my capture and return to the United States, where the prison term awaited me. Carranza declared that if I attempted to land at Vera Cruz, he would make me a prisoner and turn me over to the United States. Confronted by this situation, I got in touch with Curley, who was at Juarez, and suggested that he arrange to have the fight at Havana. This change did not meet with Villa's endorsement and he withdrew his financial support. This, however, interrupted arrangements only temporarily. Frazee and Webber, well known American theatrical men were quite willing to take over the project, and in a short time all preparations for the fight were made and April 15, 1915, set as the date.

I started training, but facilities for my preliminary work were lacking and there were many other circumstances that prevented me from getting into first-class condition. On the day of the fight, my condition was fair and I could have defeated Willard and retained the title, but temptation had come to me and as I was stirred by the irresistible desire to see my mother, I was trying to decide upon a course that would enable me to return to the United States. I still was hesitant about entering prison, but at times had decided that I would return and serve my sentence for the sake of seeing my mother, but never got quite to that point. While I was in Europe I received word that my appeal from the judgment of the trial court had been successful. Although I was granted a new trial, I had put myself, by virtue of my flight, into the position of a fugitive from justice. Since I was absent from the country when the new trial was granted my original conviction stood and my bonds of $15,000 were forfeited. Preceding the Willard fight it was hinted to me in terms which I could not mistake, that if I permitted Willard to win, which would give him the title, much of the prejudice against me would be wiped out. Those who chafed under the disappointment of having a man of my race hold the championship, I was told, would be mollified, and it would be easier to have the charges against me dropped, and I could again be with my folks.

It was no easy decision. It meant the sacrifice of my heavyweight title which I had striven years to attain, and which had brought me so much; it would brand me as a quitter and as unsportsmanlike and would, I knew, relegate me to an undesirable position in sport circles. On the other hand, there was held out the hope of returning home to those who were dear to me, and the possibility of finding leniency on the part of federal officials. There was the chance that I would not be imprisoned; that there would be no further prosecution of me, and that I might settle down quietly and live in peace with my fellow-men.

As I trained for the fight, these thoughts were uppermost in my mind. Day after day I reviewed the situation and the future possibilities. I did not cherish the championship title so much that I was willing to sacrifice the companionship of my mother nor peace and contentment and an opportunity to live in the country I loved so much, even though I had fled from it. Yet, if I gave up the title, I would be assailed as unscrupulous. My mind was in a turmoil. It was necessary for me of course to use some mental energy in my clash with Willard. From all sides of the ring I was being jeered and taunted, and I could not refrain from flinging back hot replies that seethed up in my disturbed mind. However, in spite of this mental struggle, I felt all the way through that I was mastering Willard. I could have disposed of him long before the final round.

Willard was declared the new champion. I came out of the ring officially the loser, but not suffering the disappointment of defeat, because I believed that I had done that which would enable me to return home and with the prejudices against me somewhat removed. My future would be devoid of the antagonism that constantly arose over my holding the championship title. As matters turned out, I had cause to regret my action, for after I had permitted the title to pass to Willard, I found that such offers or hints of leniency as had been tendered me were without substantial foundation, and that immediate prospects for my return to my own country without going to prison were so slight that I could not give them serious thought.

This realization brought upon me bitter disappointment, more intense than if I had lost the championship at the hands of a man who was my superior. The sacrifice I had made was of no avail. I could not return home and the high hopes that I had entertained at the thought of soon seeing my mother, vanished. I still was to be a wanderer and hunt my haven in a foreign country. I remained a short time in Cuba after the fight, and then began arrangement of my affairs in order to permit my return to England. In the mean-time, Rhodes, my secretary, and all members of my party who had traveled with me from Europe to Buenos Aires and Havana, with the exception of Mrs. Johnson returned to their American homes.

This was a heart-breaking experience for me and for a while I was in exceedingly low spirits. I had many friends in Cuba and they remained steadfastly by me in these disappointing hours. Having failed in their efforts to aid me in returning home, they united their efforts to promote my welfare and make my life more pleasant. Among these friends was General Mario Menocal, who was then president of Cuba and who had taken great interest in me and the fight. He had visited me in my training quarters, and after the contest renewed his friendship by showering me with many kindnesses and courtesies. His children and I had become great friends and to them I gave the medicine ball which had been part of my training equipment.

From Havana Mrs. Johnson and I returned to London and I gave my attention to the organization of a musical review, which I designated 'Seconds Out'. I engaged the best stage talent available in London, and after a successful period in the city with the pro-duction which attracted crowded houses at all performances, we took the organization on the road and filled dates in all the princi-pal cities of England, receiving everywhere a welcome and patronage that was gratifying and profitable. We continued the show until January, 1916, when we closed it, having been tendered inducements by theatrical promoters in Spain which prompted us to go to that country. In the review, I took one of the leading speaking parts, in addition to engaging in boxing exhibitions. In these parts I feel that I acquitted myself successfully. Newspaper accounts of my efforts as an actor were highly favorable, and the capacity houses which greeted us were ample evidence that the re-view met with public approval.

San Diego was the first Spanish city in which I and my party made the acquaintance of Alfonso's subjects. Here, as in every other European city which I visited, I was given an enthusiastic reception. Large crowds met us as we landed and followed us cheering as we went to our hotel. From San Diego we went to Madrid where pleasant and profitable circumstances occasioned our stay for several months. I engaged in several theatrical performances and minor ring bouts, the latter being principally exhibitions between myself and members of my party. There are few boxers in Spain and there were none at that time whose ability was sufficient to warrant serious bouts with me. The Spanish, however, take keen delight in watching a boxing contest, though they declare that it is not a sport equal to bull fighting, and consider it rather odd that a man finds enjoyment in being knocked about by another.

From Madrid I went to Barcelona, a city with which I at once developed a happy acquaintance. It appealed to me more than any other European city and I decided at one time that I would make it my permanent home, and with this in view, went so far as to purchase a house in which to settle down. At about this time I also began to consider establishing myself in some other business and looked around for opportunities outside the theater and boxing ring. The result of this was the establishment by myself of an advertising agency. Advertising was a profession which had attracted me to a considerable extent, and one which I understood quite well because of my extensive use of publicity in the theatrical and boxing world. I did not reckon with the fact, however, that Barcelona was a city which still harks back to ancient methods of doing business and my undertaking was not a very flourishing one. Clients were unaccustomed to making use of such an institution and so my venture, while not altogether a failure, was not as successful as I could have wished. The ring and theater continued to appeal to me and I returned to the stage, repeating some of the performances which had won success elsewhere across the Atlantic. I also arranged a ring contest with Arthur Craven who was an English heavyweight and had fled to Spain because of the war. A large crowd was attracted by the contest which lasted but a short time, for I knocked him out in the first round.

By this time I had become well known in Spain and frequently was urged to make public appearances. Bull fighting being the most popular sport of that country, I naturally took much interest in it and was a frequent visitor at these events. Whenever I ap-

peared in the stands a demonstration took place which was almost
equal to that accorded the matadors or bull fighters themselves,
who are national heroes to the people of Spain. As my interest increased in the Spanish sport I cultivated the acquaintance of many
matadors among whom were Joselito and Belmonte, who at that
time were ranked as the greatest matadors of the country. Both
these champions had been interested spectators at boxing and theatrical presentations in which I had taken part. They professed
much admiration for my strength and speed and planted the seed of
a new ambition within me when they declared that I would make
a splendid success in the bull ring.

I determined to acquire the art of the matador. My friends Joselito and Belmonte were delighted, and eagerly undertook to in-
struct me. I was an enthusiastic and apt pupil and they were willing
and efficient teachers. We made rapid progress and it was not a
great while until they pronounced me competent for a public appearance, and so on July 10, 1916, I appeared in the arena wearing
the picturesque costume of the bull-fighter. All Barcelona turned
out to see the pugilist turned matador. Squeezed into the tight-
fitting trousers which constitute a part of the matador's garb, to say
nothing of the flaring cape, I did not feel as comfortable as when
appearing in the scant attire of the boxer. I awaited with anxiety
the appearance of the bull which I was to fight.

I was confident of the outcome, because having drawn lots earlier in the day for the bulls that we were to fight, there had fallen to
me an antagonist of small size, and I believed I could handle him
easily. I was due for a shock, for when the gates swung open there
came tearing forth a monster bull. I thought he was as high as a
house; he was an angry, snorting creature, too, and it appeared that
the sensible thing for me to do was to let him have the arena to
himself. I was quite willing to show how speedy I was in a demonstration of how to get out of a bull ring, but in this I was hindered
by my tight-fitting trousers and the further circumstance that there
were vast throngs of humanity in the stands, through which it
would be impossible for me to flee even if I could, by some mysterious process, have flown over the high walls of the arena. The
only thing I could do was to stand my ground. I met the bull in his
onrushes in accordance with the recognized customs of the best
matadors. I found that the huge bull, though much slower than a
skillful boxer, nevertheless was equipped with many clever tricks,

and that I could not side-step him as I could the fist of a boxer. At any rate I was the victor. I delivered the fatal sword thrust at the proper time and in a manner that won for me the plaudits of the crowd. I killed three bulls on the occasion of my first appearance in the Spanish arena, and at the conclusion of the performance found that I was almost as much of a favorite as their beloved champions. I took part in other bull fighting contests and gained considerable fame. My matador friends predicted a successful future for me as a bull ring attraction, but the sport did not find high favor with me, because I preferred to return to the cushioned gloves.

My experiences in the bull ring had increased my popularity in Spain and, when I returned to theatrical work in which I appeared in several boxing exhibitions with Rhodes as my partner, I had the satisfaction of drawing large houses. I believe that my stay in Spain had the effect of creating a new interest in boxing in that country, for several efforts were made to arrange ring contests for me by Spanish promoters which efforts failed only because none could be found to engage in ring battles with me. However, I did succeed in arranging one event, my antagonist being an American named Blink McCluskey, who hailed from Philadelphia. On the night of the fight McCluskey came near precipitating a grand failure by refusing to enter the ring unless he received a greater percentage of the proceeds, his change of front taking place when he saw a house crowded to its fullest capacity, and realizing that the proceeds were to be much in excess of what he at first had expected. He held out for a long time delaying the contest, and causing the spectators to grow uneasy. The dispute and delay he had occasioned so angered me that when he did enter the ring. I was in a worse temper than I had ever evidenced in the meeting of a boxer, and I proceeded to give him one of the worst beatings I had ever forced upon an antagonist, and knocked him out in five rounds.

Boxing, theatrical engagements, advertising and bull fighting did not include all my activities while in Spain. When the United States entered the war, I found an opportunity to serve the country from which I was a fugitive by conducting investigations of German submarine operations off the coast of Spain, and I also engaged in wrestling matches, in one of which I defeated the Castilian champion.

In my work as an American agent, I was employed by the

American military attaché in Spain, Major Lang, and pursued my assignments under the direction of the intelligence department. At that time, German submarines were causing havoc with English and American shipping. The destructive boats were appearing as if by magic in numerous places on the sea. They were baffling allied naval experts by the suddenness with which they did their damage and the mysterious manner in which they disappeared. It was evident that they had bases somewhere on the west coast of Europe, or had devised hiding places so near the scene of their depredations that they constituted the greatest menace to the successful prosecution of the war by the allies. Feeling sure that the sub bases, or at least some of them, were on the Spanish coast, I was sent out to discover what I could.

I made no pretentions to military training nor had I any experience as a sailor, but the accumulated experiences of my life-time served me well in these ventures, to which were attached numerous risks including the traversing of rough water into dangerous and out-of-the-way places along the coast, infested not only by possible war enemies but by smugglers and others engaged in outlaw practices. Then, too, there was the danger of capture by the enemy and the possibility of death by promiscuous shooting which frequently took place between the furtive craft in those waters. I was in and out of various sea ports and spent considerable time at San Sebastian and San Tandier and visited several islands off the coast. I obtained much information which was of sufficient value to be communicated to the United States officials who in turn submitted it to the allies for use in resisting submarine warfare and safeguarding shipping. For my work and the information which I obtained I received due recognition from the officials under whose instructions I operated, and I had the great satisfaction of being of service to my native country, even though I was an exile.

In undertaking wrestling bouts, reference to which I made a moment ago, I found similar limitations as existed in finding boxers in my division. Wrestling in Spain, like boxing must take a secondary place to bull fighting, as a result of which there are not many skilled in the former type of athletic sport. However, Spain boasted of one wrestling champion in the person of Juan Ochoa, and with him a match was arranged for me. We met about the middle of July, 1918. The scene of our encounter was the bull fighting arena at Bilbao. It was on a holiday and festival gaiety reigned. Great crowds packed the stands and cheered the contest which was not a difficult one for me, for I took the champion for a fall in eighteen minutes.

While I am making reference to my wrestling matches in Europe, I must retrace my steps a little to a time before the outbreak of the war when I was meeting all comers in the boxing arena and was engaged in theatrical productions in France. A wrestling tournament of considerable magnitude was being promoted in Paris, and I was one of the entrants. I met several opponents and found none who were my superiors on the mat. I met both French and German twisters, and on one occasion I was billed to meet one of the latter nationality. He came recommended as a skillful wrestler and also a dangerous and tricky one. The latter quality I found he possessed to excess. He began the use of fouling tactics from the beginning. I bore his unfairness for some time, but, when he was encouraged by my patience to apply his out-ruled methods more and more vigorously, I resorted to boxing habits and applied a blow to his jaw which knocked him out. This feature of the bout was more appreciated by the spectators than any other match on the program. When it was realized how I had terminated the struggle there was a burst of cheering from that French audience that astounded me. I found out later that they were not cheering because an unfair combatant had been punished, but because he was a German.

Another wrestling event in which I took part was in Sweden, when I made a tour of that country, of Norway and of Denmark. At this time I beat Hansen, who was the wrestling idol of that country. Our meeting took place at Gothenburg, and the outcome was a surprise to the wrestling fans who believed Hansen unbeatable. However, they took his defeat in sportsman-like manner and treated me with the utmost kindness and respect.

Early in 1919 I received overtures from boxing promoters in Mexico City, who opened negotiations with me to visit that country for the purpose of getting me to appear in a series of boxing matches. After considerable correspondence two of the promoters visited me in Madrid, and it was arranged that I should leave Spain where I spent four years. But for the fact that I was compelled to forego the pleasure of returning to my own country where I had been treated with less kindness than anywhere in the world, my years in Spain would have been happy ones. As it was I was haunted by the constant wish to see my own country and to live amid the scenes that were dearest of all to me, and the unpleasant prospect of a prison term hanging over me. Then there was the added bitterness that my mother had died when I was hopelessly beyond her reach. Her death had occurred in March, 1917, and after that time I felt so much uneasiness that it was difficult for me to decide upon a definite course, yet never did the desire to return to America leave me. I accepted the opportunity to go to Mexico City, with deep satisfaction, because it would bring me nearer home and might be an important step in ultimately ending my exile one way or another. I sailed from Spain March 28, 1919. Rhodes did not accompany me, but went to New York City to make arrangements for sending boxers to Mexico City for the ring series we were contemplating. In the meantime he visited Chicago and did not join me in Mexico until the latter part of July. Marty Cutler, George DeBray and Jack Heinan with whom Rhodes had signed contracts preceded him to Mexico City, and the matches were well under way when he arrived. In these fights I was the principle boxer appearing in a great number of bouts with both visiting and native combatants and winning in every contest.

In Mexico City I made many friends among whom was Carranza, who at that time was the president of the republic. When initial negotiations for my fight with Willard were under way and Villa, the bandit chief, had promised to finance the meeting in Juarez, Carranza showed his disapproval by threatening to arrest me for the United States authorities in the event I attempted to land in Vera Cruz, which, it will be remembered, caused the fight to be staged in Havana. Soon after my arrival in Mexico City from Spain, Carranza tendered me his friendship and made every effort to make my stay in the Mexican Republic a pleasant and comfortable one, even going so far as to provide me with escorts of soldiers when I had occasion to travel in sections of the country infested by bandits or revolutionists. The president also took much interest in our ring exhibitions and frequently we met each other in private, at which times we engaged in conversations which ranged over many subjects. Carranza was a man of broad views, was well educated and despite the uncertain political situations which he faced – situations which sometimes held the threat of death for him and the overthrow of his government – he found time and the inclination to give his attention to the consideration of many things which did not pertain to his personal success. He was greatly interested in world politics and in the future relations between his country and the United States. He questioned me concerning my experiences in Europe and drew from me my views on international politics, which, although I was by no means an authority upon the subject, he seemed to believe were worth listening to. To be sure, I had in the years of my residence in European capitals gathered much information along the lines in which he was interested, and he lost no opportunity to encourage my expressions of opinion.

Following my bull fights in Spain, I had determined not to engage further in contests of this nature, but rather to devote myself intensely to my boxing, but my friends and others in Mexico City, having learned of my experience as a matador in Barcelona and other Spanish cities, frequently urged me to enter some of the contests in Mexico, where of course bull-fighting is quite as popular as in Spain. I was in no particular mood to deviate from my course as a boxer. However, I had discussed bull-fighting considerably and even had gone so far as to write newspaper articles on bull-fighting, which seemed to establish me in the minds of the public as an authority. My hesitancy in again pitting myself against bulls only increased the ardor with which my Mexican friends insisted upon my donning the colorful costume of a matador, with the result that I took part in some of the bull-fighting exhibitions which were being frequently held in Mexico City and vicinity. I had no difficulty in these events and won considerable popularity among the fans, who, like friends in Spain, sought to induce me to make this form of sport my profession. But, although it is one of the world's greatest sports in my opinion, and calls for much courage and skill, it does not hold for me the inducements that boxing does, and after several contests with the sword and cape as my weapons, I again turned my attention to ring activities. The boxing series, which had been the object of my trip to Mexico, was in the main successful, but it was difficult for me to find opponents and there were long stretches of time during which I was idle.

At about this time General Obregon was actively engaged in formenting revolution against the Carranza government, and conditions in the Mexican capital and other parts of the country for that matter were none too pleasant for Americans or other foreigners. I began, therefore, to plan for other activities. I had been urged by the governor of Lower California to visit that section where he was interested in seeing the successful promotion of boxing events in the belief, I presume, that it would prove an added attraction for tourists. He offered such inducements that I determined to change my base of operations and, accordingly, set out for Tia Juana, a journey that proved to be fraught with many hardships and dangers, and one which nearly claimed the lives of myself, Mrs. Johnson and Rhodes. An American family which had been living in Mexico City joined us in our departure, having been compelled to leave because of the activities of the revolutionists. Ordinarily, the trip would not have been a severe one, but owing to the relations that existed between myself and United States authorities, it was not practicable for me to make the trip in the customary manner which would have necessitated going to El Paso. For this reason, it was necessary for us to travel in a round about way, our course running through Guadalajara and Sonora, two Mexican states in which bandits, as well as Indian tribes, were indulging in depredations. Trains were running irregularly in this section of the country. They were being held up daily, and in many instances wrecked. Passengers were robbed and many were slain. These conditions were not inviting, but we determined to face them. Because of interrupted train service and the lack of railway facilities in some instances, part of our journey was accomplished with mules, which we rode or which pulled us over the rough roads in crude springless vehicles which were worse than the backs of the mules.

On one occasion, in Sonora, our train was stopped by a horde of savage Yaqui Indians who were supposed to be in sympathy with the revolutionary movement, but, in reality, used this principally as an excuse for pillaging trains. They were none too gentle in their methods. They did not hesitate to kill on the slightest provocation and the charred embers of what once had been railway coaches, which were scattered along the rail line were mute evidence of the lengths to which they had gone in carrying out their raids. When our train was stopped, passengers were driven from the coaches, and our assailants proceeded to search them. Some busied themselves with the baggage, and were engaged in tossing all of the passengers' possessions through doors and windows. I alighted from the train with the others and as the Indian bandits began their indignities, I began talking to them, having gained sufficient knowledge of the Mexican vernacular to make them understand. When I told them who I was, they were sufficiently interested to halt their looting, and came trooping around me, their curiosity overcoming their interest in their work of robbery. At first, they doubted that I was actually Jack Johnson. I had no idea, however, that they had ever heard of me, for I did not expect that these savages had much knowledge of what was going on in the world. I was surprised to find that they did know who I was, and for a moment, when they were convinced of my identity, it appeared that they were going to stage a wild demonstration in my honor. They manifested more interest and excitement over my appearance than they had in the promise of loot. Leaders of the band were profuse in their apologies for molesting the train, declaring that had they known I was aboard, they would not have thought of stopping the engine. What loot they had taken they restored to the passengers and told us that we might go on. I mingled freely with the Yaquis and when our train pulled out they were in a most friendly mood. I later was heaped with thanks by the passengers who had good reason to believe that had the Indians carried out their original intentions, they might not have lived to relate their experiences.

Having reached Sonora, we cut across the country westward to the Lower California coast. We found our way to Mazatlan, a small port where we sought to arrange passage northward. There were not many boats of any description sailing the route which it was necessary for us to take, and it was a difficult matter for us. Finally I came in contact with the captain of a small gasoline driven launch, who said he would undertake to carry us to our destination. The launch was nothing more or less than one used in the business of smuggling Chinese across the border into the United States, and when we went aboard we found that as fellow-passengers we were to have about 50 Chinese recently arrived from the Orient, and of a type not particularly inviting as associates. Besides them and the captain there was one deck hand and a cook. Mrs. Johnson was the only woman aboard and had she been less plucky, she would have shrunk in fear from joining such an expedition. The first day of our voyage was pleasant and smooth enough, but before midnight we ran into a storm that picked up

our small launch and tossed it about so violently that we believed
our escape impossible. The captain had been engaged in navigating along this particular stretch of water for twenty-five years and
was well acquainted with the coast. Knowing of sheltered strips of
water, he managed to turn the launch toward shore and succeeded
in nosing it into a small bay in which we were free from the dangers of the storm. Here we remained the rest of the night and until
late in the afternoon of the following day while the gale on the
gulf continued to rage. We were glad enough to go ashore from
the launch when daylight came, because we had had an experience
that had racked our nerves. However, when we were on shore we
found that we were in a desolate, barren and apparently uninhabited section of the country, but as we explored further
inland, we discovered that it was not uninhabited, but that it was
the camping place of a tribe of Indians, the name of which I never
learned. Perhaps they had never acquired any designation for they
were without doubt the lowest in the human scale that I had ever
seen. They had human forms but other than that they were animals. They were even worse than animals for I have never seen
animals so unclean and so lazy as they were. They were naked and
their skins were filthy with slime. They lay about their camps like
vermin, men, women and babies piled up together with dogs who
had the same privileges as the others – privileges which permitted
them to nurse at the breasts of the human mothers who lolled list-
lessly about, a suckling babe on one side, a dog on the other. These
Indians, I was told, were of a ferocious nature and had attacked
strangers who had ventured among them previously; but we were
not molested by them, and because of their filthiness, we did not
remain near them long.

In the afternoon the storm abated, and the gulf waters appeared
to be quiet enough for us to resume our voyage. We left our sheltered spot and took to the open again. Scarcely had we reached the
gulf proper when another gale struck us. It was more intense than
the one from which we had fled on the day before. The waves
rolled upon us mountain high and were gigantic enough to swal-
low boats, much larger than our own. The launch was tossed from
the crest of one wave to another with as much ease as a couple of
stalwart athletes throw a football about. The wind blew at a terrific speed and threatened to strip the launch of every shred which
it bore and suck its human freight down into the surging waters.

The captain sought to turn about for the coast again, but was unable to do so. The storm was so furious that his only possible means of safety was to keep the nose of the craft straight ahead. To attempt to turn meant that it would be dragged down. Assailed by the roaring winds and the tumultuous water, we found ourselves headed for the open sea. The storm raged for hours. Our captain said it was the worst he had ever encountered in all his years in those waters. I do not hesitate to say that I was frightened; both Rhodes and myself concluding that this would be our last earthly venture. The Chinese passengers were panic stricken with fear and the captain, though determinedly battling for the safety of his craft, declared more than once that we were lost. There was nothing any of us could do either in navigating the launch or adopting some means of safety. We were helpless and every minute we expected would be our last. In all this tumult of water and wind and human fear, Mrs. Johnson was the calmest one aboard. I never knew such gameness in man or woman. The storm continued the better part of two days and every minute of those two days was one of agony. Wave after wave rolled up and against us; the wind howled about us, slapping the launch about as it pleased, and tore furiously at the water.

How that little craft survived I do not know, but it did. When the storm subsided, we were many miles out of our course. As soon as the wind and water quieted we tacked about and eventually were on our way again, but at no time did the gulf become smooth. We had a constant battle with the rough waters and were never out of danger until we reached the Colorado river, into which the launch was steered. I have never experienced a moment of greater relief than I did when, for the first time after several days, I realized that we were safe. I was more or less astounded to find that we were out of danger, for when I thought of the raging wind and water through which we had come I was unable to understand how, with such a frail craft, we had escaped.

We chucked along up the Colorado river for a day or more, when we reached an isolated landing, without a name, as far as I could determine. It was at this landing that the smuggled Chinese left the boat, hiking from there for many miles to the Texas border where at an equally isolated spot they crossed into the United States. At this landing, we were compelled to lay-to for several hours awaiting rising of the river tide, so that we could continue our journey. During the wait, we decided to go ashore because we were stiff and sore as a result of our long stay on the boat and the terrific knocking about which we had suffered. We effected the landing and began to explore about, rejoicing in the good fortune and the thrill of touching land again. Our happiness, though, was to be short lived for within a short time after leaving the boat, and as we were busying ourselves with the things of interest about us, a regrettable accident occurred, when a gun which I carried was accidentally discharged, the bullet striking Rhodes in the arm. It caused a serious wound. There was no doctor at hand and no other facility for giving him aid. Tia Juana was 150 miles distant. We were unable to float our launch and delay was dangerous. The only thing for us to do in an effort to obtain the necessary aid for Rhodes was to start the trip to Tia Juana overland, and we lost no time in setting out with the wounded man. I had succeeded in getting a message to a telephone and over that I had sent a call to Tia Juana for an automobile. In the meantime, Rhodes lay in an abandoned cabin. Upon the arrival of the auto Rhodes was rushed to a hospital at Mexicali, where he lay several weeks but where he made a successful recovery, joining me at Tia Juana. The drive across the desert with Rhodes was a nerve-racking experience. The patient with a gaping wound in his arm suffered tortures, but he showed remarkable courage, without which he doubtless would have died from loss of blood and lack of attention which, though we were eager to give, was impossible.

As soon as I reached Tia Juana, I found that several bouts had been arranged for me. The sportsmen, tourists and others apprised of my coming awaited me anxiously and gave me quite a welcome on my arrival.

In spite of the gruelling experiences through which I had been – the storm at sea, and the drive across the desert with the injured Rhodes – I was in excellent physical condition, and lost no time in taking on several boxers who had been engaged to meet me. There were none, however, in the group who proved difficult as antagonists and the bouts were of so little importance that they do not merit description, though I may add that I won all of them easily. Boxing in Tia Juana served only temporarily to occupy my time and attention. It was not a profitable occupation and I sought other means of assuring my income.

Soon I opened a café, which was popular from the start and well patronized by visitors from the States and other parts of the world who were flocking into Tia Juana because of the lack of restrictions prevailing at that time. But I was not satisfied with my lot in life. There was nothing, I felt, which would compensate me for continuing as an exile from my home and friends, so I thought constantly of returning but was at a loss as to how I should proceed.

While this question was uppermost in my mind, after a stay of six months or so in Tia Juana, Tom Carey, a well known Chicago politician and one time candidate for Mayor of Chicago, and for many years a close friend, arrived in Tia Juana to visit the races. We were not long in renewing our oldtime acquaintance, when I picked six winning horses for him out of seven races. During his stay we spent much time together and visited most of the places of interest. During our association I confided to him my wish to return to the United States and discussed with him the difficulties which confronted me. He understood my wishes, and insisted that I should return, offering his service both as a bondsman and mediator, promising to make the way for my return as easy and generally satisfactory as he could. With the assurance of his good offices, I decided to surrender myself, and communicated with the Sheriff of Los Angeles county and federal officials, telling them that I wished to cross the border into the United States. I was instructed to go to San Diego where the proper officials met me, and where I arrived after surrendering the passports of myself, Mrs. Johnson and Rhodes. I was back on American soil again and the realization thrilled me quite as much as though I were entering the realms of a strange and unexplored land. I was filled with the thoughts of again seeing loved and familiar faces and of walking among scenes that were old and dear in my memory. There were many formalities to be disposed of before I could begin the journey to Chicago — a journey which I anticipated with more eagerness than any journey which ever before I had contemplated even in the most enthusiastic days of my youth.

7
The World Through Prison Bars

It was arranged that I should make the trip to Chicago virtually as a
free man. Carey and Rhodes had preceded me, and were making
preparations for my arrival when I left San Diego. Newspapers all
over the United States blazoned forth the news that I had crossed
the border, surrendered and was on my way to Chicago to stand
re-trial. Consequently all along the route, wherever my train
stopped, railway stations large and small were jammed with
crowds waiting to see me. They swooped upon my train almost
threatening forcible entry into my coach in an effort to see me, if I
failed to make an appearance. It was a memorable journey. All the
way I rejoiced in the realization that I was back on my native soil.
That I probably would be compelled to serve a prison term, after
all, was incidental. Of that I thought very little. That I was back in
my own country was enough, and I was willing and capable of
paying all the penalty that might be exacted from me for the privilege of regaining the home and friends that I so treasured.

It was originally intended that I should come to Chicago, but
when it was learned that an unusual demonstration might take
place on my arrival, plans were changed and arrangements were
made to have me leave the train at Joliet. The demonstration
which interrupted the program would not have been a hostile one.
As it was, thousands of people gathered at the railway station
where it was thought I was to leave the train. Many of these
awaited me merely out of curiosity and were eager to see the ex-
heavy-weight champion and the man who had caused such a stir in

court and ring circles. Others however, composed of those of my
own race and of white people were friends, intent on seeing that I
had a fair deal and meaning to aid in preventing any undue persecution that might develop as a result of my return. It was not a mob
as some newspapers hinted. The crowd was an orderly one and it
was also a disappointed one when it was learned that I had been
taken from the train at Joliet.

I was placed in prison at Joliet to await trial at Chicago. Newspaper writers, photographers and amusement promoters flocked
about me. They invaded my prison quarters. The newspaper men
were eager for interviews with me from which they constructed
stories for the public that often were vastly contrary to the information I had given them. The promoters were anxious to sign me
up for various stage and public appearances. Many of them apparently thought that I was soon to be freed of the charges against me,
and some of them even went so far as to announce that they had
made contracts for me to appear under their direction. These were
mis-statements and were responsible in large measure for the court
dealing with me more strictly than might have been the case. Judge
Carpenter, in passing sentence upon me, later hinted that these an-
nouncements smacked of too much assurance that I had nothing to
fear from the court. The newspapers printed many garbled stories
concerning me, among them being those to the effect that I was not
treated in the Joliet jail as a prisoner, but was permitted such privileges and freedom of conduct as to make the action of the prison
officials illegal. These stories aroused bitter criticism and complaint, and as a result I was removed from the Joliet prison to
Geneva. As a matter of fact, I was treated better in the latter prison
than in Joliet. I was made a trusty at the outset and assigned duties
that often took me outside the prison, where I remained at my own
discretion. I also was made a turnkey, in which capacity I had
charge of several prisoners, whose liberty in the jail increased or
diminished according to my judgment. I remained in this jail for
about three months or until October, 1920, when I was taken to
Chicago for trial, the nature and result of which I have related in
another chapter. The sentence imposed upon me, as I have said, I
considered unjust, and the shadowing and persecution that followed had originally precipitated my flight.

Soon after the sentence, I was placed in charge of a United States
Marshal, and accompanied by my friend, Jerry Brown, taken to

Leavenworth to begin the prison term of a year and a day. The trip
to the federal prison was made by way of Kansas City, Missouri,
where there was a wait of several hours. During this period, on my
promise to meet him at train time, the Marshal allowed me to
make some hurried visits to friends in the city unaccompanied, and
true to my promise to him, I joined him at the Union station, re-
suming the last leg of the trip that was to place me behind prison
gates.

Prison officials were not surprised at my arrival, but I found that
many surprises awaited me. Preparations had been made in advance for me, and after I had gone through the formality of 'check-
ing in,' I was assigned to my quarters and supplied with the
regulation prison garb and other equipment. My first surprise
came when I was presented with the suit of blue denim which was
to be my prison uniform. The man who had planned its dimensions
must have used his imagination rather than a tape measure, and
there must have been a liberal supply of material when the suit was
constructed, for it was large enough for a tent and would have held
me and several others like me. It was necessary to put through an
emergency order for another suit before I could be properly
arrayed.

Soon after my entrance, Warden Anderson and Deputy
Warden Fletcher summoned me for an interview with them, in
which they questioned me concerning my talents and the manner
in which I wished to occupy my time inside the prison walls. From
the outset both wardens were kind to me and I shall never cease to
be grateful for their consideration and help. I was told by them that
they wished me to keep up my physical condition, and to direct
my efforts during the term I was to serve in a way that would benefit myself and the prison as well. Warden Anderson assured me
that it was his wish to discharge me a better man physically and
otherwise than I was when I entered the prison. In this purpose I
believe he attained a signal success. By this I do not mean that the
prison discipline improved me morally, but my stay in the prison,
cutting me off as it did from the perplexities and strife of life, gave
me time to take stock of my friends and my enemies. I came to the
conclusion that one of my greatest errors was my flight to Europe,
that I might avoid the disgrace and ordeal of prison. While to all
intents and purposes, I had a delightful time in my travels and
learned much concerning the world, I was, nevertheless, an

unhappy and restless individual. During the years in which I was a
fugitive nothing came into my life in the way of adequate compen-
sation for the stings and grief I suffered over my separation from
my friends and relatives, and particularly keen was the regret that I
had not remained with my mother, or as close to her as I could. I
was not given to melancholy contemplation of my situation, because there was much within the prison that stirred my interest and
kept me alert.

After a day or two in the prison Warden Anderson introduced
me to a man who, he said, was an old acquaintance of mine. At first
I did not recognize him, but a word or two stirred pleasant recol-
lections which echoed from one of the very important events of
my life. The friend referred to was former Governor Dickerson of
Nevada, who was the chief executive of that state when I fought
Jeffries at Reno in 1910. Mr. Dickerson was serving in the capacity
of prison superintendent, in which connection it proved later, I
was to have much association with him. Dickerson, like the
warden and his deputy, manifested much interest in me and prof-
fered me his aid if ever I should need it. It was doubly pleasing to
have his assurance of friendship, and to recall that we had formerly
met at a time when I was facing a severe contest. On that occasion,
too, he had extended me his friendship. My first meeting with
Governor Dickerson came soon after my arrival in Reno, and
while I was in training for the fight we met often. The governor,
an ardent sportsman, was interested deeply in the training camps of
both Jeffries and myself. He visited me frequently and discussed
with keen interest the fight in which I was about to engage. He
asked me if I thought I would win. I replied that I intended to do
my best, and that I would win even though I broke an arm. He also
asked me if I had any fear of Jeffries to which I answered with an
emphatic 'no.' He questioned me also concerning rumors to the effect that they were 'going to get me, even if it was necessary to use
a bullet.' I assured him that I was not frightened over these alleged
threats, and that I placed no credence in them. He was not so sure
however, and insisted on providing me with a guard of five state
rangers. During the period of my training some of these rangers or
all were constantly near me, and they with others were at the ring
side on the day of the fight in order to forestall any attempt that
might be made on my life. Governor Dickerson was determined
that I should have a fair chance in that fight, and he left nothing

undone that would provide it. Shortly before the fight, he told me, he had placed a bet on me. Later, I learned this bet amounted to several thousand dollars.

Throughout my prison term, the former Nevada governor was a staunch friend and adviser, and I was impressed through his interest in me, with the fact that one of the greatest things in the world is friendship. There is nothing which brings deeper satisfaction than the assurance of possessing loyal friends. They are rare and valuable, and there is nothing that should be more carefully guarded than these friends, particularly those whose confidence remains intact when circumstances place you in an unfavorable light and give room for criticism which seems unanswerable.

It did not take the prison authorities long to decide in what manner I should occupy myself in the prison. The post of physical director was soon created for me, and I was given charge of all athletic work. All prisoners wishing to engage in field or gymnasium activities were assigned to me. There virtually was none over me and there was no one to whom I was answerable in the performance of my duties in the prison excepting the executives. I had supervision of the baseball field, the prison track area, the gymnasium and all forms of athletics. I sought out those interested in boxing and gave them special training, and there were many snappy bouts staged between the more clever of the glove wielders in the prison. From this it will be gathered that whatever else I may have been denied as a prisoner, I was not compelled to give up the work which had been my chief concern in life.

In all, my imprisonment was in no wise as severe as I had anticipated. In many ways, I believe, I was the means of doing much good among the prisoners and for the prison. As a rule a man has no cause for congratulation over the fact that he has been compelled to forfeit his liberty, even for a short time. There is, at best, no attraction in prison life,and the thought that one is living under such discomforts and inconveniences as prison discipline imposes is not comforting. Yet I do not feel that the months I spent in Leavenworth were wasted.

My work as physical director kept me busy and interested. I had many duties and obligations, notwithstanding which, I gave considerable attention to the conduct of my personal and business affairs outside the prison. My business interests I did not neglect at any time, for I was looking ahead to the day when I would have paid the price, regained my freedom, and resumed my place in normal activities. Rhodes continued to act as my secretary and manager. He spent much time with me in my prison quarters, making many trips back and forth between Chicago and Leavenworth. In this manner I was enabled to keep in close touch with world affairs and such matters as pertained to my personal welfare. My wife, too, who made her home with my relatives during the time I was behind the walls, watched my business affairs closely and successfully. The combined efforts of Mrs. Johnson and Rhodes kept matters in satisfactory condition, so that when I was liberated I was ready to take up and carry on in such a manner that I was scarcely aware of any loss that might have been occasioned because of my enforced absence. Mrs. Johnson also was a frequent visitor at the prison, and her presence and continued confidence in me was a source of strength and inspiration that contributed greatly to my patience, and maintained my hope.

Without wishing to boast, I am tempted to record that my conduct in prison won for me a shortening of the original term. My record for good behavior was such that I was discharged after serving eight months of the year and a day for which I was sentenced. On the day I left prison, many close friends came to meet me at the gates, but further than that there was a sort of general celebration, the extent and nature of which surprised and disconcerted me. There were four bands taking part in the demonstration. Hundreds of people whose cars were parked all over the prison grounds awaited my appearance and swarmed about me, once I had re-entered the outer world. They cheered and congratulated me, and if I had ever felt that my life had been a failure or that there was nothing further for me to accomplish, I changed my opinion at that moment and found myself rejoicing, eager and confident.

One outstanding event of the period of my imprisonment took place on Thanksgiving day when I appeared in the ring especially built within the prison walls, and fought two men, over each of whom I was the victor. It was not the fight particularly which impressed itself upon me, for fights have been so numerous in my life that they, with some exceptions, were only incidents. The Thanksgiving day event, however, was a gala one for the prison, and I am told that nothing ever took place in the prison's history which was characterized by more ceremony or excitement. My opponents in the ring were Topeka Jack Johnson, a former sparring partner and George Owen, a 227 pound boxer who had been brought from Chicago for the occasion. Attending the fight were more than a thousand inmates of the prison and several notable persons of Kansas and Missouri, many of them state officials. The fight took place in mid-afternoon, but guests and spectators began arriving before noon. An hour before the preliminaries began, the seating capacity was entirely exhausted and improvised seats, gathered from every corner of the prison, were hurriedly placed. The prison bands were out in force and played march tunes as the spectators took their seats. The bands also, blared forth when I took my place in the ring. As I looked about me I saw that several special guests were present and that among them were well known sportsmen and newspaper writers. According to the latter my skill and form was equal to any former occasion on which I attempted to entertain the public. I knocked Owen out in six rounds. The go between Topeka Jack Johnson and myself was more of an exhibition affair, and it was said of us by those who were competent judges, that our bout was a fast and classy one. Certain it is, the old prison had an awakening that day unlike any that had gone before it.

There were no particularly unpleasant incidents during my imprisonment, at least none in which I was concerned. I found little cause for complaint and outside the fact that I chafed under the ordeal of restriction from the outside world, my life was pleasant and comfortable. Only once was my temper aroused and that was occasioned when a man, actuated by the desire to make a dollar, substituted a roasted cat for an opossum which I had asked him to obtain for me. I had, with the permission of prison authorities, arranged with a hunter to get the opossum. He was unable to find one, and rather than lose the dollar which I had promised him, killed and dressed a cat, being careful to remove all parts of the animal which would reveal its identity. The cook who was delegated to prepare the animal for me was unfamiliar with opossum meat and unwittingly served the feline flesh with approved opossum trimmings. I had invited two or three friends to dine with me, but before we had partaken, of the delicacy which we had anticipated with watering mouths, the deception was discovered. It was a disappointing dinner affair, but my disappointment was not as

severe as my anger. Had I been able to lay my hands on the hunter
at that moment, I fear that I would have treated him rather roughly.
When my anger had subsided I tried to view the matter as a
joke, but I failed in this. I was too big to deal with the offender as I
wished, but I made arrangements with a smaller man to deal with
the hunter, and according to reports which reached me, he paid
dearly for the dollar which he had pocketed.

I left the prison in June, 1920[1] On the evening of the day on
which I was liberated, I found myself in a role quite different from
any which I had previously carried. I had been a boxer, a bull-
fighter, a wrestler, an advertising man, an actor, a promoter, a
clerk, a mechanic and a musician – now I was to be a lecturer. The
lecture took place in one of the large halls of Leavenworth, and
was under the direction of one of the prison chaplains. I had no
particular subject but wandered around in a rather extensive field
having for my topics religion, squareness, courage and successful
living. As large as the hall was, it was unable to hold all who
sought admittance, a large crowd having been turned away. In the
audience were both white people and those of my own race. Just
how well I acquitted myself, I will not attempt to say. However, I
was conscious of the fact that I held the interest of my auditors, and
I was assured that my talk was a good one.

I found material for my address in the information I had gained
and the observations I had made while in prison for I was much
given to study the men and conditions about me. I made the
acquaintance of many types of men in prison. There were
criminals of all degrees and they were paying penalties for offences of
many kinds. Some were hardened, bitter and dangerous; others
were gentle, patient and without the slightest evidence of baseness.
Some had served many terms, and some were serving their first
term with the prospect, judging from their conduct within the
walls, of serving additional terms. I learned that men who are
criminals by instinct or inclination, always will be criminals, and
that prison discipline will never deter them from being criminals. I
also learned that men who are criminals by accident or from force
of circumstances, and in whom there are no natural tendencies
toward crime become criminals, as a result of imprisonment and

[1] This date is entirely wrong as Johnson surrendered on July 20, 1920. He was
sent to Leavenworth on September 14 and released on July 9, 1921, his sentence
having been reduced.

their contact with other criminals.

Long and repeated prison terms have no effect in turning the evil doer from his path. His confinement only gives him opportunity to nurse his bitterness and to plan new exploits when he is out of prison. He is actuated by a desire to repeat his offenses believing that he can escape future capture or punishment by profiting by whatever mistakes he might have made in covering up former crimes. He has the constant desire to outwit the police and courts, whom he considers his enemies bent on accomplishing his destruction. His association with other criminals implants new ideas within him and he is always on the alert to obtain information from those of his kind, which he believes will prove helpful to him in his activities as a law-breaker. For men who have chanced into prison through a temporary lapse, because of a mistake, or due to unfortunate circumstances, and in whom there are no natural germs of criminality, long prison terms serve only to arouse bitterness. They have time to contemplate their misfortune, and most men of this class feel that they have been so thoroughly disgraced that they never again can appear in decent society. They are unwittingly influenced by the hardened criminals, and when they are once liberated, they have been saturated with ideas that will ultimately prove their undoing, and defeat the purpose of punishment or discipline as established by law. For a man who has committed an offense, the penalty for which is prison, if it is his first, and is committed without intent of criminal practice, a very short prison term will prove as efficacious, and will do more to protect society and himself than a long and arduous sentence. I believe there should be a schedule of prison terms devised which will enable courts to impose sentences according to individual temperaments, and the past records of accused persons.

After my discharge from prison, several business propositions demanded my attention. I had been considering numerous plans prior to my release but had not decided on a definite course. I was offered several theatrical engagements. Some were rather attractive, but I was not eager to leap into the limelight such as would mark my return to the stage. However, after my lecture in Leavenworth, I filled a short engagement at Kansas City and then went to Chicago with my wife. I received a splendid welcome on my return but did not remain long. I visited with my relatives and friends a few days and went to New York.

Upon my arrival there, I was accorded the greatest ovation by the people of my race and the public in general that I had ever received. A grand ball sponsored by Barron Wilkins and Dick Ellis, well known sporting men of the city, was staged for me and thousands of people were in attendance. My presence in the metropolis was for the purpose of lecturing in some of the churches, and I fulfilled several engagements discussing political, racial and other topics. At the conclusion of these lectures, I signed some vaudeville contracts covering a period of two months and calling for my appearance in New York City, Philadelphia and Pittsburgh. When these were finished, I returned to New York and organized an all-star vaudeville show, in which all the performers excepting myself were white. In this show I did some comedy and exhibition boxing and did other stage work in conjunction with the other members of the troop. Our show was on the road twenty-five weeks, during which time we visited Chicago and most of the larger middle western cities. The venture was a prosperous one, but I was urged by an inclination to retire from the stage, and in casting about for another line of business, selected one which was not only entirely new to me, but which differed vastly from my previous experiences and associations. My new venture was in the brokerage field. I opened offices at 49th and Broadway, and engaged in selling stocks and bonds. I was more successful in this undertaking than might have been expected, inasmuch as it was a business the nature of which was entirely foreign to either my experience or temperament. In spite of these limitations, my efforts were not without success. I established no unusual records and the profits of the enterprise were not so large that I could not handle them. But when I gave up the business after several months, I did so with a clear conscience and with no liabilities hanging over me, which was more than could be said of many others whose capital and experience was much greater than what I had invested.

After my release from prison, I made no serious efforts to arrange any boxing matches, though I was by no means doubtful of my ability, and I lost no opportunity to emphasize my willingness to meet any man in the world. I had had my triumphs and the bitterness which accompanied them in my case. Yet, had circumstances been so arranged as to make a meeting between Jack Dempsey and myself possible, I would eagerly have gone into the ring with him. At no time in my life had I neglected my physical health, nor had I failed to maintain a regular schedule of physical culture and gymnastic work. I had reached an age when popular belief assumes that a man must retire from ring or athletic exploits, and this belief was against me. But, as I said, I had not entertained serious intentions of engaging in spectacular ring contests, though I knew myself capable of doing so. My efforts to engage in other lines of business were only half-hearted, because I could not bring myself to ignore boxing, nor cease to believe that I had the old-time speed and punch.

Early in 1924, though I had reached the age of 46, the Montreal boxing commission after a thorough examination of me, declared that I was fit for ring work and issued me a boxing license. Armed with this, I signed for a ten-round go with Homer Smith of Kalamazoo, Michigan, who had whipped several heavyweights and who was acquiring a reputation for a 'pile driving punch.' The fight took place before the Montreal Athletic Club and was attended by one of the largest crowds ever patronizing a fight in that city. It was a sorry failure, however, and added nothing to my prestige, because Smith would not fight. Throughout the ten rounds he was at my mercy, and it would have been inhuman for me to take advantage of his weak efforts. I coaxed him to fight and the crowd jeered, but it was no use. After I had knocked him down sixteen times the contest ended quietly with the decision unanimously in my favor. One thing, however, was established by the fight and the training I did preceding it. Newspaper writers conceded that I had disproved the fact that age is a disqualifying element before youth in athletic contests. Sport writers who were prejudiced against me, grudgingly conceded that despite my long years in the ring, I had my old time skill and still wielded my famous punches with as much vigor as ever. That they were correct in their surmises, I confirmed more than two years later on May 3, 1926, when at the age of 48 I won the decision over Pat Lester, a 24-year-old fighter, much larger than myself, whom I fought with comparative ease through fifteen rounds. The fight took place in Nogales, Sonora, Mexico, and I shall have something more to say concerning it in another chapter.

Following the Homer Smith bout, I appeared in several exhibition matches in Montreal and other parts of Canada, but there were no fighters in that country of sufficient experience or skill to make a satisfactory match with me, and I was confronted again with the lack of contestants and a consequent necessity of turning my attention to other lines of endeavor. This new enterprise took me for the second time into the advertising field in which capacity I was employed by a Canadian Brewery Company.

If I had begun to think that my troubles and griefs were over I was due for a rude awakening, for while it seemed that I was steering into quieter and smoother waters than had ever before characterized my life, some new domestic griefs reared themselves in my path. Echoes of the old wrath which my mother-in-law, Mrs. Cameron, nursed against me, came out of the past and Lucille, after twelve years of a marriage that had been a happy and successful one, obtained a divorce in New York City. Another romance had come to a sudden end. Our love, after many years of trials and tests through which it endured, was destined to fade. She had been in my life longer than any other woman and had enjoyed with me some of my greatest triumphs and suffered with me some of my greatest hardships and sorrows. She was always loyal and steadfast and she possessed a pluck and courage that enabled her to stand up bravely under many arduous experiences.

8
Adventures on Highways
and Byways

There are few countries in which I have not traveled. I have not
only loitered along the beaten paths of the old and new worlds, but
I have gone into many strange and out-of-the-way corners of the
globe and mingled with strange and little known people. I have
rubbed elbows with the aristocrats of the European capitals;
mingled with the frivolous in the noted cafés and restaurants of the
continent; I have disported on the French and Italian Rivieras; I
have been a guest in some of the finest homes of Mayfair, in
London, where the élite and semi-royalty gathered in staid and
dignified receptions. I have frequented exclusive clubs in St. James
Street, London, and attended gatherings of notables in Paris. In
Moscow my associates were Russian field marshals and aids of Czar
Nicholas; in Budapest, Bucharest and Vienna my haunts were
among some of the most wonderful clubs and restaurants in the
world, where I met artists, scientists, writers and idle rich; in
Australia I was the guest of notable men of that country. Having thus
often found myself in the most exclusive circles of men the world
over, I have on the other hand leaped to the other extreme and
lived side by side with the aborigines and savages of the South
Seas, of the Fiji Islands, and the Hinterland in Australia; the pro-
vincials of French and English possessions; the semi-savages – the
Yaqui of Mexico; ruffians and adventurers of South America and
the West Indies. I have been on the seas with smuggling crews and
been a fellow-passenger of Chinese coolies who were being

smuggled across the border from Mexico into the United States. I have
had opportunities to observe denizens of the underworld in nearly
every country of the world; I have witnessed scenes among them
that have no parallel even in the most imaginative fiction of melo-
dramatic writers.

It is not my purpose to enter into a routine account of my travels,
nor to attempt any description of the geography, commerce, races
or customs of the lands and peoples I have learned to know. That
has been done too many times by others more accomplished than I
in the art of the narrative, and there is nothing I could add that
would be new or interesting. Since this, however, is a personal
account of my experiences I shall dwell only on certain outstanding happenings and situations in which I was concerned, not
that they depict me in any particularly favorable light, or brand
me as a globe-trotter, but because I believe they will entertain and
amuse my readers.

There is much I could write about the great World War, because I was in close contact with events immediately preceding
that catastrophe and situations which came to pass in the first few
months of the conflict. But of this, I am going to say little more, for
that subject has been discussed and written about so voluminously
that there is not much left for me to say. Elsewhere in this volume I
have related my experiences in Moscow, where my party and I
were arranging a series of public engagements when the war suddenly was precipitated upon the world. I have told of my close
contact with military leaders and confidential advisors of the
czar, of our sudden leave of that country and the adventurous
journey through the war-frightened countries back to Paris and
London.

When we were back in the French capital from the Russian
center of war preparations, we found the country in chaos. Everything was being turned to war and its demands. Private citizens
were being deprived of their automobiles and everything that
could be used to resist the threatened invasion of the Germans.
Being an American citizen, I was permitted to retain my automobiles, and as a result, we were able to travel extensively over
France, and to see at close range the intense process of preparing
for war.

Not long after our return from Moscow, we determined to go
to London, and, loading our two cars with what possessions we

had left, we started for the French coast from where we were to embark for England. For several days we had been within sound of the terrible gun-fire on the battle front, and not infrequently we had been directly under fire, having more than once traveled within a short distance of the battle lines. When we reached Boulogne, we realized the vast proportions the war was assuming because we encountered the first British troops to arrive on French soil. They were disembarking upon our arrival, and the sight was one that will never be forgotten. Speed was one of the factors entering into the war at that time, for the Germans were getting dangerously near. Regiment after regiment of English soldiers which had been hurriedly mobilized were leaving the boats with their equipment, and were immediately being marched away to the front.

It was at Boulogne that we had an experience that I can number among the many which nearly cost our lives. Cavalry and artillery horses belonging to the English troops were being unloaded from the boats and herded into every possible vacant space. It was pitch dark, lights having been strictly prohibited because of the dangers of air raids. It was almost impossible for the troops to pick their way from their transports, and the handling of the thousands of horses under these circumstances was a difficult task. There was a high pitch of tenseness on the part of both men and beasts. Everywhere there was an anxiety and an awe that was overwhelming. Suddenly, we became aware of a terrific disturbance. There was a rush of horses and human beings in the dark; thousands of hoofs were heard pounding in every direction, and at the same time there arose the shouts of alarm and fright of thousands of people.

The next minute there was added to this din the shrieks and groans of those who were in pain. We were in our cars, and about us came swirling masses of horses. More than 4,000 artillery and cavalry horses had got beyond control of the troops and were in mad stampede. The brutes, frightened as a result of their rough trip across the channel during which they had been unmercifully tossed back and forth across the stock decks of the boats, were in a highly excited state when it came to unloading them. We had noted previously that they were rearing, kicking, plunging and tearing about, but now with a suddenness that bewildered their herders, the thousands of troops, and a large proportion of the population of that French section, they had broken away and were roaring and milling about in the dark, trampling everything before them. They raced snorting over a wide territory, plunging into the troops and groups of citizens, many of whose bodies were mangled under their hoofs. Many persons were killed and hundreds were injured in the mad rush. Though we were in the midst of all this chaos, we were uninjured, being fortunate enough to be protected by our cars, but there were times when we feared they would either leap into the cars or turn them over in the furious jam.

While we were waiting at Boulogne for the boat that was to take us to England, news came to us of a terrible slaying of French soldiers which had taken place near us. The conflict in which they died was one in which they had killed one another by the thousands, their own artillery having raked the infantry and other units with deadly results. This horrible event was due to a trick which the Germans had planned. They had arrayed several of their own troops in French uniforms, the purpose being to get within the French lines, upon which they would have turned and dealt an overwhelming defeat. The French, however, discovered the deception. They had become aware of the approach of the enemy in their own uniforms and had turned their guns upon them. In the confusion that followed, the movement of the struggling regiments brought several units of French soldiers within range of their own guns, and the defending troops believing that the soldiers surrounding them or attempting to surround them were Germans proceeded to pour death upon them.

In this trap, thousands of Frenchmen were slain and wounded. Many of the latter were brought into the Boulogne section, and hearing that one of the wounded was a friend, I obtained permission to search for him. I found him in one of the emergency hospitals. His name was Cerf, a well known Paris sportsman, who with Theodore Vianne, another Paris man, had first intended to promote my fight with Moran. My erstwhile sporting friend was mangled by bullets, and the lower half of his face had been entirely shot away. It seemed impossible that he could live, and yet he did, though the disfigurement he suffered was most awful to look upon. On my visit to Cerf, I found with regret that many of my former Paris friends and acquaintances were among the wounded who had survived the trap. How many of my former associates had been killed I do not know, but I imagine there were many.

On reaching London after this experience, I signed a contract to appear at the South London Theater in the Elephant and Castle district, and hardly had our show been under way when the theater became a favorite target for air raiders. One night shortly after the opening of the show, bombs began to drop all around the theater and my audience was in panic. They attempted to rush from the house, but I stopped them. Hurrying to the footlights, I begged them to be still a moment. I told them that rushing from the theater as they were about to do, would cause more deaths than the bombs.

'Stay inside,' I told them. 'It is safer in here than out in the open.' They were quieted and resumed their seats, but the situation was a tense and unpleasant one. Fear gripped the audience, and although we tried to continue with the show in order to distract their attention from the bursting bombs which were falling all around us, it was more or less of a failure. Finally the raiders departed, and the audience was dismissed. When we ventured out, we found the streets full of wreckage. Thousands of windows had been shattered and many buildings had been demolished. I had a dinner engagement that night after the show with some Americans who were visiting in London, and, entering my car, I attempted to reach the scene of the appointment. I found it impossible to travel over the course necessary for me to take because of the great piles of glass and other debris in the streets which blocked my car. Everywhere we looked we saw windowless buildings.

Unable to reach the home of my friends, I turned the car toward my home in the Haverstock Hill section. But the trip was not to be made undisturbed, for suddenly there came roaring out of the black sky more bombs. The raiders had returned. Between blasts of bombs which were falling all around us, we could hear the whir and swish of the Zeppelin overhead. I speeded the car up in an effort to get outside its bombing radius, but was surprised to learn that no matter how fast I traveled or in what direction I turned, the bombs were close upon us. It was then I learned with considerable alarm that the Zeppelin was following us. My car was a white Benz, and must have loomed up conspicuously to the raiders, who found it a tempting target. They persisted in the chase until I reached home, and I scrambled under shelter with all the haste I could summon. It was a miracle that we were not blown to bits. How we escaped I do not know. When we were under shelter, the

Zeppelin did not desist, but remained over that section of the city for a long time, dropping countless bombs. When we ventured out the following morning, we viewed a scene of desolation. Many homes and public buildings had been hit by bombs, and a railway station a few blocks from us was completely demolished. That night, many persons were killed in several parts of the city, many of them in the neighborhood in which my home was located. The horrors of that night remain indelibly impressed on my memory and I still have a few shudders when I recall them.

In my travels throughout the world, I have been caught in the turmoil of several revolutions, in which warring elements were striving for control of governments, and in which blood-shed took place on a far greater scale than the American people realize because of the meager news-reports which they have concerning them. I have been in revolutions in Spain, Portugal, Brazil, Mexico and Cuba. In most of these clashes I have been recognized as a neutral because of my noncitizenship, and was not purposely molested nor deliberately subjected to danger, but notwithstanding this, I have had some hair-breadth escapes and frequently have come near being the repository for a bullet intended for some other person.

On one occasion, in Barcelona, Spain, when that district aspired to secede from the Spanish government and set up an independent state, I was caught in the fire between the rebels and the government troops. Bullets whizzed about me with a recklessness that made me decidedly uncomfortable, and I saw myself stretched out like a human sieve. There is no doubt but that I would have been had I not been accompanied at the time by Chicorita, a well known Spanish bull fighter, who, incidentally, in the early part of 1927 was a visitor in Chicago. Chicorita knew how to conduct himself under such emergencies as we had encountered, and when the bullets commenced to spin about us, he jerked a white handkerchief from his pocket and waved it aloft. With the handkerchief waving above our heads, signifying that we were neutral, or at least ready to surrender, we sprinted down the Barcelona street with a speed that would have broken all running records, if there had been an official scorekeeper to make a note of it.

During this particular revolution, I was accorded every courtesy by the contending factions, and was afforded all possible protection for my home. I was the only resident in Barcelona who was permitted to draw his window curtains, all others being compelled to keep their shades up so that soldiers could look within the houses when they wished, and to prevent snipers from hiding behind curtains and picking their opponents off in the street by gun-fire. In other revolutions I was considerably inconvenienced at times and compelled to remain under cover, but never was I in such danger as when Chicorita and I sped to cover under the protection of the white handkerchief.

On another occasion, when my party and I were in Montevideo, Uruguay, a revolution broke out. Although it was being waged for political control, each of the contending sides had fixed their interest and attention upon the banks and cash depositories of the country. I had been taking part in several profitable boxing exhibitions, and had at this time accumulated a considerable bank account. Learning the precarious conditions of the Uruguayan banks, I made haste to withdraw all my money. I had about $20,000. I could find no place of safety for it, because there was no place beyond the reach of the revolutionists who were pillaging right and left. As a result of this situation, I carried my money about with me, wherever I went. I placed it in a bag and devoted my entire time and attention to guarding it. When I visited friends or took part in business engagements, I retained a firm grasp on that bag. It was near my finger tips when I sat down to eat in the restaurants. When I went to the theater, I held fast to it; when I slept, the last thing I did was to fasten my fingers firmly about it. Wherever Jack Johnson went in that disturbed country, that money bag was close at hand, and when he left the country its contents were intact.

During my stay in Barcelona, I signed a contract to produce a moving picture, or rather to play a leading role in the picture. A Spanish company made the picture, and mindful of the popularity of American films sought to imitate some of the thrillers which had found their way into Spain. The title of the picture was 'False Nobility.' It was planned to have numerous sensational and breath-taking scenes. I had to rehearse scenes in which I, as the hero, had many narrow escapes from death. Some of these events proved more realistic than was intended and there were several times when I was considerably in doubt as to whether I would live to appear in the final scenes.

In one scene in which I was supposed to have been beaten and cast by my enemies into a jungle to die, a boa constrictor came near putting an end to my earthly existence. The snake had been obtained by the producer purposely for the scene. It was a giant, twenty-eight feet long, and had been an object of much interest on the part of members of the cast and others permitted to see it when 'off stage,' and to all intents and purposes seemed rather tame and gentle. In the picture scene, the reptile was supposed to crawl from its jungle home and come upon me lying helpless in the jungle waste. The plot of the scenario called for me to suddenly awake to the grim danger threatening me and to have a fight with the snake for my life. When the constrictor was released from his cage, he was not in a particularly energetic mood and resented being compelled to move out. It was necessary to prod him considerably and to drive him into the synthetic jungle at just the right spot. The result was that by the time it was necessary for our titanic struggle to take place, the snake was consumed with a grouch. He was in an ugly mood, and when he saw me in my lethargic position, he suddenly determined to vent his spite on me. As he emerged from the grass and under-brush, I was seized with chills and fever, and the cause was not the imaginary wounds which I was supposed to be suffering from. That snake did not look as kind and agreeable to me as he had when I had viewed him in his cage. I read a sinister intent in his flashing eyes as he fixed his gaze on me, and forgot all about the instructions I was to follow. I was supposed to battle the monster for my life. It was said that when coiled, he was nine feet high, but as I looked at him preparing to lunge at me, I made a hurried calculation to the effect that there must be some mistake in the figures, and that instead of being nine feet high, he was sixty-nine. I also calculated that my skill as a fighter had suffered a momentary lapse, but I found that I could sprint; I got away to a quick start, and Olympic track stars, had they seen me on that occasion, would have felt themselves disgraced. It was necessary for them to get another man for the part, and after serious contemplation I came to the conclusion that film making wasn't such an enjoyable occupation after all.

After a few days, when I had recovered from my meeting with the snake, I appeared on the picture lot again and was informed that I was to have a lion for a playing partner. I did not relish this idea, but I believed that a lion was much more companionable and susceptible to reasoning than a boa constrictor. My part with the lion was to take place in the jungle too. I had sought to put myself on friendly terms with him and whenever I made a social call at his cage, he seemed to be possessed of a sweet and kindly disposition. I was assured that he was docile and would enter into his part of the picture-making with the utmost gentleness. But I had my doubts, and as it turned out these doubts were well founded. His cage was moved into the jungle scene and concealed by trees and shrubs. I, for the time being a nomadic wanderer, was supposed to be resting at the edge of the jungle, contemplating the beauties of nature or some such noble subject as that, when the lion was to spring upon me, and a fight was to take place that would bring movie spectators out of their seats gasping. I assumed my position as per instructions and awaited the leap of the lion, which was to be liberated from his cage behind the jungle growth by an attendant. But when he leaped, I was utterly unable to perform in a manner expected of moving picture heroes as they appear on the screen. When I saw that monster with his glaring eyes and wide open mouth flying through the air at me, I changed my mind about being a hero. A long wooden staff such as lion tamers use was to have been near at hand for me to seize in my tussle with the jungle king, but the property man had forgotten it, so I had nothing but my bare hands. But what I lacked in courage and muscle for that occasion, I made up in vocal demonstration.

'Get out,' I yelled at the lion. I yelled some more and very loudly and excitedly too; in fact I yelled so loud that the lion took fright, changed his mind about devouring me and turned his tail, hiding himself in nearby woods, where he remained for several hours. As for me, I traveled in the opposite direction, and did not slacken my speed until assured that the lion was not on my trail. I told the director that I believed he would be able to play the part better than I. He thought the matter over a little while and decided that that particular part was not necessary for the success of the picture anyhow, and I heartily agreed with him, having been of that opinion from the beginning. To whatever extent that picture was finished, and however successful it proved, there is one thing certain – the waiting public did not see me vanquish the boa constrictor or choke the lion to death, as the director no doubt intended.

I have always been an ardent motorist. I have driven a car nearly ever since the first models were available to the public. Never have

I been without one, and during my ownership and operation of cars, a sample of nearly every good car manufactured has at one time or another been in my possession. I have owned nearly every make of American and many models of European cars. I have shipped my motors across the Atlantic and the Pacific as I engaged in traveling. With few exceptions, these cars were built for speed and the court records of several American cities and not a few European cities will attest to the fact that I took advantage of these qualities countless times. I never had an ambition to be a real speed demon, but I must confess to having a weakness for fast driving. I decided, however, that I was not cut out for a race driver, when on one occasion I entered a race with Barney Oldfield. The manner in which he out-drove and outstripped me, convinced me that I was not meant for that sport, but nevertheless I have been near death many times in auto clashes, and on five occasions my cars have turned completely over with me, each time demolishing the car, but always I escaped uninjured as did everyone riding with me, except once when my head was torn open and it was necessary for me to have twenty stitches in my scalp. Four of these turtle turning experiences were in 1925. One took place at Benton Harbor, Michigan, when I was driving Chicago-ward in a rain-storm, my speedometer indicating a speed of sixty miles an hour. In attempting to take a highway curve, my car refused to turn. Instead it plunged straight ahead. The front wheels caught and wedged in a culvert, and remained there, but the rest of the machine with myself and a wolf dog in it, was hurled forty feet. The car was splintered but I did not get a scratch. The wolf dog squirmed out of the wreckage some way, and I found him later several miles from the scene.

At another time my car turned over near Elgin, Illinois, three men riding with me were unhurt, but I suffered the injury in this accident which necessitated the several stitches I mentioned previously. When I was thrown some distance away from the wreck, I lighted near a small pile of pebbles, and when my companions came to my aid, one of them exclaimed:

'My God! His brains are running out.'

This exclamation aroused me from my daze, and I felt my head to make sure that I was alive. I was hurried a short distance down the road to a doctor. When we arrived, he said he could not attend me because a man was dying in an accident near-by.

Galveston Giant in his prime

Burns and the title about to part company

Lucille Johnson and the Heavyweight Champion of the World arriving at Folkestone, 1913

Etta at ringside for "The Battle of the Century"

The black panther stalks a diffident Frank Moran

Two legends entwine at Reno

The black man rides the white man's best punch

A quiet holiday in the Nevada sunshine

Punish the body and the head will fall

Weighing-in for Willard

Cowboy Jess and a few supporters in Havana

A rare photograph shows Johnson seemingly in command during the Willard fight

Finale: defeat or abdication?

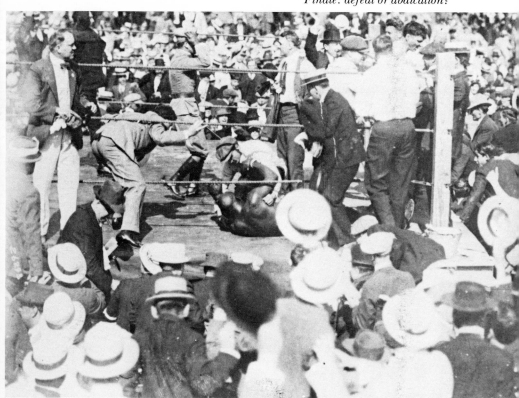

'I'm the accident,' I replied. 'They brought it to you.'

The car was smashed to smithereens, as another car was near Cleveland when it turned over on the highway, when I took to the ditch to escape a collision. In this smash my passengers and I were uninjured.

In 1924, while driving between Bridgeport and New Haven, Connecticut, my big touring car, traveling at top-steed, leaped from the highway and turned over several times. There was none injured at this time. In France in 1914 when I was on my way from Paris to Boulogne driving an Austin car at seventy-five miles an hour it left the road, went over a bank and plunged fifty feet. Neither myself, Mrs Johnson nor Rhodes, who were with me at the time, were hurt, but there was not enough left of the car to tell what it had ever been.

9
Chasing the Champion

I chased Burns around the world in order to get him into the ring with me. It was a two-year job. When I finally faced him in Sydney, New South Wales, December 26, 1908, and won the championship, the occasion was a notable one in the history of the prize ring. It was unlike any other event in the boxing world, because it marked the first time that a man of my race had ever won the title. It was the first championship contest ever waged off American soil, and for the first time in ring annals, the promoter of the fight and the manager of one of the contestants served also as referee. My suggestion that Hugh McIntosh serve in the latter capacity was one of the last of countless concessions that I had made in my effort to get at Burns, who had side-stepped me for months, and who had imposed conditions, some of which were almost impossible, and none of which a man less eager than I, would have considered for a moment. I trailed Burns from New York to London, from London to Paris and back, and from London to Australia. Always he made excuses or whenever he did show a willingness to meet me, it was under terms which denied me any possible advantage, and virtually removed every inducement excepting the possibility of gaining the title. I was the object of much ridicule on the part of Burns and his friends and he had openly insulted me so many times by uttering unprintable remarks and by calling me 'yellow,' that, had I met him personally, he would have fared worse than he did in the ring at Sydney. But he was careful to avoid a personal meeting and hurled his insults at long range. For

123

many months prior to the fight, there had been much bitterness between us. As the fight approached the tension increased, and a day or two before the ring meeting, came near assuming a rough and tumble clash, when he attempted to hit me with a chair.

My intensive chase after Burns began when I left San Francisco early in 1907, and went to New York, where Burns then was. I sought to arrange a meeting with him for the purpose of discussing a match, but he declined to meet me and soon afterward left for England. In the meantime, I engaged Sam Fitzpatrick as my manager, and we launched our campaign to go after the world title. Hattie McLay had joined me, and financed by her father, she, Fitzpatrick and I took up Burns' trail and followed him to London. He deftly escaped meeting me, but indulged in a lot of ill flavored remarks and threats concerning me. Soon after my arrival in London, I made several music hall engagements, which kept me so busy that I had little opportunity for training or keeping myself in shape.

Fitzpatrick was busy in planning bouts for me, and despite the unfavorable fighting condition I was in, made a match with Ben Taylor, who was then England's most promising heavy-weight, having defeated every possible contender. This match was based upon the craziest terms under which I ever fought, and in view of the important prospects at stake, I thought Fitzpatrick had suddenly lost his senses. Taylor was in fighting trim and was much heavier than I. I was in poor shape, yet Fitzpatrick had consented to terms which provided that to win, I must knock Taylor out in ten rounds; that the rounds were to go only two minutes each; and that we should use six-ounce gloves. Had I lost this fight, and there was a chance that I might, it would have meant a sudden end to my theatrical engagements, for I would have ceased to be an attraction. Furthermore it would have placed me in a class which would have prevented serious consideration of me as a contender for the title.

There was nothing for me to do but abide by Fitzpatrick's silly arrangements and I entered the ring with Taylor with my chance at the championship at stake. Fortunately, I was able to comply with the terms and knocked Taylor out in the eighth round. Hardly had I finished this fight when Fitz had another ready for me. It was Fred Drummond[1] whom I beat in a fairly fast go at Ply-

---

[1] No record exists of this alleged bout.

mouth. The results of these fights were to raise me considerably in the esteem of the British public, which began to sit up and take more notice of me. The press and boxing authorities, if they ever had favored Burns, now became more friendly toward me, and recognized my claim on the privilege of meeting Burns, and backed me in those claims, taking occasion to direct much severe criticism upon the title holder.

I filled a few more theatrical engagements in London and Paris, while Burns left for Australia. I did not linger long in England, for my quarry having flitted, it was necessary for me to resume the pursuit. Accordingly, my party and I also set sail for Australia, where I eventually cornered Burns and arranged for our fight. It was my second visit to the Antipodes, and there were many friends to greet me. On my first visit, I had polished off Felix and Lang, two Australian fighting boys who were well thought of. This had won for me the respect of boxing enthusiasts, but there were not many who believed I had a chance with Burns, who was a prime favorite, because on two occasions he had knocked out Bill Squires, another Australian, who at one time had been a seven-days' wonder to the kangaroos. Because of his two defeats of Squires, Burns was considered unbeatable and was the prime betting favorite, the average odds against me being two to one.

In addition to Burns' popularity, and the belief that I could not defeat him, the rumor became prevalent that there was some crooked work abroad; that it was framed that I should lose, and that I was not to have a fair chance in the ring. These rumors helped sustain the betting odds, and friends and others who really believed I could whip Burns, bet their money on my opponent in the belief that the decision would go against me, despite whatever showing I made. I felt too, that there was something astir and knew that I should have to watch my step in the selection of the referee. This was no pleasant combination of circumstances under which to contest for the championship in a strange country, but I was determined that nothing would prevent me from going through, because I already had sacrificed most of the usual rights and privileges accorded a challenger, and had agreed to accept a trivial sum of money — $5,000 whether I won or lost, while Burns was to get $35,000 win or lose.

My, but I did train for that fight! My training camp was at Botany bay, and in my camp were Duke Mullins, chief adviser and

second; Bobby Bryant, Leo O'Donnell, Rudolph Unholz, the
Walker brothers, Jack and George, and other boxers, all of whom
served me well as sparring partners, seconds and general aids. My
condition was superb. I do not recall another pre-fight period in
my life when I felt better or was more fit to enter the ring. My
lungs were in especially fine condition, and no matter how
strenuously I exerted myself it seemed that I never got winded.
Although we were engaged in the serious business of preparing to
fight the world champion, we had a gay time at that camp, and
indulged in strange and at times rather frivolous amusements. We
performed stunts that amazed the Australians and caused them to
shake their heads as if they doubted our sanity.

In two of these stunts, I was the sole performer, and the manner
in which I performed indicated the excellent condition of my
breathing equipment. Half in jest, I had wagered with some of my
friends that I could outrun a kangaroo. The wager was taken and it
was up to me to back my assertion. Accordingly, we stirred up a
kangaroo and the chase began. These animals, it is generally
known, are able to cover distance with ease and the one with
which I raced was no exception. How far I chased him, I do not
know. Both of us were developing high speed, and each was determined to endure, but the poor kangaroo finally gave up and top-
pled over dead. He had completely exhausted all his strength and
vitality. As for me, I was little the worse for the chase.

On another occasion, a greased razor-back pig was turned loose
for me to catch. He was a long, tall and lanky member of his species,
built like a race horse. Furthermore, he was undomesticated and
valued his liberty exceedingly high. He had no wish to be coddled
and manifested a rather vicious nature. Once turned loose, he
endeavored to put as much space as possible between himself and
mankind. But as speedy as he was, he was unable to out-run me.
After a pursuit that included many turns, twists and other
maneuvers, I grasped his oily body, and despite his struggles
subdued him.

Imitating hounds in speed and cunning, Duke Mullins, Bobby
Bryant and myself ran a jack-rabbit to death. These rodents are
considered about the last word in animal speed and are used in
Australia in hound chases. Our race with the rabbit took place on a
half-mile dog racing track within an enclosure. The rabbit was
turned loose with the three of us in pursuit. Our victim resorted to

all his clever tricks in eluding his enemies, and traveled so fast at times that he looked like a streak, but he was not clever nor fast enough to escape us, although he ran until he fell exhausted.

These are not imaginary tales but are actual occurrences and were reported in the Sydney newspapers. These and other events at my camp were a source of much discussion among Sydney folk and because of the unusual things which we did in the course of enjoying ourselves, attracted many people daily to our camp, wondering what we would do next. They got a lot of entertainment out of it and my friends and acquaintances increased in number. Most of my training was done in the early morning. I did lots of road work but comparatively little boxing, giving my attention largely to ball and bag punching. This method of training also caused the Australians to marvel. They were not accustomed to such procedure. They were certain that I was not training properly and that I was most neglectful. They were convinced that I could not possibly be in shape for the fight, and this belief having gained circulation, also added to the conviction that Burns would have the best of me.

I never was sure of getting Burns into the ring until I faced him inside of the rope. After the fight agreement was signed and our training camps were established, Burns continued his old tactics of sidestepping and making excuses. He was not satisfied with the terms of the contract, even after he signed them. He had many complaints to make, and persisted in opposing various details of arrangements for the fight. I expected him to call the fight off any day. I myself remained silent and either ignored his objections or consented to measures that would remove them, so eager was I to insure his presence in the ring at the appointed time. I do not exaggerate when I say it was almost necessary to drag him into the ring, but once in the ring he was a game and determined fighter and he took the punishment I gave him gamely and tried hard to defend his title.

The selection of referee was one of the most difficult tasks in connection with the fight and sometimes assumed such proportions as to threaten interruption of the fight. It was the subject of much bitter controversy and afforded Burns much opportunity for stalling. There were referees whom Burns would have accepted, but sensing the possibilities of trickery, or at least of an arrangement that would not be to my advantage, I, too, became more cautious for I knew that there were men in Australia who, especially when the welfare of a favorite was at stake, would make decisions according to instructions, if the inducement was sufficient. We had several meetings for the purpose of discussing the referee and most of these were heated affairs.

One evening I went to the office of Promoter McIntosh to take up the troublesome subject. The meeting was by appointment and those attending were Burns and his manager, Fitzpatrick, and myself. Accompanying me was Phyllis Bain, the seven-year-old daughter of James Bain, manager of the National Amphitheatre. Accompanied by her parents, the little girl was a frequent visitor at my camp. They were my dinner guests most every evening. Phyllis was quite fond of me and I of her. She insisted on going with me whenever I went to the city, on a drive or elsewhere. It was a rather unusual meeting for a child to attend. As our discussion progressed Burns became very angry.

'You used to be a good fighter,' Burns said to me, 'but you are all shot now; you might as well take your medicine.'

I only smiled at this and other insults which he uttered, but when he began to use profanity and become obscene I ceased to smile and warned him to stop.

'Burns,' I said, 'the newspapers are describing you as a gentleman, so be careful what you say. If you swear any more before this child, I shall give you a lacing right here.'

This angered him beyond endurance, and springing to his feet he made a gesture as though he would pull a gun, and I moved toward him. As I advanced, Burns grabbed a chair which was snatched from him by McIntosh. He then seized an inkwell which was standing on McIntosh's desk, but before he could hurl it, McIntosh grabbed his arm and attempted to hold him.

'Let him loose,' I said to McIntosh. 'He's tame and harmless.' Then, turning to Burns, I said: 'I'll remember this when I get you into the ring.'

We came to no agreement that day. I returned to my training wondering what the outcome would be. In the following few days, Burns three times threatened to declare the fight off unless he could select a referee. As the day of the fight approached, they sent for me three times to go and discuss the referee, but I declined. I had decided that nothing was to be put over on me and had been working out a proposition which I proposed to spring at the proper time. Two days before the fight when all parties to the contract, the newspapers and the public were in suspense as to who would be the referee, or whether or not the fight would take place, I took Fitzpatrick with me and went to talk over the problem with McIntosh and Burns. I had been battling for time and still was, my intention being to delay the selection of the referee until the last possible moment. On the occasion of this, our last meeting I permitted the conversation to go on for several hours. I felt that Burns was seeking to call the fight off, but I did not intend that such a disappointment should ensue.

I knew that I could whip Burns in a fight staged on merit, regardless of whom he might pick as referee, and if I had been convinced that there would be fair play in the contest, I would never have bickered. I knew that Burns and McIntosh were the closest of friends and that each had the fullest confidence in the other. I knew that McIntosh, as promoter of the fight, would not dare give an unjust decision such as might be given by an outsider, and so after the futile discussion had gone on for some time, I sprang my proposal which was a surprise bomb to those present. I turned to Burns, who was sitting across from me, and said:

'Before going any further with this match, I want to know if you and McIntosh are good friends.'

'We are friends, the best of friends,' replied Burns.

Turning to McIntosh, I inquired: 'How about it; are you and Burns good friends; do you have confidence in each other?'

'We are great friends; there are none better,' he answered.

All this time, Fitzpatrick stood by without uttering a suggestion or comment. I addressed McIntosh again, saying,

'If you and Burns are such good friends, then you must referee this fight.'

Fitzpatrick gasped in astonishment and began to frame a protest, but I interrupted him.

'I am fighting this fight and am going to have some part in naming the referee.

'Is it all right with you, Burns?' I asked.

He replied that it was. When I addressed the same query to McIntosh, he hesitated declaring that he had never had experience as a referee, and expressing his doubt as to whether or not he could qualify. I insisted that he should, and before we left the room, he had consented.

The next day it was given out to the newspapers that McIntosh was to referee the fight. At first, neither the papers nor the public believed the statement was true, and hundreds flocked to the training camps to ascertain for themselves whether or not it was so. The arrangement did not please the public and there was much sarcastic comment. When the announcement was confirmed, it had the effect of changing the betting odds. Burns, who had been a 5 to 4 favorite during the last few days before the fight now became a 7 to 4 favorite, which clearly showed it was believed that the naming of McIntosh meant an advantage for Burns. Fight fans were never quite reconciled to the selection, and on the day of the fight when McIntosh entered the ring, he got a noticeably cool reception, compared with the cordial receptions given both Burns and myself. However, while my appearance created a ripple of applause, it was nothing compared to the ovation that was given Burns.

The fight was the greatest ever held in Australia. Twenty-five thousand spectators attended, thousands of them having formed in line twenty-four hours before the fight began in order to get seats. Although in the midst of strangers, many of whom were semi-hostile toward me, I was not in the least perturbed. I felt no doubt of the outcome, and had I not intended to give the crowd its money's worth, I could have finished Burns in the first few rounds. Then, too, I figured that Burns had something coming to him, and I proposed to extend his punishment over a considerable length of time. I certainly wished to give him his $35,000 worth. He found out after the first few blows that he was done for, but he kept coming, and I heartily commend him for his gameness. His blows had no strength and I do not recall that they as much as stung me. Certainly he never jarred me. I hit him at will, whenever I wished, but I never exerted my whole power on him.

In addition to his gameness Burns fought cleanly. Neither of us used any foul or tricky tactics, which made it easy for the inexperienced and somewhat nervous referee. Once or twice he tried to separate us in the clinches, but lacking the strength for such effort, he gave it up and left us to work out of them of our own accord. Once in a clinch, he grabbed my wrist, which enabled Burns to land a blow on my face, but since it did not hurt me I made no complaint. Burns on the contrary complained many times and frequently appealed to the referee. My defense completely baffled

Burns. I led brisk lefts and rights to his body and face, and administered an awful punishment to him.

I found my opponent easier than I had anticipated. I kept up a continual conversation with Burns and with those at the ring side, as I usually do in the ring. Once with my hands at my side, I extended my chest and chin inviting Burns to hit me. I made openings for him and called his attention to them. 'Find that yellow streak,' I told him. 'You have had much to say about it; now uncover it.' At first, Burns tried to answer my sallies, but he soon desisted, his remarks being scarcely audible.

The intervals between rounds gave me a chance to scan the crowd and pick out unusual types of faces, or watch the changing expressions that flitted across the countenances of the spectators as they concentrated their attention on us. I even had opportunity to examine the outlying landscape and the immediate structure around the ring. As my gaze wandered out into the surrounding territory, I saw a colored man sitting on a fence watching the fight with open mouth and bulging eyes. My glance returned to him again and again. He was one of the very few colored people present, and he became a sort of landmark for me. I became more and more interested in him, and soon discovered that mentally, he was fighting harder than I was. Whenever I unlimbered a blow, he, too, shot one into the air landing it on an imaginary antagonist at about the same spot where I landed on Burns. When I swayed to avert a blow from Burns, the fighter on the fence also swayed in the same direction and at a similar angle. When I ducked, he also ducked. But his battle came to an inglorious end when it was necessary for me to make an unusually low duck. He attempted to follow the movement and fell off the fence. This incident so amused me that I laughed heartily, and Burns and the spectators were at a loss to know what had so aroused my mirth. Jack London, the late story writer, and Mrs. London were ring-side spectators and I think it was at this time that London got the idea of the golden smile with which he often described me later and which was so frequently mentioned in after years.

In the ninth and tenth rounds Burns was in a bad way. It would have been easy to have disposed of him, but so long as he invited more punishment I ladled it out to him as thick as he could stand it without going under. I eased up considerably in the last rounds, but in the fourteenth I decided to put an end to it. Just as I stepped out with this intention, I caught the eye of the police inspector. He had said nothing, but I felt that he was going to and I desisted from any further attack on Burns. I was not mistaken about the inspector's intention. 'This has gone far enough,' he said, and the fight came to an end. I had gained the title of champion of the world.

Friends and acquaintances, many of whom had lost money on Burns because of their fears that the fight would be unfair to me, swarmed upon me as I left the ring and poured forth their congratulations. Burns' friends helped him from the ring and hurried him to a doctor. I had suffered no discomforts in the bout and there was scarcely a scratch on me. After leaving my dressing room, I took a plunge in the surf, followed it up with a motor drive, and that evening entertained friends at dinner.

10
The Great Jeffries Bows

It was virtually necessary for me to wage two ring battles before I established undisputed claim to the championship. My fight with Burns really gave me the title, for he was the recognized champion. When I acquired his laurels, the question suddenly arose as to whether or not Burns was the champion. It was stoutly declared by some that Jeffries was the champion, because he actually had not lost the title in the ring, merely having voluntarily relinquished it to Hart, who had been defeated by Burns. It was upon this basis that Burns claimed the championship, and it never was questioned until I established my claim. At any rate I was not permitted to rest secure in the title. I was constantly harassed and criticized. Those who conceded, but resented my rightful claim to the title, started a turmoil by hunting a 'white hope' or one who would regain the title for the white race.

This hunt was a long and bitter one. All kinds of condemnation was heaped upon me — originating from no other cause than that I was not white. A large proportion of the public, or that part interested in boxing, at least, insisted that Jeffries still was the champion and that I must defeat him if I wished to retain the belt. I did not object to this proposal. I was willing to defend my claims against any man in the world. I lent my efforts and willingness to arrange a bout with Jeffries. It is interesting to note that Jeffries himself laid no claim to the title. He had retired from the ring and wished to remain out of it. At first, he declined to fight and much pressure had to be brought upon him to induce him to consider a match. An insistent cry went up from the country – a demand that he fight. It was said he was the only 'white hope' available and that he must meet me in order to keep the title in the possession of the white race. He had not fought for a long time, but he finally agreed to meet me, and it was arranged that we should fight July 4, 1910, at San Francisco.

This fight, too, was an historic one and stands out as one of the most unusual ring events in the world. A one-time champion – one of the greatest fighters in the history of pugilism, had been coaxed back to contend for the title in order to satisfy jealousy, hatred, and prejudice.

I deeply regretted this phase of the affair, but I was determined that I would defend my title and demonstrate that I was worthy of it. I knew that I could whip Jeffries. I was so willing to meet him, that I made many concessions, just as I had in the Burns fight, but being the title holder I did reserve the right to dictate some of the financial terms, as a result of which I was able to obtain a modest fortune which was really the most substantial returns I had ever received from my ring ventures. The fight was promoted and managed by Tex Rickard, and both he and I had our troubles with the affair. Throughout the whole business there were many difficulties and disappointments. It seemed that fate was working over-time to stop the fight or to make it a failure. Rickard at first wished to stage the fight in Salt Lake City, but Californians brought so much pressure upon him that he agreed to hold the mill in San Francisco. After he had obtained the license, built the arena and sold $300,000 worth of tickets, and Jeffries and myself had estab-lished training quarters in the San Francisco district, Governor Gillette suddenly forbade the fight giving no explanation for his action. Rickard lost $50,000 by that move, but undismayed he set out to find another site, and negotiated for holding the contest at Reno, Nevada, to which place it was necessary for us to move our training quarters. As the plans for the fight progressed, strained relations developed between George Little, my manager, and myself. He had carried on the negotiations for the fight in my behalf, but while I was training events came to such an issue between him and me, that we separated and from then on, until the day of the fight, he carried on a campaign against me, based upon misunderstanding and falsification, that in the end proved disastrous to him and all who had listened to him.

Jeffries was very bitter toward me and indulged in many hateful and venomous remarks concerning me. He condemned me in scathing terms. For a long time he declared that he had drawn the color line. He attacked Burns for fighting me, saying that he was money-mad and that he had sold his pride and the pride of the Caucasian race by fighting me. Jeffries' father, a minister, said he would disown his son if he appeared in the ring with me, forgetting that his son, Jack, had been in the ring with me in 1902 and that both Jim and his brother, Jack, had previously fought men of my race. During all this long period while discussion of our fight was carried on, the ex-champion was engaged in the theatrical business. He devoted much time to denying that he would meet me, or informing the public what he would do in the event he did meet me. This talk, which filled the sporting pages, was good advertising for him and made his show business profitable, and when the articles were finally signed by us, he proceeded to make as much capital out of it as possible and there was no doubt but that because of his forthcoming meeting with me the public paid more willingly and liberally to see him on the stage. I bore no bitterness towards Jeffries; I said very little in reply to his taunts and criticisms further than to reiterate my wish and willingness to fight him. As the fight neared, ugly rumors were afloat concerning the 'fixing' of the fight, and frequently it was declared that I was going to 'lie down to Jeff.' To these I paid little attention, though I admit that many circumstances developed which made the outcome seem doubtful to me.

My break with Little, my manager, coming as it did during the training period, caused the public to indulge in much speculation, and when he hinted that he had information to the effect that the fight was 'fixed,' letting it be known that this was the reason for splitting with me, the public was more than ready to believe it. Little circulated about freely at Reno, and became very friendly with members of the Jeffries camp. More than that, he bet heavily on Jeffries and that was the signal for many others, who originally intended to back me, to switch their money to Jeff. This also shot the betting odds upward. The fact is that the things that caused Little and me to separate were insignificant. They concerned the fight in no way and were not even based upon business relations. I liked Little, for he was a splendid fellow in many ways, but subject to erratic and hot-headed actions. When I learned that he was betting on Jeff and hinting at crookedness on my part, I was not resentful as much as sorry for him and sent him word cautioning him not to be silly. 'I am going to win this fight,' I told him, 'and if you do not want to lose your money you better not bet on Jeff.' My warning had no effect upon him. He continued to put all the money he could raise on Jeff and urged his friends to do the same. The consequences to him and his friends, in a financial way, my readers can easily guess. Opposition to me was heightened and belief in the possibility of crookedness was increased when Sam Langford arrived on the scene and intimated that he had information to the effect that I was going to let Jeffries win. Perhaps Langford did think that Jeffries would win, but neither he nor any other had any except an imaginary reason to believe the fight was not on the square. Langford, however, disliked me, principally, I think, because I had defeated him, having given him a good beating at one time. At any rate, he bet on Jeff, and his friends and others followed his example. The results were disastrous for them, but preceding the fight, Langford's activities lent color to the rumors afloat concerning me.

Recently he was reported to have said in an interview for a magazine article that he found me an easy opponent, in spite of the fact that I defeated him. I have no desire to exaggerate my ability as a boxer nor to minimize the capacities of my opponents. Langford calls attention to the fact that he knocked me down to indicate that I did not have the best of him. If Mr. Langford really gave this interview, all that I can say is that, in the language of the prize ring, he is punch-crazy, for no such knocking down of me occurred. The fact is that I dropped him a few times during the encounter. The boxers and sport writers who witnessed the event, among whom I recall the names of Joe Walcott, Mike Twin Sullivan, and John Twin Sullivan, Stephen Mahoney, a noted Boston sport writer, and Alec McLean, fight promoter, will attest the truth of my remarks.

Now to go on with the story of the Johnson-Jeffries fight, because of the bitterness entertained by Jeff toward me, and the persistent hints concerning the fairness of the fight, and the importance with which it was fraught for me, the selection of the referee for the contest, like that in the Burns fight, was a difficult problem. The press and sporting authorities gave it much attention. It was a matter of lengthy daily discussion by sport writers. Countless men were suggested for the task, but neither Jeffries, his manager nor myself could decide upon one that would be mutually satisfactory. We held many conferences over the proposition, and at times this phase was a troublesome one. It became the source of much speculation, and fight fans were considerably on edge because of the suspense that ensued. It was necessary for me to proceed with caution in the selection of a referee, because not only were the championship and a fortune at stake, but my reputation was involved. However, I brought this controversy to a satisfactory conclusion by suggesting that Rickard be the referee. He was acceptable to Jeff and his manager and consented to act in that capacity. Thus, for the second time in the history of prize-ring contests, the bout promoter was the referee, the other occasion being, as I have described, when I won the championship from Burns. Tex, I am pleased to say, proved entirely satisfactory and his decisions and his conduct of the fight throughout were such as to please all concerned. Despite the hatreds, jealousies and several small fortunes which were involved in this contest, it was as clean and square a fight as ever was staged, and I do not think there is any one who will say otherwise.

The manner in which I fought certainly vindicated me of any charges of 'crookedness,' and disproved the countless untruths and damaging hints that were bandied about preceding the fight. There have been charges in recent months that Jeffries was doped,[1] and that he entered the ring in a dazed and helpless condition. These charges are absurd, and were raked up by those desiring to revive a controversy which will do neither boxers nor the ring any good. Perhaps they were concocted for no other reason than to please sensation mongers. Certainly, if Jeff was doped, he would have realized it at the time, and even though he might have kept silent as the fight began, hesitating to say anything that would worry his friends, surely he would have said something concerning it after the fight, if for no other reason than to explain his downfall. But he said nothing, and so far as I can learn has not entered the controversy, either to confirm or deny the declarations. Even though Jeff had failed to realize his condition, had he been doped, the expert trainers, sporting authorities, and others about him would have recognized any condition in him resulting

[1] Jeffries himself repeatedly made this claim, and it appears in his book *Two-Fisted Jeff*, 'ghosted' by Hugh Fullerton.

from dope or poison of any kind. He was an object of great care and solicitation on the part of those about him. They were watching his condition constantly, and when the hour of the fight arrived, pronounced his condition perfect, because he had been thoroughly examined physically a short time before the bout began. Had he been doped or dazed, I certainly would have recognized such a condition when he got into action. Instead, I found him as alert, energetic and vigorous as any fighter I had faced. There was absolutely no indication of any condition that would impair his mental or physical ability. The charge that he was doped, I must assert, was absolutely unfounded, and I believe Jeff is of like opinion.

That there were those willing and capable of doping either Jeffries or myself, however, I do not doubt. One thing of which I am certain is the fact that an effort was made early in my training to poison me, and had not one of my associates swallowed the poison which was meant for me, the Reno fight might have had an entirely different ending. As it was, Frank Sutton, a member of my training staff, became deathly ill, and was constantly under the care of a doctor. The effect of the poison was just as one might wish, had he planned to disable a boxing contestant, for it left continuous ill effects and it was almost a year before Sutton had recovered, and then only after he had been almost constantly under the care of a physician. The poison was swallowed in a bar-room at the Seal Rock Hotel, San Francisco, where I had established my training quarters. I, myself, and members of my party often went into this particular bar-room for a glass of wine. Sutton, who purchased all my food and superintended its cooking was cautious and watchful. He subjected everything to close scrutiny. On the day he was poisoned his suspicions were aroused and without saying anything to me, he shifted the glasses of wine which had been poured for me and my friends. He got the glass intended for me and it proved to be heavily loaded with something as poor Sutton could well attest for many months afterward. However, he did not slacken in his duties toward me nor relax his vigilance, for, after we had moved to Reno, there were numerous rumors about to the effect that they were going to 'get me,' and all of us observed the utmost caution in eating, or whenever we were in public. Rumors that gunmen were on my trail were prevalent, and because of this, Governor Dickerson detailed five state rangers to guard me.

Happily, no other attempt was made on me; I finished my training, defeated Jeff and left the Nevada town hale and sound.

I feel that I was even in better condition when I stepped into the ring with Jeff than I was on the occasion of the Burns fight. My physical condition was perfect. My training had proceeded to just the right point, and I never felt more fit nor confident than I did on that memorable July 4. My training had begun at Seal Rock but had been interrupted by the stopping of the fight by Governor Gillette. We then moved to Reno, transferred in a special car. We set up our camp at Ricks' roadhouse, and we worked earnestly. In my camp as trainers, sparring partners and seconds were Al Kauffman, Monte Cutler, Kid Cotton, Tom Flannigan, Frank Sutton, Barney Fury, Stanley Ketchel, Bill Delaney and Watson Burns. Bill Little, at the beginning, was my manager and Owen Sighart was business agent.

In my training periods I never maintained a particular chief trainer. I never left it to my trainers to devise methods nor did I look to them for instructions. I had worked out my own system which I believe surpasses all others, and my trainers and others were directed to follow this to the letter. They worked under my directions, and they co-operated in a manner which made our associations pleasant and successful. In developing my system, it was only necessary for me to have substantial and dependable men around me, and in this matter I was exceptionally fortunate in my work at Reno. The men I had with me knew the game. Any one of them was capable as a trainer and any one could have worked a boxer into superb condition. Watson Burns was one of the greatest trainers of all times. Delaney was my chief second, and what a second he was! Others in my corner as seconds were Watson Burns, Harry Foley, Jack Lehay and Barney Fury. Sutton, as I have said, purchased my food and engineered the kitchen. He went to Reno daily, obtaining supplies and never did he buy twice at the same place, if he could help it. He established no permanent purchasing place because he did not intend to give possible food poisoners a chance to do any of their tricks. He watched the kitchen like a hawk. He inspected every food ingredient and all food after it was cooked before I was served.

Every member of my party had confidence in my ability and in my integrity. All thought that I would win the fight and they backed their beliefs to the fullest possible extent. Of all these staunch fellows who aided me in preparing for the fight, none has ever had reason to desert me. All of us, to this day, have remained the closest of friends. Four of them, I regret to say, are dead, but I recall their presence with the tenderest of memories. The four who have gone are Foley, Delaney, Ketchel and Cotton. They, together with those who are still living, made training worth while, and association with them was a privilege and a pleasure. Our lives in training were happy and cheerful. We had good times after some of our initial troubles and disappointments were disposed of, and I suppose that one reason that Little, Langford and others were sold on the idea that I was going to lie down was because I took life easy; I did not worry much, and sought always to extract for myself and others whatever enjoyment life offered.

So sure was I that I was going to win over Jeff that I lost no opportunity to urge my friends to bet on me, and one time when Hector McKenzie, who was a member of the Jeffries staff came over to my camp, I told him that I knew he was a friend of Jeff as well as a friend of mine, and that I did not wish him to lose any money, and that the best thing for him to do, if he did not wish to bet on me, was to keep his money in his pocket. However, I offered to bet him $5,000 that I would win, to indicate to him my certainty of the outcome of the battle.

Governor Dickerson visited my training camp often and we came to be excellent friends. Our friendship, it proved, was one that was to endure many years. He has always been staunch and loyal, and was one of my closest advisers when I was in prison, where he was superintendent. He took great delight in watching me train. I shall never forget a remark he made one day after watching me spar with Kid Cotton. He said, 'I have never seen a man who can whip Jack Johnson as he stands today, and I am forced to bet on him.' This observation by the governor followed a bout which I had just finished with Kid Cotton, two days before the fight. I did not wish to box Cotton on that occasion, preferring to polish up with Kauffman, who was more of Jeffries' style and manner. Cotton, however, was anxious to be seen in action that day, because a notable crowd was watching us. The kid was unusually active and aggressive and once butted me on the lower lip with his head which caused me to bleed – something that had never happened to me in boxing. Cotton seemed to be trying to make a grandstand showing, so I gave him his chance. For five rounds, I beat him severely and in the sixth he went down and out. He never was the same Cotton after that. He did not regain his senses until late that afternoon, and once he broke away from those who were caring for him and jumped into an irrigation ditch full of water, and in which he would have drowned, had not Fury and some of the other boys pulled him out. Noting that my lip was bleeding so freely, Governor Dickerson tried to get me to cease training for that day, for, knowing what was in store for me in the next two days, he feared it would not be a good thing for me. The cut caused by Cotton started to bleed again when Jeff hit me, and the fight fans roared with delight, for the thought that Jeff had drawn blood on me was a sign to them that he had the best of me, but it was not Jeff's tap which caused the flow of blood.

A dispute over a poker hand, and a disagreement over a play in a baseball game were the trivial causes of the breach in association between George Little and myself. Never once did we have any misunderstanding over the fight, its terms, or any other business affair as many supposed. It was an unfortunate circumstance, arising, as it did, in the midst of my training and preceding my meeting with Jeffries in a fight that was to be significant in ring annals. It caused much uneasiness on the part of all concerned. It disrupted my camp for a while, and had I been more temperamental it might have had more serious results.

The disagreement over the card game took place on a train on which we were enroute to San Francisco, preparatory to my training. There were three of us in the game, Little, Sighart and myself. Little did not like Sighart and often criticized him. I liked both of them and had confidence in each, and often found it necessary to adjust their differences. In the game Little sat between Sighart and me. During one hand, Little obtained a straight. My hand was no good and I had laid it down. Sighart had a better hand than Little but the latter having more money was able to bet so strong that Sighart was forced to quit. The situation nettled him and he was not in a good mood, feeling, as he did, that Little was deliberately trying to make things unpleasant for him. I dealt the following hand and Sighart opened the pot; Little raised and I staid; Sighart raised Little who again boosted; the pot was raised 15 or 20 times before the draw, the tussle being between Sighart and Little, I being content merely to stay. Little had three kings to start with;

Sighart had four jacks and I, although I did no betting had four
aces. Sighart drew one card, Little two and I stood pat. Both
thought that I had a straight. Little thought that Sighart had tried
to fill a flush or straight; he, himself drew his fourth king, and was
sure he had both Sighart and myself beat. He raised the bets of
Sighart and myself many times. The latter hated to lay down his
four jacks, but began to figure that Little had him beat. He accused
him of trickery and a hot argument ensued. With the betting, the
accusations and quarreling it was more than two hours before the
show-down, an unusually long time for deciding the merits of a
poker hand. In the quarrel that had taken place, each had accused
the other of doing funny things with the deck. I had remained
silent throughout the whole proceeding; neither Little nor Sighart
had figured me in the game, so when I won the pot, which contained about $1,500, Little became more enraged than ever and
accused Sighart of manipulating the cards so as to give me my four
aces. Of course he had done nothing of the sort, but nothing which
either Sighart or I could say could convince him that the deal was
square. A little while later Little and I clashed again, Sighart
having remained out of the pot. When, after considerable raising, I
beat Little, he threw his cards down, declaring again that Sighart,
who had dealt me the winning hand, was crooked and vowed that
he would 'get even.'

A few days afterwards I hurt my back while training at Seal
Rock, and was compelled to take up light exercise. We organized
two baseball teams composed of the men in my camp. I was the
captain of one and Little of the other. Sighart was playing on my
team and during a game one morning, Little and Sighart got into a
row over a play at third base. They had come to blows when I
stepped in and separated them. After that, Little declared that
Sighart would have to go. I told him that he would not – that I
would keep him. For a week or more we wrangled over Sighart.
Things were in a turmoil and, added to the difficulties occasioned
by the Governor's action in preventing the fight, my training was
not proceeding very pleasantly or satisfactorily. I told Little that if
any one went, it would be he and not Sighart. This was like
throwing kerosene on a blaze. Little became vicious and accused
me of intending to lie down to Jeffries. At about this time Rickard
was visiting me frequently, at which time we talked of how the
campaign preceding the fight might be carried on, in order that the

public might learn that I was training faithfully, was in good shape, and that none of us had any intention of fooling the public. These talks, into which Little was not invited, made him insanely jealous and he became more and more bitter. He pretended to believe that the talks between Rickard and myself concerned some crooked plan, and accused me of many things. I had borne all his tirades patiently, believing that he did not mean all he had said, but at this juncture I felt I had to get rid of him. After he left my camp, I settled down to real training and things went pleasantly. Flannigan succeeded Little as acting manager.

The day of the fight finally arrived. It was a beautiful one – the weather, excepting for the intense heat, was superb. The atmosphere was clear as crystal, and one could see for miles. More than 25,000 people had gathered to watch the fight, and as I looked about me, and scanned that sea of white faces I felt the auspiciousness of the occasion. There were few men of my own race among the spectators. I realized that my victory in this event meant more than on any previous occasion. It wasn't just the championship that was at stake – it was my own honor, and in a degree the honor of my race. I was well aware of all these things, and I sensed that most of that great audience was hostile to me. These things, while they impressed me with the responsibilities that lay upon me, did not disturb or worry me. I was cool and perfectly at ease. I never had any doubt of the outcome. Outside of a contemplation for a moment of the auspiciousness of the gathering, I was thinking for the most part of getting home. That had been my thought when I crawled through the ropes, and as Fury was tying my gloves I saw in the audience the yardmaster who had charge of the special trains. I sent Fury to ask him to come and speak to me. When he did so, I told him I wanted to leave right after the fight and that I wished him to make arrangements for my immediate departure. He said it would be impossible – that it could not be done. I said it must be done, and that if he would do it I would give him a tip that would make plenty of money for him. He stared at me for a moment, then said that he would get me out on a special.

'Do you mean that?' I asked. He said he did.

'All right, then,' I told him. 'Bet on me; I am going to win.'

I do not know what his winnings were, but he was as good as his word, and two hours after the fight, I was on my way to Chicago on the train which he arranged for me.

I was the first to enter the ring. There was one shady corner and in this I seated myself. Jeff followed a little later with his seconds, and proposed that we toss a coin for the shady corner. I declined to toss, but offered to relinquish the shade to him, an offer which he accepted, and I moved over into the sun. The crowd gave me a very hearty reception, but that given Jeff was twenty times greater than mine. When the fight started Jeff was a 10 to 4 favorite, but in the fourth round I was the favorite by the same odds.

Hardly had a blow been struck when I knew that I was Jeff's master. From the start the fight was mine, and, as I have just observed, the fourth round brought the crowd to a realization that Jeff had little chance to win. He fought in his usual style and I think with as much of his vigor, speed and endurance as ever. If he had not been fit, and if there had been the smallest particle of dope in him, as some have contended, he never could have stood under that hot sun for fifteen rounds withstanding the punishment I gave him. He fought his best. He brought into play some of the old swings and blows for which he had been noted. His brain was working keenly, but he found it almost impossible to get through my defense and at no time did he hurt me. He landed on me frequently but with no effect. He devoted his attention to fighting and did not take much part in the run of conversation which was going on. About all he said, was, once, when I struck him on the head:

'Say, but that's a tough old head,' he remarked.

As for me, I took part in the palaver that went on, addressing myself particularly to Jim Corbett, a member of Jeff's training staff, who took occasion to send a few jeering remarks in my direction. I told Corbett to come on in the ring, that I would take him on too. At the same time I was demonstrating, that, contrary to Jim's disparaging remarks, I was putting over a good, fast fight. I hit Jeff at will. There was no place that was beyond my reach, and I landed some stiff jolts on him, but not as stiff as I might have, for I really did not have any desire to punish him unnecessarily. The cheering for Jeff never ceased. The spectators urged him on and gave him every possible encouragement, but their cheering turned to moans and groans when they saw that he was suffering as he was. There came up to me from the ringside gasps of astonishment that turned to cries of pity, and more than once I heard them shout:

'Stop it! Stop it!'

The great crowd cheered Jeffries for his grit and supreme effort and they pitied him in his suffering, but they did not for a moment lose their admiration for him. As for me, they learned that I was not a quitter; they realized that I had not entered into any crookedness, and that Little, Langford and others who had swung much of the betting against me had let them in for a good trimming. However, it was not enough that the fight should be a meritorious one and that the best man had won on his worth or that the entire mill had been clean and square; the crowd was by no means pleased. The 'white hope' had failed, and as far as the championship was concerned it was just where it was before the beginning of the fight, except that I had established my rightful claim to it beyond all possible dispute. But from that minute on the hunt for the 'white hope' was redoubled, and when it proceeded with so little success other methods were taken to dispose of me, as I have related in former chapters.

The Reno fight probably was attended by more famous sporting men, boxers and promoters than any other. Prominent among them were John L. Sullivan, whose name stands out boldly in world fight records – the first holder of the recognized championship of the world. Hugh McIntosh, the Australian promoter who had backed my fight with Burns was present, and Burns, too, had made a long trip for the occasion. Another promoter present was Jimmy Coffroth. Frank Gotch, the famous wrestler, was in Jeffries' camp. Billy Jordan was the announcer and George Harding was the time-keeper. Bill Lang had come from Australia for the event. Tom McCarey was present and so were Fitzsimmons, Sharkey, Ketchel, Kauffman and hosts of others who had made and were making sport history. There was an army of photographers, newspaper writers, telegraphers. Prominent men from all walks of life had come from England, France, Spain, Mexico, Australia, Canada and every corner of the world to see what they hoped would be the return of the heavy-weight crown to the head of a Caucasian.

Since writing the above, there has come to my attention additional comment concerning the alleged doping of Jeffries for this fight. I have been told that Jeffries himself has said that he was doped and that members of his party have risen to express a similar belief. I am unable to verify the truth of these statements, but I am led to conclude that such men as Bob Edgren, James Corbett,

Sharkey, Choynski and other notables in sport circles who were with Jeffries at the time, all said to be experts and authorities upon points relating to a boxer's condition and capabilities, certainly had a part in misleading the public if, knowing that Jeffries was in no condition to enter the ring on July 4, 1910, because of the effects of drugs, they permitted him to attempt the fight. I am sure that their claim to expertness and trustworthiness must be considerably weakened if what they say is true and they knew it on the day of the fight; and they must have known it that day, for certainly there would be no way of discovering it after the fight – several years afterwards, at least. About the only dope which Jeffries suffered from was that administered by myself in the form of jabs and uppercuts to the jaw.

11
Challengers

Reposing in a Paris bank are something like 300,000 francs under court supervision, 250,000 of which belongs to me; the other 50,000 belongs to Frank Moran, an American boxer now living in the West. This bank account equivalent to about $60,000, together with interest, since June, 1914, Moran and I expect to have paid over to us within a short time. The money represents the gate receipts of a fight which took place in Paris between Mike and me in the above month and year. It was placed in the bank at the direction of a court in which an attachment was brought against the gate by McCarthy, an American publicity man, who obtained the order following a disagreement between him, Moran's manager and myself, a disagreement occasioned by McCarthy's greediness in trying to obtain more money than his contract with us provided for. Pending a decision by the court, the war came on, delaying matters at first; later McCarthy died and court action was further delayed. Information which recently reached us is to the effect that the money is to be paid to us shortly.

My fight with Moran was for the championship of the world, and because of that fact and other circumstances connected with it, it is one of more than passing interest. I was at the time a fugitive, which accounts for the fight taking place in Paris. Moran had ambitions to try for the title, and his manager Dan McKetrick of Pittsburgh opened negotiations with me. Acting as my own manager, I accepted Moran's challenge and made the necessary arrangements in the French capital for the meeting. This fight, while by no means the greatest, was one of the most interesting of my career, and for some reason I recall it vividly – more vividly than any other similar contest.

I trained earnestly and faithfully for this fight, because I knew that Moran was no commonplace contender, and I desired that, taking place as it did in a foreign capital, it should be a successful and satisfying public event, because boxing is a popular sport in France, and spectators like to get their money's worth. Only a few were aware of the intensity with which I trained, because most of my training was done under cover. It was said of me that I did not take the fight seriously and there was considerable doubt as to whether or not I would be in condition. It was my custom to arise at 4:30 o'clock in the morning and hit the road for a long and hard sprint. It was at this time that I discovered that France was preparing for war, though the public was unaware of the approaching conflict. Each morning along the route which I followed in my road work, I saw large masses of French soldiers maneuvering. It was said they were only engaged in periodical training, but there were signs in their movements which caused me to know that there was something more serious astir. On returning to my quarters, I would relate to members of my party what I had observed and many times declared that France was preparing for war with Germany. My assertions were laughed at and much joking was indulged in at my expense over what was termed my unnecessary alarm.

One morning while taking my usual run, I met a German who engaged me in conversation. He manifested deep interest in me and the approaching fight, and asked permission to visit my quarters. He lost no time in presenting himself. He inquired concerning my morning road work, asked about the hours and the routes which I took. These questions apparently were harmless and I answered them unsuspectingly. He next asked permission to accompany me on the runs, and I assented to his proposal. He went with me several mornings. It was a terrible ordeal for him. He could not keep up with me and spent most of his time and breath begging me to go slower. I could not accommodate him on this point because I was eager to carry on my training to the utmost. I was in splendid condition and, despite his appeals, I traveled at top speed leaving him far behind. He would come up panting and exhausted when I stopped, but he was game and tried hard to cover the ground with me. He soon dropped out of the early morning trips, however, and began a program of questioning seeking to find out what I knew about the movements, numbers and intentions of the French troops which I had observed. I told him little because I knew little. I afterwards learned that he was a spy in the employ of the German government.

As I continued my training, neither Moran nor the public knew much of my movements. I would finish my work by 7 o'clock in the morning and rest until 9 o'clock. I would then have breakfast and later I would make a round of the cafés, loiter along the streets or visit with idling friends. My apparent idleness caused everyone to believe that I was giving little attention to training and I frequently was reproached by those concerned in my success for my laziness or lack of interest. Meanwhile, Moran was doing much hard training and in a manner which impressed the public with his earnestness and skill.

One afternoon when I was engaged in ball punching McKetrick, Moran's manager appeared at my training quarters accompanied by McCarthy whom he introduced as an American publicity man who had lost most of his money in Paris, and who was seeking some means of recuperating his fortune. I always was ready to aid Americans, especially when they were in distress on foreign shores, and when McKetrick suggested that we might engage McCarthy as a publicity agent for the fight I readily assented, and we signed a contract giving McCarthy 5 per cent of the gross gate receipts.

The arrangement was a satisfactory one all round and none appeared better pleased than McCarthy himself. All plans for the fight proceeded smoothly. McCarthy did good work. The public was deeply aroused over the battle and the advance sale of tickets was huge. More than 25,000 spectators attended the fight. When McCarthy noted the exceptional flow of gate money he became dissatisfied and sought to change his contract to provide for a payment of 10 per cent instead of 5 per cent. I would not agree to this, and I was backed up in my stand by McKetrick. We engaged in a row of considerable bitterness, the upshot of which was the resignation of McCarthy followed immediately by his attachment of the entire gate receipts, a step which, as I have previously related, tied up the proceeds of the fight.

Moran and I fought twenty rounds. I do not believe that he hit

me a half-dozen times. From the tenth to the twentieth, I cut him
to pieces. During the first ten rounds I made little effort in the
fight. The public thought my training had been insufficient and
that my condition was poor. Moran thought I was doing my best
and figured that if he could stay ten rounds he would beat me. But
in the eleventh round, I unlimbered and began punching harder
and faster than ever, much to Moran's surprise. I literally slashed
him to ribbons. The crowd livened up and yelled with glee, because the French certainly like to see athletes punish each other,
and flowing blood to them is the sign of something worth while.
When the fight ended several doctors sprang into the ring to
examine Moran and give him first aid. He was under the doctors'
care for more than two weeks.

I believe that on the night of that fight, Moran was in the best
condition of his life, and that he could have whipped any white
man in the world. He put up a wonderful fight and struggled
every minute to land a telling punch on me, but in vain. I also believe that the fight was one of the best Paris fight fans ever witnessed. As for myself, I was in splendid condition mentally and
physically and got much entertainment out of Moran and the
crowd. As I write this, I am recalling in the most vivid manner
every detail of that fight. I can see myself jabbing with my left,
uppercutting, occasionally stopping right swings from Moran and
sending my right to his jaw. I can hear myself kidding Moran and
telling him what a nice fellow he was. I told him it did not look
right for him to have black eyes and a scarred face. He didn't waste
much time kidding back, but kept coming at me with blows
intended to be wicked, but all of which failed to connect. Once, he
slipped me a glancing punch and the crowd screamed with joy. At
this time, I dumbfounded Moran and the spectators by stepping
back and joining with the spectators in the applause, pounding my
gloved hands with all the energy I could and raising my voice in
the shouts of approval. As the fight went on, I carried on a conversation with McKetrick, asking him when he intended to sail for the
United States, and whether or not he wished to become my manager. I told Moran he was a great fighter – that he was putting up a
great fight, but that he would never again be the fighter he was
that night. When the fight ended I did not bear a scratch and was
not in the least fatigued. I went to the dressing room, donned my
evening clothes and went to a dinner and dance. Moran went into

the fight confident that he would win, and bet heavily upon himself, basing his confidence on his belief that I had not trained sufficiently, and on the further contingency that I had broken my left arm in a fight a while before with Jim Johnson, a tough boxer from the States.

The crowd before which we fought was, I believe, the best dressed I ever saw gathered about a boxing ring. Everyone in attendance was in evening clothes, with the exception of the Dolly sisters who then were appearing in a Paris theater, and who had come to the fight because of their former acquaintance with me, when I appeared with them on the American stage in a fifteen-weeks' engagement. Moran and McKetrick left Paris shortly after the fight and just preceding the war. I never saw the former again until May, 1926, when we met in Juarez, Mexico, where we had a jolly meeting, talked over the Paris fight and discussed our chances of getting the money held in the Paris bank.

My fight with Stanley Ketchel, who aspired to the heavyweight championship took place in Colma, Calif., October 16, 1909. Ketchel was an excellent fighter in the ring and a fine fellow out of the ring. He was, at the time of our contest, world's champion middleweight boxer. To my mind, he was far too small and light ever to have defeated a heavyweight, but the fact that he was game enough to try it proved his courage and confidence. Those who saw the fight or the pictures know that I played with Ketchel as I liked and that I refrained from punishing him any more than was necessary. I write this portion of my autobiography with regret and sorrow because Ketchel is dead, and he was one of my best friends and one whom I admired for his many excellent qualities. Because he is dead, I shall try to write not only truthfully but most respectfully of Ketchel's part in my life. In making the match with Ketchel I had a clever fellow to deal with in the person of Willis Britt, Ketchel's manager. I was my own manager in this event and between Britt and myself there was considerable argument over percentages. However, Ketchel was a great drawing card and I knew it. I knew that he and I together could draw a record gate. Because of this I did not wish to pass up the opportunity afforded by this match because of a few cents difference in percentages, and I finally assented to a percentage for Ketchel which was greater than I would have granted any other living fighter. I figured that I must get a large proportion of my money out of the pictures and was determined to make the fight an interesting and exciting one. Both Ketchel and I were trained to the minute and were in excellent trim for the contest. With the ability he had, I knew he would make a good showing and I, being so much larger, decided to give him a chance for the purpose of affording the spectators as much thrill and entertainment as possible. I was hoping for something of a sensational nature and tried to devise a plan to that end.

On the day of the fight, I started in my car with my seconds and personal party to the Colma arena. I was driving a six-ninety Thompson Flier and traveling at a rate of speed that enabled me to pass Ketchel and his party who were going to the ring in a white Lozier, at that time considered America's classiest cars. He was going 62 miles an hour he told me later. Despite the speed I was driving I was busily thinking how I could make the fight picturesque, and a plan occurred to me. This plan I did not divulge to any of my party though I told Bob Armstrong, one of my sparring partners, that if he should see me down in a certain round he need not get excited. We arrived at the arena 20 minutes before the fight and found that every ticket had been sold. We caught several men on the gate knocking down on us. We made them shake loose their cash and put it in the cash box, fired them off the gate and replaced them with others.

Once in the ring I looked about me and was surprised to find that every possible space that could hold a human body was filled. A few minutes afterward Ketchel entered the ring and I turned my attention from the crowd to him. I looked him over as he sat in his corner, and saw a man whom I recognized as a great fighter. I figured to myself that Ketchel was a good puncher and a game man, and that I must carry on the fight in a way that would make the pictures snappy and worth seeing. I decided that I would take him along for several rounds and let him make a good showing, so that the spectators would not tire of the fight. However, I did not propose to let him hurt me. I followed this plan throughout the fight and as it neared the end, I had Ketchel well in hand and could do with him as I wished. He sent over a punch which landed on my jaw. It did not hurt nor disconcert me. My brain had been working rapidly – so rapidly that I recognized this to be a clean cut blow with apparently much force back of it. I said to myself, 'Now's your time! Now's your time! Here's your chance,' and so I hit the canvas. All the time I was watching Ketchel and the referee. I was watching the latter so that he would not count me out and I watched Ketchel so that he would be in the position I wished when I arose. In order to do this, it was necessary for me to get up at a certain angle. It would cause him to move into the position I desired. As I got to my feet, I pretended to be groggy, but in reality I was ready to deliver the knockout. Ketchel rushed me with determination to put me out. I met him with a murderous blow that put him out instead. It was a right uppercut and the fight was over. Stanley lost several teeth, and when I returned to the dressing room I found one of his teeth embedded in my glove. After the fight we became fast friends and continued so until the day of his death. He was a member of my boxing party when I fought Jeffries and was an able assistant. When he was shot to death by a cowardly assassin on the farm of Colonel Dickinson in Missouri, there was no one who grieved more than I, because I admired him and counted him as one of my most valued friends.

12
The Frame-up for Freedom

Definite arrangements for my fight with Willard began when Jack Curley came to London to talk it over with me. The selection of Willard came about in the process of hunting the 'white hope.' The result of the fight ended that search, which had been carried on so intensely and bitterly that it had caused me much trouble and sorrow, because of the persecution to which I was subjected. On his arrival in London, Curley asked me if I meant business in meeting Willard. I told him I certainly did and that he would not find it difficult to make terms with me. The first night of Curley's stay in London, we visited the Coliseum where Oscar Ash and Lillie Braton were appearing. We did not talk shop that night. The next day we went to lunch and the preliminaries began, and in the evening at dinner we began to talk more freely. I told Curley to put all the cards on the table and to deal from the top of the deck. I had known him a long time. We had been close friends and had met in previous mutually satisfactory business deals. At one time in my life, when I was in serious trouble, he had stood loyally by me. As a result of this, I had the utmost confidence in him.

He frankly told me that if I lost the fight to Willard I could return to the United States without being molested. He said that I would be able to engage in a prosperous occupation and would gain new friends and please old acquaintances who were anxious to see me comfortably and peacefully settled down at home. These hints were inducements of course, but the greatest inducement of all was the opportunity it offered me to see my mother, for all who

know me and who have read about me, know that whatever other
failings I may have had, the love I had for my mother was so deep
and sincere that I would have done anything to end the separation
between us. After Curley had talked a while, explaining the
chances I would have and mentioning my mother several times, I
became more anxious than ever to get back home. After that first
conversation with him, I did not care any more for the title of
world's champion than a child does for the stick from which the
lollypop has vanished. In fact, I despised it.

Curley explained that Frazee and Webber, amusement promoters, were associated with him in arranging with me to meet
Willard. The fight, he said, would be held in Juarez, Mexico, and
Villa, the revolutionary bandit leader who then controlled
northern Mexico would finance the fight. Curley remained in
London a week or so, and when he departed we had reached an
agreement, as far as I was concerned, which would give Willard
the championship and permit me to return home. He gave me sufficient money to defray transportation expenses to Mexico and I set
about making preparations for going to the scene of the proposed
fight. I did not tell my wife nor Gus, my nephew, that I had agreed
to lose the fight, but pretended that I had entered into the deal with
the hope and expectation of winning.

Taking our leave of London, we embarked for Rio de Janeiro
early[1] in 1914. We made a brief stay on our arrival at the South
American port, and then departed for Buenos Aires, where we
remained for six weeks and where I put on several boxing exhibitions. When it came time for us to leave the latter city, we
found great difficulty in arranging passage for a trip back to Rio de
Janeiro, and after much search were compelled to board a freight
vessel which took us to Barbados in the West Indies where my
party remained three weeks, and where I did much exhibition
boxing and made many friends.

It was our intention to go from Barbados to Vera Cruz or
Tampico, Mexico, but owners of vessels and crews were dubious about
venturing far out to sea because of the submarine danger which
they believed existed, because of Germany's threats to carry on
'ruthless sea warfare.' We finally persuaded the owner of a small
sailing vessel to attempt a trip to Havana, Cuba, a port which we
reached after a hazardous trip during which we were driven by a

[1] Must have been after June 27th.

gale and nearly wrecked. After I reached Havana, I learned from
the newspapers that it was the intention of Carranza, president of
Mexico, to capture me if I sought to land either at Vera Cruz or
Tampico, and turn me over to the United States authorities,
whereupon I got into communication with Curley, who had gone
to Juarez to arrange for the fight. After several cable messages, I
induced him to come to Havana. Upon his arrival, I explained my
predicament and sought to have the scene of the Willard fight
changed to Havana, because I was eager to go through with my
part of the bargain. Then I intended to surrender to the United
States, but I did not wish to risk capture by Carranza, because I
foresaw that such a circumstance would involve me in official red
tape and delays which I was in no mind to contend with.

On his arrival in Havana, Curley said that Frazee, Webber and
himself had made arrangements for me to return to the United
States if I lost to Willard, but first I was to take the films of the fight
and exhibit them in South America and Europe, which sections of
the globe were to be my exclusive territory. I collected the fight
percentage due me just before the fight, but an additional percentage, which Willard's managers owed me if I lived up to my agreement to lie down, was not paid until the fight was almost over.
They tried hard to renege on payments to mè and even went so far
as to try and deprive me of the films which were to be given me,
according to contract. Pictures of the fight were made by Mace,
and when I learned that the situation was not ripe for my return to
the United States, I immediately left Havana for London. I was
told when my boat was ready to leave that the films were not in
readiness but that they would be sent to me in London as soon as
they were finished. I waited for the pictures several weeks and
when they did not arrive, I cabled to Curley asking why they had
not been sent. He replied that they were on the way. I watched
eagerly for their arrival, and when they did arrive, I was astounded
to find that they were blank – that they never had been on a spool.
I cabled demanding an explanation and in reply was told that the
deception or mistake was due to Mace, the maker of the films.

This turn of affairs enraged me and I started other inquiries by
cable, the result of which, among other things, brought me the information that Curley and his associates had made no move whatever to provide for my return to the United States. The failure of
the films to arrive had not caused me to lose faith in my supposed

friends. I tried to believe in them and to charge the delay in the films to other causes, but when I found that they had not kept their word in paving the way for me to return home I became not only cognizant of the fact that I had been flim-flammed but that I was up against a pretty raw deal. Therefore, I kept silent, but was not inactive. Inquiring at the office of the American Express Company, I learned that a film of the Willard-Johnson fight was being shipped to London from the United States. I knew that some plot was under way and I hired detectives to trace and watch the shipment. When it arrived I stayed close around the express company's office, knowing that some one would call for it.

I was not mistaken in this. A young man named A. Weil, who now lives in Chicago, appeared on the scene to claim the films. When they were transferred to him, I snatched them from him and obtained possession, though not until after a heated argument and various attempts to get them from me had taken place. I contracted with Barker & Company, one of the largest film firms in England to make prints of the films, and these I put on exhibition throughout England. I also sold the rights to the pictures to a South American company and with the proceeds from this sale and the display of the pictures in the United Kingdom was able to realize very satisfactory returns — returns which were ample enough to make me feel somewhat repaid for the manner in which Curley and his partners had bilked me. I also sold the Australian rights to the pictures to Rufe Nailor.

Preceding the fight with Willard, I did no serious training. I engaged in a few boxing exhibitions and did a few 'strong man' stunts, such as pulling against horses and permitting a horse to stand on my stomach. This was about the extent of my training. I had no wish to undergo the ordeal of strict training knowing as I did how the fight was to terminate. Mrs. Johnson, my nephew Gus, my sparring partners and friends were curious and alarmed over my failure to train properly and several times demanded to know what my object was in being so indifferent. I boxed occasionally with Bob Armstrong, Sam McVey and some other American boxers whom I had previously fought in America, but as I always had been able to box rings around all of them, they never knew whether or not I was in shape.

On one occasion Mahoney, an American contractor who had played a big part in the Spanish-American War, and who then was living in Havana overheard me talking to Willard and repeating 'Hit me! Come on, hit me!' I was then a big favorite in the betting. What Mahoney heard caused him to take quick leave of the arena and re-enter by another way, when he laid a big bet on Willard. He won a big sum of money, of course. It just happens that today Mahoney is a very close friend of mine. I have visited Cuba three times since the Willard fight, and on each occasion Mahoney has met me and been my host.

I did not tell Mrs. Johnson I was going to lose the fight until a few moments before I entered the ring. Curley had paid me my fight percentage before I left my home. No one knew that the money was there, and I employed four policemen to guard the home, though they did not know that it was because of the money, and with the understanding that they merely were to watch the premises. I instructed Mrs. Johnson to sit at the ringside and watch the fight; that there was more money due me, and until this money was paid to me, I would not let the fight take the course agreed upon. Delay in paying this money was due to the incomplete count of gate receipts, which was under way when the fight started. Mrs. Johnson was to signal me when she had received the additional money, and I was to signal her so that she might leave the ringside. The fight was originally intended to end in the tenth round, but when that round arrived the money had not been paid. It was nearing the twenty-sixth round when the money was turned over to Mrs. Johnson. I had specified that it should be in $500 bills in order that the package should be small and the amount quickly counted. After examining it she gave me the signal. I replied that everything was O.K. by a pre-arranged sign and she departed. In the twenty-sixth round I let the fight end as it did. I felt very sorry for Mrs. Johnson, to have to relinquish the belt, but I was not sorry that I had lost the championship – or rather permitted another to attain it. On the contrary, I was happy, because I hopefully looked forward to my speedy return to the United States, where I would again be with my old friends and above all, with my mother. It was this expectation of my return to my native land, my friends and my mother that determined my part in the historic Johnson-Willard fight and explains why and how I lost it.[2]

[2] Most contemporary critics declared that Johnson had been fairly beaten, but Jack always maintained that he 'lay down' and Nat Fleischer, editor of *The Ring* magazine paid him $250 for a signed confession that the fight had been faked.

13
Looking at Life at Fifty

I am about to reach my fiftieth year. So far as I am able to determine, there never has been in the history of pugilism, or other athletic endeavors, a man whose career has been longer than mine, and there has been no one to reach my age with his skill and strength intact. Men ten to twenty years younger than I have retired from the ring and are forgotten. As for me, I am continuing daily, my physical development and the care of my body with the same conscientiousness that I observed when engaging in the arduous work of meeting all boxers. More than that, I have in recent months engaged in some severe ring battles and won all of them. Only the restrictions of boxing commissions because of my age, prevent me from becoming a contender for the highest ring honors. Yet a large percentage of the public, I believe, feel that I still am capable of standing up against the best of the boxers. Friends who know me best believe that I can defeat any of the present heavyweights.

The three members of the Illinois boxing commission, John C. Righeimer, George Walter and Paul Prehn, have told me that personally they believe I can defeat nine out of ten of the leading present-day ring men, but the commission's rules prevent them from confirming their opinions by issuing the license which is necessary, and which I believe I merit.

Denied this privilege, I am deriving much satisfaction from persistent training of myself, and also by contributing my efforts to the training of young men who are daily working out in my gymnasium. I am teaching them to train their bodies, their muscles,

their nerves and their eyes so that, whether they become professional boxers, merchants, bankers, doctors or lawyers, they will
have strong bodies and good health which are assets that every
man should have to make him a useful and successful citizen. If I am
instrumental in helping a few of the younger men – men who must
soon assume more important places in life – if I can, by my own
experience and methods direct them into channels of success, I
shall do more than I would in merely producing a boxing
champion.

I, least of any, should speak lightly of the successes I have had and
the good fortune that has been mine, notwithstanding the bitterness and tragedies that have crept into my life. I am by no means
unmindful of these successes and the kindly way in which fate has
treated me. Yet I believe that today I am serving in a more useful
capacity than at any time in my life. My place in the world is no
longer as spectacular a one, as it was a few years ago, because I have
chosen to direct my path into quieter activities. These activities, I
have the satisfaction of believing, are more useful to the world and
my fellow-men. As for myself I am happier; I have plans and pro-
jects for the future which I think will reveal the real Jack Johnson
and I am sure will redound with even greater credit to me than the
things which I have done in the past.

In August, 1925, I was married for the fourth time, when Mrs.
Irene Pineau became my wife. While we have been married
scarcely two years this union is proving a most happy and inspiring
one. Mrs. Johnson is a woman of many splendid qualities. She possesses, besides her feminine charm and grace, an unusual intellect.
Her accomplishments are many and varied. Our ambitions, our
likes and dislikes, our contemplation of life and its purposes, and
our desires to live and live right are mutual. Between us there has
developed an understanding that makes our lives peaceful, enjoyable and content, and together we are striving to attain as best we
can. We have faith in and love for each other, and we look to the
future with keen anticipations of the happiness and success it holds.
I am intimately acquainted with the domestic life of people from
all ranks of society in Chicago, in America and elsewhere, and I
can truly say that there is no home filled with more sincere mutual
love, peace, contentment and co-operation than my own. Mrs.
Johnson represents to me the highest and the best that a woman and
a wife can possibly be. At the present time I am happier than I have

ever been in my whole life. My wife and I share each other's interests whole-heartedly, and these interests are not merely professional but cultural. I have every reason to believe that our love and happiness which binds our lives together is lasting. My love for my Irene is a love that knows no parallel either in my own life or that of any man I have ever known.

The more that is written and said concerning one who has held public interest, the less the public knows about that person. Of me there has been much written and much said. My enemies have never neglected an opportunity to place me in an unfavorable light before the world, which is more ready to believe the evil than the good. I do not mean this as a condemnation nor as a criticism; it is merely force of habit, a sort of instinctive desire for the sensational. Furthermore, when favorable reports concerning one's behavior or accomplishments are chronicled, they are couched in simple and unadorned terms; when a person of prominence deviates from the beaten path or even an unfounded rumor of transgression of the conventions of society arises, discussions and descriptions flare in impressive and suggestive news-stories and headlines. Sly hints of something more serious are deliberately injected and misstatements pass unchallenged. From this prevalent practice have come circumstances which have caused me many undeserved difficulties. I have been the subject of untruthful and unjust statements. I have been accused of many evils in which I had no part. When there was occasion for unfavorable report, those reports were grossly exaggerated and were accepted as true. On the other hand, when I did anything of a worthy nature or performed a distinctive service, oftentimes nothing was said of it, or, if it did receive attention, it was only of a casual and indifferent nature. I am not thin-skinned, nor do I chafe under criticism or condemnation. I have born much of it without obvious resentment. I either maintained silence or laughed it off. Yet it is not comforting or pleasant to realize that I have been misunderstood, and that my motives in many instances have been misinterpreted. I am discussing these things not in defense of myself, for I need no defense, but because I believe I am entitled to explain some incidents, the truth concerning which I know my many friends will appreciate, and which it would be good for my enemies to know.

I must admit that my profession as a boxer and my interest in kindred matters have brought me in contact with a plane of life, the nature of which gives rise to more doubt and suspicion than attaches to ordinary pursuits. I have had associations with classes of persons who do not rank high in the social scale. For this reason it has been comparatively easy to arouse suspicion concerning me and to aggravate rumors of my alleged misconduct. Then, too, I have been the victim of prejudices and jealousies aroused because of my racial origin, and these have kept adverse criticism fanned to a heat that sometimes was intense. In all candor and without fear I ask any fair-minded and unprejudiced person or organization, if they can cite a single instance in which I have in any way been guilty of a crime or shown any inclination to criminal conduct, other than accusations arising out of conspiracies planned for the sole and selfish purpose of blocking my legitimate and rightful efforts. I challenge mention of a single instance in which I have been guilty of dishonesty, theft, bodily injury to anyone with malice, or any other crime or charge which could be sustained in a court of law.

I have been severely criticized because of my several marriages and because of my love affairs, but in none of these did I go beyond my legal privileges or conduct myself differently from prevailing customs, observed by thousands of my fellow citizens. They have involved me in scandal, it is true, and imaginative newspaper writers and maliciously minded persons have seized on them to bring condemnation and misfortune upon my head, while others doing exactly as I have, were dismissed with little more than a knowing and forgiving gesture. My marriages and my loves have been sincere. They have been clean. The women who have come into my life have been honored, and lovingly protected by me. To them I have given the utmost consideration and kindness; to none of them have I been cruel, and never was I lacking in my responsibilities for their welfare and happiness.

A pugilist is not presumed to have high ideals. By some he is believed to have brutish tendencies, and at best to be concerned only with material things. The possession of muscular strength and the courage to use it in contests with other men for physical supremacy, does not necessarily imply a lack of appreciation for the finer and better things of life. Brutish qualities and base inclinations are prevalent in all classes. A man's vocation is no measure of his inner feelings nor a guarantee of his earnest desire to live right and attain the highest standards.

Fate made me a boxer. My home surroundings when a child and growing youth were such that I might have been expected to adopt most any other means of gaining a livelihood other than boxing. As I have previously remarked, my father was a pious man and earnest in his church activities. He did not neglect to impress upon me and my brothers and sisters the importance of religious life, and I at one time was deeply concerned in the Bible and its teachings. Throughout the eventful years of my life I have never lost my faith in those teachings, but I never professed to be religious or to have church affiliations.

When I had attained distinction as a boxer and was enjoying the acclaim accorded celebrities, I found that there was much bitterness mixed with the sweetness of triumph. When prejudiced and vindictive persons and organizations began pouring their wrath upon me, and I found myself beset on every side by unjust condemnation and accusations, I sometimes wondered if there was a God. I also wondered, what, after all, was the use of attaining something if its possession was to bring persecution and cause for regret.

Everywhere I saw hypocrisy in its most deplorable forms. I saw men and women quite willing to trade their honesty and character for wealth, power or fame. I came in contact with those ready to risk their own souls and to sell mine if some worldly prestige were to be gained. Discrimination and inconsistency I found prevalent everywhere, and I began to study human nature and life in every phase that was presented to me. My attention was drawn to the churches in this study, and in following my profession as a boxer I was by no means separated from church members. In fact, they made it their business to impress me with their existence and influence, and I discovered, I am sorry to say, more hypocrites in the church and more people of church membership who were dishonest in their conduct than among all the care-free, thoughtless and irreverent spirits in the world of sport and questionable living.

In 1898, when I was twenty years old, I began to make money in quite large sums. As the years went by I made more and more money. Several small fortunes came into my possession. Altogether, I estimate that my earnings reached one and a half million dollars; yet there were many times when I was broke and found it difficult to obtain the merest necessities. It was said of me that I

was a spendthrift; that I was plunging into dissipation and living a
riotous life. Such stories follow in the wake of champions. My excellent health and physical condition today certainly refute these
charges, because there is no more obvious fact than that dissipation
and health are mutually incompatible.

But I will admit that I disposed of my money freely, sometimes
wildly and foolishly; I probably spent some of it for things of no
tangible value. I gave much money to churches of all denomi-
nations. I frequently was solicited by them for contributions and
never, when I had money, did I fail to give regardless of creed or
color. I gave my money to men and women in my world who
were sick and unfortunate. I did not give in dribs nor content
myself with merely giving to a special fund, but I took it on myself
many times to defray the hotel-, hospital-, grocery- and rent-bills
of persons whom sometimes I did not even know, but who had
been reported to me as in need.

My friends and associates less fortunate than I, never lacked for
anything when I had funds at my disposal, and I never thought of
enjoying life, or indulging in pleasures unless those about me were
as well provided for as I. I did not do these things because I wanted
to be a 'good fellow,' I did them because I enjoyed seeing people
happy and comfortable. It is with pride and satisfaction and not
with boastfulness that I say that other people have enjoyed more
benefits from my money than I have.

I might digress here sufficiently to mention the conventional
mode of living prevalent in the prize-ring world. I seldom, if ever,
traveled alone, but was generally accompanied by a number of
friends and camp-followers whose expenses were paid out of my
income. In this I was merely following the established custom,
although I probably was sometimes not as attentive to my own
financial interests and ready to cut myself loose from parasitic indi-
viduals who were taking advantage of my generosity. But looking
back upon my expenditures, I do not regret the pleasures that my
money has brought to those about me.

When I was accused of crime and misconduct and suspicion was
being cast upon me, some of the persons to whom I had been the
kindest, were the first to desert me, and others for whom I had
done little proved my staunchest defenders. The churches and their
members censured me severely and made people who did not
know me despise me. Before I had been tried on charges, of which

I was not guilty, the churches were vicious in their attitude toward me, and were responsible for much of the prejudice that arose against me. If the troubles of Job were compared with the troubles of Jack Johnson, I think that mine would be found the more intense, for they struck at my soul, while Job's greatest cause for complaint was that he had been deprived of his wordly possessions and his health, and he was moved to curse the day he was born, but I did not become so desperate as that. It was probably because I saw in the story of Job some parallel to my own experiences that he became my favorite Biblical character.

My faith was unshaken, for I believed, and still believe, that there are honest, fair-minded and decent people in the world, though I have a vague feeling that they are in the minority. Although ancient in origin and reduced to a common-place level by constant repetition, there is no greater moral or religious precept than that which urges us to 'Do unto others as ye would have them do unto you,' and I believe that the greatest test of our morality is to help those who are in trouble and in need, even though their own misconduct has brought their troubles and their needs upon them. I thought at one time that this was a basic ideal of Christianity, and that it was exemplified by the church and religious organizations, but I was forced to question this belief in 1913 when persecutors were hard upon my heels, and were led by the churches. The latter tried to stop me from boxing which was my profession, and they went so far as to try to stop my appearance in theaters which meant nothing more nor less than preventing me from making an honest and legitimate living. I did not mind so much that they should seek to stop the prize-fighting, for I can readily understand that churches might not believe in that form of activity. But why should they wish to stop exhibition boxing on my part in the theaters? How did they expect me to live? Should I become a thief by night, a gangster or a murderer? It was this persecution, this discrimination against me, and the insistence that I was a wicked and undesirable person which was the cause of my deeper contemplation of life, of people and the conditions that give rise to their strange behavior.

I cannot recall that I have ever been an enemy of society, nor that I have ever corrupted any one, yet here was the hand of fate in the guise of Christianity turned against me. I did not feel myself humbled, nor did I suffer a slackening of courage, but there were times when I felt that perhaps, after all, if I relinquished my career in the prize-ring I could avoid some unjust criticism. This thinking took a definite course when I was in prison. I always had given much attention to the Scriptures, and actuated by the manner in which I had been treated and concerned in solving some of the problems of existence, I gave the Bible more serious study. I became deeply interested in some of the narratives of this sacred book, because I found in them parallels applicable to present-day conditions. The result of this study was that in 1922, a year or so after I had been discharged from prison, and following the completion of a theatrical tour I addressed congregations from the pulpits of several Eastern churches.

In undertaking to address church organizations, I became the object of new attacks. They questioned my sincerity in appearing in churches. I was ridiculed and many flippant jibes were hurled at me. I was described as a prize-fighter turned preacher. To the humorists and satirists it was incongruous, and supplied their wits with sweet morsels. I was reproached with having selfish motives and accused of capitalizing the curiosity which people entertained concerning me. But if I were bent on money-making in my pulpit adventures, I could certainly have employed my time in a more lucrative manner.

In addition to questioning my sincerity erroneous reports were spread abroad concerning what I had said, and at one time I was charged with an attempt to rouse the members of a colored congregation to rebellion by advising them to use 'force,' if necessary, to gain their rights. In this particular instance, I had discussed casually the relations between the white and colored people, but it was from the standpoint of more harmonious living and mutual understanding, for I do not countenance racial antagonism. I would be the last one ever to appear in the role of an agitator upon this subject.

I have given much thought to the great problem of the relations of the white and black race in America. I believe that the discussion of these questions has not helped greatly to clarify the issues. White people often point to the writings of Booker T. Washington as the best example of a desirable attitude on the part of the colored population. I have never been able to agree with the point of view of Washington, because he has to my mind not been altogether frank in the statement of the problem or courageous in the formulation in his solutions to them. On this point Frederick Douglas' honest and straightforward program has had more of an appeal to me, because he faced the issues without compromising. Personally I cannot say that I have ever been in doubt as to my own policy. Although I have often encountered prejudice on account of my race I have always, when I met people personally, been able to win their confidence by honest dealing and by straightforward and disarming face-to-face contact. I have found no better way of avoiding racial prejudice than to act in my relations with people of other races as if prejudice did not exist. A glance from eye to eye instantly does away with mutual suspicion.

While I was termed by some to be engaged in 'preaching,' I prefer to define my church engagements as lectures. In these lectures I departed entirely from the subjects of boxing, sports and such matters as had constituted the principal concern of my life, and had for my subjects Biblical characters and narratives. My several lectures were woven around Job, Saul, Esau, Jacob, Esther and Revelations. I devoted several weeks to these lectures and occupied the pulpits of several New York churches as well as those of Jersey City and Pittsburgh. My auditors were both white and colored congregations. Wherever I went on those missions, I was received with the utmost kindness and consideration, and I have reason to believe that my efforts were not without good results.

I have taken occasion to emphasize somewhat the tendency of newspaper writers to utter untruths and ridicule concerning me when my conduct seemed to be not strictly in accord with moral and social precepts. I have alluded to the avidity with which the public pounced upon me when I was accused of deviating from established custom, and to the exaggerated statements, loaded with malicious hints that were made whenever it was possible to present me publicly in an unfavorable light. The press was eagerly bent upon reciting anything savoring of the sensational where I was concerned. But when I performed some worthy service there usually was complete silence. Thus, when I was in Spain during the World War, and gave my services to American and allied officials in obtaining information about the activities of German submarines along the coast of Spain, there was only slight mention of my efforts. During the war, there were a number of stranded Americans in Spanish cities, many of whom I aided financially and otherwise, and who, but for me, would have been subjected to much suffering and discomfort. But my part in these little tragedies so far as I know, has never been recorded.

I saved many lives when the tidal wave engulfed Galveston September 8, 1900. In this disaster, the greatest of modern times, thousands of persons lost their lives. As the water rose, thousands of homes were threatened and most of them were destroyed. Great numbers of persons were driven to the upper stories and the roofs to escape drowning. Avaricious men appeared on the tragic scenes with boats and wagons charging a fee of several dollars to convey these unfortunates to safety. When I encountered them, I either compelled them to go to the rescue of the victims, or brought my boxing proclivities into play and took possession of their rescue conveyances myself and piloted the threatened to safety. I spent many days in relief work after the catastrophe feeding the hungry, caring for the sick and injured and burying the dead, but industrious newspaper writers in seeking topics concerning me never chronicled these events. The records of Galveston authorities, and of the relief committees will substantiate what I have related in this connection.

A few years ago in southern Illinois a cyclone laid waste a large stretch of country. Millions of dollars' worth of damage was done and there was a large death toll. My friend, Johnnie Conners, sponsored a boxing program for the Elks lodge of Springfield, the proceeds of which were to go to the fund for the relief of the cyclone sufferers. Conners asked me to take part in the program and inquired as to my charges for the occasion. I offered my services without charge, paid all of my own expenses, and in addition paid another well known boxer a substantial sum, together with all his expenses to appear with me in the boxing exhibition. The show netted several thousands of dollars, and was one of the greatest single amounts contributed to the relief fund. Conners and the Springfield Elks lodge will confirm me concerning my part in this. To newspapers, it was only of minor interest; they would have preferred something more salacious.

At Bridgeport, Connecticut, I put on a boxing exhibition not long ago for the benefit of a sanitarium where wounded and tubercular World-War veterans are being treated. Many entertainments and other methods of raising money for the benefit of these sufferers had been tried. My boxing program made more money for the sanitarium than all the previous entertainments combined. The trustees of the sanitarium will vouch for the truth of this statement.

In an exhibition boxing contest with Sam Langford in a Boston theater I was instrumental in raising one of the largest sums of money contributed from the New England states to the sufferers in the San Francisco earthquake and fire. By donning the gloves, I was able in the unmanly and unrespected sport of boxing, according to the definition of some, to raise more money than any other single entertainment or club event conducted for the same purpose in Boston. The relief committee to whom the proceeds of this fight were turned over will substantiate the truthfulness of this statement.

Various organizations and war relief committees in England will give favorable reports of my activities during the World War period when I was in England. I appeared in numerous boxing exhibitions, the proceeds of which were used to procure comforts for crippled, blind and tubercular soldiers. In these events I not only tendered my services without cost, but I defrayed my own expenses.

A few years ago in Chicago, while I was driving through Washington Park in an automobile, accompanied by Barney Fury, a huge car overturned pinning four people underneath. I attempted to life the car off the victims, but injured my back so severely that I was compelled to give it up. I hurried to the Del Prado Hotel and turned in a fire alarm which brought a company of firemen to the scene. They aided me in rescuing the injured motorists. One of them, a girl, had suffered a fractured skull, and placing her in my car, I sped to Washington Park Hospital. Hospital authorities refused to admit the patient unless I agreed to defray the cost. I readily assented to this, although the girl was a stranger to me. I paid the entire hospital bill, and as far as I know, the injured girl never learned who had aided her. Records of the hospital will bear me out in this narrative.

When Sam McVey, the noted pugilist with whom I had several ring contests, died in New York City of pneumonia, I was playing a show in Cincinnati, Ohio. I learned of his death, and that a fund was being raised for the purpose of burying him. I wired to New York and stopped the raising of the fund, closed my show and followed my message to the metropolis, where I paid all of the funeral expenses and disposed of the bills that had accumulated during

McVey's illness. Friends of McVey and the attending undertakers will confirm me in this statement.

During a visit in San Francisco I learned that a former well-to-do Galveston family had met with misfortune. Their only daughter had died and they were without funds with which to bury her. I went to their aid, tendering them sufficient money for the funeral and other expenses which they had been unable to meet. The mother and father, and Catholic priests who had been aiding the family, and others will speak for me in this instance.

These brief references are only a few of the many cases in which I have given my time and my money to persons and causes, in the hope of having some part in reducing suffering and misfortune. I could cite many others, but I do not wish to invite accusations of self-praise. It never has occurred to me to mention them previously, and I do so now only to present the contrast that has marked my life, and to strengthen my assertion that the world is ready and willing to make much ado over one's delinquencies, but slow and negligent in recognizing worthy qualities and deeds.

As I am writing this, almost six years have elapsed since my release from prison. These years have not been spectacular or eventful ones, but they have been modestly successful and very happy ones. When the prison gates opened, and I again found myself facing this erratic world, a new era had dawned for me. Including my prison term, I had been absent from my old haunts nine years, but I soon picked up the raveled ends. As I have intimated, I had an inclination to turn my attention to fields other than boxing, and therefore went on the lecturing platform, sold stocks and bonds for a while, devoted several weeks to theatrical work, acted as advertising representative and fostered a few small investments.

But whatever course I followed, it inevitably led back to the boxing profession in some form. In these six years, I have fought in several contests, the principal ones being outside the United States because, in this country, boxing commissions mainly animated by prejudice feel that I must retire. Besides my bout with Homer Smith in Montreal, I engaged in some exhibition work in Cuba, and also fought two men, each of whom had gained some reputation and recognition as heavyweight contestants. One of these was Jack Thompson whom I beat in seven rounds, and the other was Farmer Lodge, who was expected to gain more than passing distinction in the ring. I won over him in four rounds. Each of these fights, while not of great importance, received much notice, and they were attended by large crowds of both Cuban and American fight fans. Returning from Cuba, I filled a few more lecture dates, one being under the auspices of the Ku-Klux Klan organization at Danville, Illinois, where I was given a lively and friendly welcome. At this event, hundreds were unable to enter the hall where I appeared. My lecture topic was 'The Golden Rule,' and the approval of those who sponsored and heard the lecture was expressed in an emphatic manner. This again demonstrated to me that personal contacts can break through official prejudices.

My outstanding ring contest of the present period was on May 2, 1926, when I fought fifteen rounds with Pat Lester at Nogales, Sonora, Mexico, a mile or so south of the American border. I easily won the decision. This fight was not a spectacular one, nor did it mean much in ring history, except that it removed Lester from the ranks of contenders for the championship title. He was rated as the West's most formidable fighter, and prior to meeting me, he was considered a logical antagonist for Dempsey,[1] who still held the heavyweight title. But whatever this match lacked in importance to world ring affairs, it was one of the most notable of its kind in boxing history, because one of its combatants was the oldest boxer ever to have entered the ring in a legitimately staged bout for a decision. That oldest boxer was myself. I was forty-eight years old and Lester was twenty-four. But whatever he lacked in experience, he made up in size and pounds. He was 6 feet, $3\frac{1}{4}$ inches in height, and weighed into the ring at 235 pounds, exceeding me in height by $2\frac{1}{4}$ inches, and out-weighing me fifteen pounds. He had had three years of intensive fighting, and had put away some of the best men on the coast. He was being coached and managed by Spider Kelly, a veteran fighter and manager, said to be one of the world's greatest trainers and seconds. He had developed Lester thoroughly and carefully, and not only believed him well on the way to championship honors, but considered the fight with me only an incidental affair. The fight was promoted and directed by Dan Cole of Nogales, Arizona, and was staged in the bull-ring. More than 8,000 spectators were in attendance, special trains having been run into the Mexican town for the occasion.

Lester was a two to one favorite in the betting, because of his

[1] Jack Dempsey, World Heavyweight Champion, 1919–26.

reputation in the west and southwest. He had shown unmistakable signs of being a formidable boxer in several hard fights. Being sponsored as he was by Kelly, of whom it was said that he seldom picked a loser, his Arizona friends wagered heavily on him. His record was good; he had a remarkable physique, strength and youth. To them he looked like a sure winner. Regardless of the odds, my friends had faith in me, and took the offerings of the Arizonans in liberal amounts. My training camp was with the 25th United States Infantry at Nogales, Arizona. All of the boxing skill of the regiment aided me in my training and officers and enlisted men backed me confidently with their money. Major Bliss, physician and surgeon of the regiment subjected me to a thorough physical examination, and watched my training carefully. He was so impressed with my condition that he wagered all the money he could raise on me to win over Lester. Because of the faith in me as manifested by these troops, and their loyalty as evidenced by their tangible backing, I had increased reason to rejoice over the outcome of the fight.

I formed a close association with Col. A. J. Dougherty, regimental commander, who extended to me many privileges and facilities for my training, and when I departed after the fight, he wrote me a letter which I greatly prize. This letter commended me for my clean sportsmanship before and during the fight. He complimented me for my 'clean shooting,' and declared that the facilities and courtesies of the regiment would be extended to me again if occasion presented. My training at the regimental headquarters was one of the most pleasant and successful of any similar period in my career.

Preceding the fight, sport writers had much to say about my attempt to stage a 'come back.' They went back into history and elaborated considerably on my unusual ring record, emphasizing my tremendous past fighting ability and unanimously crediting me with being 'the world's greatest boxer and the most skillful defensive fighter ever known.' The writers and boxing authorities had watched me train, and all agreed that I appeared to possess the same punch, skill and speed as when at the height of my career. They marveled at my appearance and said that I looked to be no more than thirty-two. They declared that I was the picture of health and vigor, and decided that rumors of my alleged dissipation and careless living were unfounded. 'It makes no difference how strong and speedy he may appear to be, he is nearing the fiftieth mile-stone, and it is unreasonable to expect that he will be able to stand up against the strength of youth as exemplified by Lester,' they wrote before the fight. How quickly they changed their tune I will show by quoting, verbatim, some of their expressions after the fight. J. F. Weadock, in a press dispatch said:

'Battling gamely, but uselessly, Pat Lester of Tucson lost every round of fifteen in his bout with Jack Johnson, former heavy-weight champion, in the bull-ring in Nogales, Sonora, yesterday. Johnson's punishing left to the body and right to the head, alternated at will, landed consistently as the men clinched. Constant clinching and infighting featured the entire bout, with Lester unable to lay an effective glove on the dusky battler. Laughing at friends at the ring-side, Johnson played through the bout, never in danger, although Lester gamely tried to land.'

The report of the fight sent out by the Universal News service said:

'Jack Johnson, former world's heavyweight champion, won a 15-round decision over Pat Lester of Tucson, Ariz., in the bull-ring here this afternoon. Johnson won every round by a wide margin, hitting Lester at will uppercuts to chin and body. Lester proved himself one of the gamest of fighters by absorbing the ex-champion's punches and punishment and forcing the battle throughout. He was cut to ribbons in the third round, but kept coming. Johnson emerged uninjured and apparently fresh. The fight was fought beneath a blazing sun and before 8,000 people one mile across the American border. Spider Kelly, Lester's manager and second, failed to outwit the cagey negro, who fought as of old, apparently in wonderful physical condition and showing his teeth in a broad grin at all times. He seemingly took a delight in toying with his opponent after he found him possessed of a concrete chin and body. Lester, who has been fighting for three years, and who has never been stopped, was considered the best heavy-weight in the west, but he was helpless today before the old master. As the last bell rang, Johnson requested the Universal Service correspondent to announce through Universal Service that he is back on the boards and that he challenges Dempsey or any other heavyweight in the ring.'

From these accounts, it is obvious that the news writers and sport critics were compelled to eat their own words concerning the handicap of age in general and my own in particular. These accounts also indicate that Lester was no dub, and that he was not only an able fighter but a game one as well. As for myself, I came out of the ring no more fatigued than when I entered, for at no time was it necessary for me to greatly exert myself.

The fight was wholly upon merit. Both of us fought earnestly, and it proved that I not only retained all my former boxing qualities, but also that despite my age, I was a fit contender for the championship had I wished to push any claims upon that point, and had I not been prevented from doing so by the prevailing boxing regulations in the United States. I was sincere in challenging Dempsey, or any of the other heavyweights. And as I write this, I am of the same mind, but I realize that the private regulations and prejudices of boxing commissions prevent me from making a serious effort to arrange such a bout. Furthermore, I am content to remain out of any controversy that might throw the boxing business into an uproar that would do the game no good. I am willing to remain in my present place, satisfied with the successes I have achieved, but none the less eager to train and develop prospective boxers, and lend my service and experience in whatever manner I can to the welfare of the sport.

Luis Angel Firpo had challenged me to a bout in the event I was victor over Lester, and I readily accepted the challenge agreeing to meet Firpo any time, any place that promoters might arrange. But nothing came of this prospective contest. If it had been arranged, Firpo would have presented no difficulties for me. When he was training for his fight with Dempsey in 1923, I boxed with him, gaining a full measure of his skill and ability. Newspaper accounts of our boxing were meager. The event was considered merely incidental in the preparation for the Dempsey-Firpo match, yet boxing authorities were aware of the fact that I was the master of the South American. Firpo made such a poor showing in the ring with me that Rickard, the promoter, fearing that publicity of this would injure the gate-receipts, stopped further boxing between Firpo and me.

Since my fight with Lester, a new champion has acquired the title in the person of Gene Tunney, who defeated Dempsey September 13, 1926, at Philadelphia. Dempsey, a masterful fighter, had held the championship for seven years, a few months less than marked my own claim on the belt. Jeffries also held the title seven years. I may, therefore, lay claim to the distinction of having held the belt longer than any other fighter. Tunney is the eighth man to gain the heavyweight title since John L. Sullivan, who was the first to be recognized as the champion boxer of the world, gaining that pinnacle in 1899, by defeating Jake Kilrain in the last championship battle fought with bare fists. This contest lasted seventy-five rounds, and was one of the fiercest on record. Of the eight men, I am the only one of my race in the history of professional boxing, ever to have held the title. All of the title-holders have been Americans except Fitzsimmons, who was a Cornishman, and Burns, who was a Canadian. With the possible exception of Hart and Willard, all the champions have been of Irish extraction.

With the passing of Jeffries, Fitzsimmons and myself from the ring as champions, I think it can be said that the old school fighters disappeared. Dempsey was a link between the old battling system and the new. The former were at their height in the days of Sullivan, Peter Jackson, Godfrey, Maher, Sharkey and Ruhlin. Corbett, when he defeated Sullivan, foreshadowed the new school with his wit and speed, but the old school members had not disappeared at that time, and they made the going rough for the new fighters. Jeffries and Fitzsimmons, while they had the old school stamina, also had acquired some of the new tricks.

I define myself as a sort of composite fighter. I have contended successfully with both the new and old school products. My record will reveal that I had the strength and resistance of the former and the speed and mental equipment of the latter. And having had my innings with both, I am prepared to say that the modern fighter is not the machine that his predecessor was. The establishment of boxing commissions and the regulation of ring contests is largely responsible for this, for it permits the ascendency of men, who in the old days of fighting would never have been heard of. I concede that Dempsey was a superior fighter, but he never could have weathered the ring storms which would have swept upon him when some of the old boys, whom I have named, were at their zenith.

As for Tunney, the present champion, I believe that he, too, would have been unable to reach his present station against the onslaughts that he would have had to face, had his contestants been of the caliber of Jackson, Sharkey, Fitzsimmons and their class, if they were permitted to fight as they were in the days of their triumphs. Yet Tunney is a clever and fast boxer. He has good control of himself, and the ability to defend himself against hard driven blows. It was these qualities that won for him in the fight with Dempsey. Of these two, I believe Tunney the cleverest. I had, however, picked Dempsey to win, because everything was in his favor. He had had enough battles to keep him at ease. He had strength, skill and experience. But almost from the start he was out-boxed. Tunney, while not possessing the punch which still lies in Dempsey's glove was able to keep the latter from landing on him in a vital spot. Had a few of Dempsey's connected as he intended them, the fight would have had a different ending.

I believe I can speak as authoritatively as any one about the details of the prize-ring. It is my conviction that Tunney's defeat of Dempsey was largely due to the accidental circumstance that the canvas on which they fought was soaked by rain, which prevented Dempsey from getting a sound footing which is essential for his style of boxing. It is of course possible that Tunney might have been the victor anyway, but it does not appear to me to have been quite so probable had the boxing method of Dempsey not been so handicapped by weather conditions.

Another factor which helped to lay Dempsey low, was the form and style of his training. He was in brief over-trained. He had attempted to accomplish in a month or so what should have been attained over a period at least three times as long. He had long been out of the ring and had been engaged in occupations so vastly different from those that contribute to a boxer's form, that it was a tremendous task to get him into such condition as was necessary for the contest. His training had been intensive. Over-zealous trainers tried to restore to him all that he had lost in the months of ring idleness and neglect of training. An over-trained athlete is as sorry an object as an under-trained contestant, because he does not understand his own condition. He feels fresh and vigorous, but therein, he is tragically fooled because he lacks the co-ordination of nerve and muscle and brain, and unfortunately never realizes that something is wrong with him until he tries to achieve that which he most desires. I speak from experience. I have entered the ring in just such condition, and I am so familiar with it that I soon recognized Dempsey's handicap when his last fight started.

Charges that the Dempsey-Tunney fight was 'framed' have no foundation in my opinion. Much controversy has raged on this point, and I fear that the boxing game has suffered somewhat because of these charges. To my mind the fight was absolutely square. Both men were eager to win. There was no inducement sufficient to tempt Dempsey to relinquish his own crown, because he prized it too dearly. No man would have taken the punishment which fell to Dempsey if he intended to let his opponent win. On the other hand, any financial or other consideration large enough to sway Dempsey would have so overshadowed anything that Tunney might hope to gain as to make such a deal absurd and prohibitive.

Looking over the boxers in the heavyweight division as they stand at this time, it appears to me that Tunney has the field pretty well to himself. Outside of vague speculation and idle talk, there are no immediate serious contenders for the crown. However, the boxing game is perhaps more profitable today than ever in its history. There is a great field of potential fighters and from among them it is likely that there will spring up one who will win the right to contest Tunney's title. I doubt very much that Dempsey will seek to regain his lost glory.[2] If he does, I believe he will fail. Harry Wills continues to interest those concerned in boxing. Some persons take him seriously, but he never will get a chance at the heavyweight crown, for he does not deserve to. Although he has acquired much notoriety, he is but a mediocre fighter. There are many better than he, which was proved by Sam Langford, when the latter defeated him.

I am frequently asked if I am developing a heavyweight fighter with a view to going after the heavyweight by proxy. Perhaps I am – I do not know. It is a long way to the top, and it will take an unusual man to reach it. There are many possible contenders within my reach, and I have come in close contact with some. It is true that I am training in my gymnasium one or two men who may some day acquire the prestige necessary to challenge Tunney or some other champion. One thing is certain and that is, I am conducting a gymnasium and staging boxing bouts which offer opportunities to those with the skill and inclination. My many years in the ring and my inherent and acquired qualities seem to fit me

[2] Dempsey did in fact try to regain his title but was outpointed by Tunney in Chicago on September 22, 1927.

for the direction of boxers and athletes, and in this I am finding
congenial and successful employment.

As I am writing these closing lines of this chronicle I have had
the unexpected and unsolicited pleasure of reading the results of a
wide census of opinion as to the rank of the outstanding boxers in
ring history. The result of this census is to be found in the June,
1927, number of the leading boxing Journal, called 'The Ring,'
and shows that those competent to judge overwhelmingly nomin-
ate me as the greatest heavyweight boxer of all time. It is, indeed,
gratifying as one looks back upon one's professional career, long
after the events have lost their vividness, to realize that the highest
authorities in the profession who have no personal interests to
advance, have paid me this high tribute.

In the last half decade, my interests have been varied, but there
has never been a day when I have not in some way given my attention to boxing or the training of boxers. I have had and am having
many bouts myself, and I fail to see that I have lost either in vigor
or speed. I do not train as intensively as I did in former years, for I
have no need to do so. My principal object in doing this is for the
maintenance of my health. However, my physical condition is
such that within a short time I could prepare myself for a meeting
with any of the heavyweights, none of whom I bar, in spite of the
fact that some sport writers delight in picturing me in the act of
defying the old man with the scythe. Their talk is piffle. I have
demonstrated that proper living and attention to some simple rules
in physical training ward off illness, or at least strengthen the
system to such an extent that disease and even the weight of years
cannot make serious inroads. I have proved for myself that because
a man reaches the age of fifty, whether he is an athlete, a banker,
merchant or lawyer, he need not give up the legitimate pleasures
nor the profitable activities of life, and if in complete demonstration of this I am successful, and can aid others to attain a fuller
and better number of years, I shall have accomplished more than
the winning of the heavyweight championship. In fact, I feel that I
am getting to be of increasing use to the world as the days go by,
and surrounded by the many friends who are daily watching my
progress, who are sincerely interesting themselves in my attainments, and who have confidence in me; with a great fund of
understanding of the world and of people to draw on, and with the
penalties paid for crimes and misconduct falsely charged to me, I

anticipate the future with as much eagerness as when as a lad of twelve years, I set out to find Steve Brodie. I believe that I have much more confidence in myself than when I was demanding an opportunity to fight for the heavyweight boxing championship. My viewpoint, which was never provincial, has been considerably broadened by the varied experiences and contacts that lie behind me. My failures have made me wiser and my successes have given me great thrills and satisfaction. My half-a-century of life has been a long succession of experiences such as come to few men in our day. Between the many crises I have faced there have also been a number of short periods of calm. As I look back upon the life I have lived and compare it with the lives of my contemporaries I feel that mine has been a full life and above all a human life.

AFTERWORD

Johnson Was the Greatest

By GILBERT ODD

Until I saw Joe Louis in action, I thought Jack Johnson must have been the best of all the heavyweight champions, and when I first watched Cassius Clay (Muhammad Ali) perform, I considered he was justified in styling himself 'The Greatest'. I kept this opinion until his first contest with Joe Frazier and then returned to my first love. Taking into consideration the times in which he operated, I firmly believe that John Arthur Johnson, born at Galveston in Texas, U.S.A. on March 31st, 1878, was the superlative exponent of the Noble Art among the big men that the World of Boxing has ever seen.

In many ways Johnson and Ali were on a par. Both were extremely talkative, both were fast on their feet, both carried destructive punching power and were masters of timing. But no one had to urge Johnson to leave his corner for the start of another round, as Angelo Dundee did Ali on the occasion of the first contest with Liston, nor did Jack ever allow himself to be cornered or caught on the ropes and permit an opponent to batter away at his anatomy as his successor made a practice of doing in the second part of his career.

To an extent their fighting years were also somewhat parallelled. Both, because of their own actions outside the ring, faced a long period of inactivity; Johnson because of his contravention of the laws of his country, Ali because he refused to be enlisted in its armed forces. Jack was exiled for the best part of three years, Muhammad was absent for $3\frac{1}{2}$ years. But whereas the latter was permitted to come back and regain his title, Johnson was never given the opportunity, principally because of his colour, but also because of his advanced age – for a pugilist – Ali being only 25 when he forfeited the championship.

Again, when Jack at last managed to get a shot at the title, he was in his 31st year while Muhammad was in his 22nd. He had been boxing professionally for just over three years when he became champion. On the other hand, Johnson was an experienced warrior of eleven years standing. One last comparison. Johnson had engaged in upwards of a hundred ring battles – many unrecorded – by the time he got his big chance against Burns, while Ali's first fight with Liston was only his twentieth paid bout, although he had been boxing as an amateur for a number of years prior to winning a gold medal at the 1960 Olympic Games.

Physically, Ali is a bigger man altogether than was Johnson; $2\frac{3}{4}$ ins. taller, eight inches longer in reach. But Jack would have stalked him and a man going backwards loses any advantage he may have in reach, while if Ali had retreated into the ropes or allowed himself to be cornered, he would, in my opinion, have been cut to ribbons.

The boxing lives of most world champions are divided into two distinct parts, the prelude to winning the title and the aftermath. In Johnson's case this is more defined because the majority of his early opponents were coloured like himself; in fact, a negro in his day had little opportunity of securing a match with a white man unless it was pretty certain that he would lose.

In Jack's time there were some very formidable coloured heavies in circulation, three notables being Sam Langford, Sam McVey and Joe Jeannette. Johnson went fifteen rounds with Langford to win on points and although the famous Boston Tar Baby was Jack's most persistent challenger, the pair did not have a second meeting simply because that while the thought of having a coloured champion was bad enough, the idea of two negroes contesting the title was unthinkable. Moreover, as the astute Johnson well knew, an all black championship bout would not have been a box-office draw.

Before becoming champion Johnson fought McVey three times and Jeannette nine times. To record that Langford met McVey on fifteen occasions and Jeannette fourteen times, while McVey and Jeannette clashed five times, gives a good idea of how coloured boxers had to fight one another over and over again in order to keep employed in the days up to the First World War. The fact that Jack only once defended his title against a black man, and that by circumstance more than choice, gives an indication of the times as compared with today.

Johnson's accession to the heavyweight throne came about because of two outstanding, but entirely unassociated circumstances. The first was James Jackson Jeffries' retirement whilst the undefeated champion in 1905 having run out of challengers after a reign of six years, thus leaving the title vacant; the second was the fact that his ultimate successor, Tommy Burns, was, and still remains, the smallest man to become world titleholder.

When Big Jeff decided to call it a day, he refereed a contest between Jack Root, from Chicago, and Marvin Hart, of Jefferson County, Kentucky, and declared the winner as the new holder of the heavyweight championship. This happened to be Hart, who won decisively in twelve rounds, and seven months later was outpointed by Burns, who hailed from Hanover in Canada.

Tommy (real name Noah Brusso) was 25 at the time. He stood only 5ft. 7ins., weighed 179 pounds (12.11), but had extremely long arms that gave him a reach of 74½ inches which he used to every advantage. Besides being a clever boxer and a powerful puncher, Burns was a keen business man. He had acquired the most valuable of all the boxing titles by sheer good fortune and proceeded to make the most of it.

Although the biggest purses to be obtained at that time were in the United States, he decided to go on a world tour, partly to establish his claim to the championship, but also to escape the prospect of having to defend his crown against one or more of the menacing black quartet who regarded themselves as his foremost challengers, Johnson in particular.

He defeated in turn, the champions of England, Ireland and Australia, boxing in London, Paris, Sydney and Melbourne, thereby becoming universally accepted as world titleholder. Johnson followed him to London and the National Sporting Club was eager to stage a match between them, but its Committee was aghast when Burns demanded the hitherto unheard of guarantee of £6,000 for himself, win, lose or draw. They paid him what they considered an adequate amount of £2,400 to defend the title against Gunner James Moir, the British champion, and were prepared to go to £3,000 for meeting Johnson. But when Tommy asked for double that amount and refused to take a penny less, he was told in no uncertain terms that it was nothing short of blackmail, so he departed for Australia.

Johnson was eager to follow, but lacked the necessary funds to do so, whereupon the N.S.C. management advanced his travelling expenses on the strict understanding that, in the event of winning the title from Burns, he would return to London and defend it against Langford. That he failed to honour this agreement was the start of the unpopularity he was to build up against himself in the forthcoming years.

In Sydney, Hugh D. McIntosh, a promoter of various sports, including boxing, willingly paid Burns the required sum for defending his title against Johnson, erected a large roofless arena, paid Jack £1,500 and made a handsome profit. The fight itself was one-sided, a case of David and Goliath in reverse. Johnson, like a statue in ebony, towered over the champion, taunted him, hit him at will and punished him severely.

Burns was down in the first twenty seconds of the contest and dropped again before the opening round was over. Then, having clearly demonstrated his superiority, the coloured challenger played a cat-and-mouse game with the courageous Canadian; a monotonous slaughter, flooring him several more times, jeering at his futile attempts to retaliate and gradually reducing him to a mere animated punching-bag. Finally, in the 14th round, when Jack had set up his dazed opponent and was about to administer a spectacular knockout victory, the ringside doctor spoke to the Police Superintendent sitting beside him, whereupon the officer climbed into the ring and ordered the referee to stop the contest.

If the National Sporting Club expected Johnson to return to London and fulfil his obligation, it was doomed to disappointment. Jack returned to America where he found to his delight that money now flowed towards him instead of having to be sought after, often in humiliating circumstances. There were promoters eager for him to appear in 'no-decision' contests for which there was no necessity to train and he made the utmost use of these abortive bouts with which the American public appeared to be contented. All Jack had to do was to make sure he did not get knocked out and there was little likelihood of that happening in six-round events against men of inferior class. It was merely a matter of going through the motions, and Jack carried this to extremes when he undertook to face Al Kaufman, a big but inexperienced Californian, over ten rounds at 'Sunny' Jim Coffroth's arena in San Francisco. Wearing a roll of fat round his midsection, Johnson made no effort to dispose of a man so obviously his inferior in every department of boxing but size. He merely thwarted his opponent's efforts to land a punch and the affair became nothing more than an exhibition bout which was heartily booed by the fans who naturally expected to see something more exciting from the man who had defeated Burns so easily and effectively.

Five weeks later Jack again boxed for Coffroth, but this time at the promoter's large outdoor arena in Colma. His opponent was the reigning middleweight champion of the world, Stanley Ketchel, who had the reputation of being a kayo king. Of course, he was a lot smaller than Johnson, but about the size of Burns, so that he was considered to be in with a chance, and that is all his supporters, and those who hated the coloured champion, could expect. They called Ketchel 'The Michigan Assassin' and the whole white population of America were hoping that he would land one of his swiping rights and so remove that 'golden smile'.

There is reason to believe that when the match was proposed, Ketchel's manager, Willus Britt, approached Johnson and suggested they should fight for the title over 25 rounds and that Jack would carry his challenger through to the finish in order to provide a full-length movie which could be exhibited throughout the States and provide a substantial source of income. Neither Ketchel nor Coffroth would know anything about this arrangement and the promoter would put up a purse of 40,000 dollars, of which Johnson would receive sixty per cent. Stanley would provide all the action and Jack the science. With the right publicity it would provide a capacity attendance of 12,000 spectators and with such a plan Johnson would save himself the trouble and expense of training and, having got away with the affair with Kaufmann, Jack readily agreed to Britt's suggestion.

Actually it was intended by Ketchel's manager that Johnson would be double-crossed; that they would catch the coloured champion out of condition while the challenger would be trained to a hair. At 23, Stanley was in his prime, eight years younger than Johnson. He was used to long distance battles, having gone 32 rounds to win the middleweight championship two years earlier.

Britt had visions of his boxer bringing off a sensational victory that would restore the heavyweight title to the White Race. Stanley would be a national hero.

Things went as the plotters planned with Ketchel chasing after his big opponent, swinging viciously to try and bring him down. Jack parried his wild punches with ease, smiling at what he imagined was Ketchel's way of making the 'pictures' look exciting. Then, in the 12th round, an extra mighty swipe from the middleweight champion just grazed Jack's jaw. Immediately, Britt called out: 'Now, Stanley', and Ketchel swung again.

The shout aroused Johnson's suspicions and he glanced to see who had made it. For a split second he took his eyes off his opponent and received Stanley's second punch fully behind his left ear. A shade lower and he might have been knocked out. As it was, the power behind the blow sat Jack on the canvas with a bump. The vast crowd broke into a tremendous roar, Britt was yelling, Ketchel was grinning, and Johnson realised that he had been tricked.

He sprang up, a look of fury on his face. He stepped back and Ketchel dashed in, his right hand cocked for another knockdown punch. He never landed it. As soon as he got into range, Jack calmly let fly with a right uppercut that caught the contender under the chin, lifted him off his feet, and sent him crashing to the boards on his back. He did not move a muscle while the referee counted him out.

The onlookers had seen the real Johnson; the man who could finish a fight with one punch when it pleased him to do so. Now those who had been urging Jim Jeffries to make a comeback and considered he was big and strong enough to dispose of Johnson despite a lay-off of six years, were given cause to have second thoughts. But the overwhelming desire to have Jack dethroned induced them to lure the 35-year old ex-champion out of a happy retirement in a vain effort to bring down the coloured titleholder.

There was no question of an 'arrangement' about this one. Jeffries would be in earnest and so would Johnson, in fact, if never at any other time, he was determined to show his superiority over every other boxer in the world – to prove that he was indeed the champion heavyweight; that no other man had the right to be in the ring with him.

In defending his title against Jeffries, Jack was opposed, not by a

single man, but the whole white world. Of the 15,760 persons who
paid to see this fight that shook the world, very few were
coloured. Tex Rickard, who promoted it and also refereed it, was
white, as were all the other officials. Most notable is the fact that
while Johnson received a total of 145,600 dollars as defending
champion, Jeffries was paid 192,066 dollars. In both cases this included the fighter's share of the motion-picture receipts. The
scheduled distance was 45 rounds, but no one expected it to last
that long.

It can be stated categorically that this particular prize fight
enjoyed the widest possible publicity the world had ever known
and has remained so despite the arrival of the television era. Boxing
in 1910 was restricted to the United States and Canada, Australia,
South Africa, France and, of course, Great Britain where it had
originated. In all these countries there was the widest interest, even
among those who had never seen a glove contest.

For the year and a half since Johnson had defeated Burns, hardly
a day passed without some mention in the newspapers about the
inevitable clash between the coloured champion and Jim Jeffries.
As the months went by public concern increased, even more so
when various puritan bodies in America and England protested
and tried to have the contest banned on religious and racial
grounds. The coming fight became the talking point in sport and
journalistic space was steadily enlarged, especially when the venue
was finally decided upon and the men set up their training camps.

Day by day reports were published and editors sent their representatives to be on the spot and provide up-to-the-minute accounts
of how the contestants were shaping. By the end of June it is
estimated there were more than 300 sports journalists in Reno who
between them sent out a million words a day to their respective
papers. Denver S. Dickerson, Governor of the State of Nevada,
paid a visit to both Jeffries and Johnson during their preparation
for the contest and enlisted a strong force of deputised citizens of
Reno to keep order in a town that had grown suddenly from ten to
twenty thousand in a matter of days. He also engaged the services
of detectives from New York, Philadelphia, Chicago, Denver and
San Francisco, plus a detachment of State Rangers and a patrol
from Arizona.

Saloons and places of bawdy entertainment sprang up overnight
and, apart from the fight enthusiasts that came by rail and road,

hordes of gamblers, professional tricksters, tramps and drunks, came in a continuous stream. Every available space in the hotels and boarding houses was taken and thousands were forced to sleep in the open air for several nights. Fortunately it was July. Promoter Tex Rickard took the precaution of relieving the spectators of their knives and revolvers before permitting them to pass through the gates into the hastily-built wooden arena.

The world-wide interest that had been aroused had to be met by the newspaper proprietors. The presses were held up to await the cabled result and crowds in London, Sydney and other far-off cities stood patiently outside the offices to learn the outcome of a fistic contest that had thrilled the universe with excited expectancy. In America the fight fans could be better acquainted as to the course of battle. The *Kansas City Star*, for example, hired its large Convention Hall for a crowd of 14,000 people to hear a blow-by-blow account telegraphed from the ringside and relayed to them by megaphone. Round by round bulletins were posted up outside the offices of the *New York Times* and similar means of spreading the news was adopted by other newspapers throughout the length and breadth of the United States.

Even though it was only 1915, it was acclaimed the Battle of the Century and although this title has been given to other important heavyweight contests since then, it is doubtful that any surpassed the Johnson v. Jeffries fight for the widespread intensity of interest it aroused. This, I regret to say, was mainly due to its colour aspect. Johnson had taken the championship that in the minds of all whites was their sole prerogative. Now, a former great champion, who had never been beaten by anyone, was to try and put it back where it belonged. On this and no other count, the Johnson v. Jeffries clash, coming at the time it did, created an atmosphere that can never again be repeated. It was a unique situation that involved two men who were to settle the supremacy of one race over another.

From the start Johnson allowed his burly opponent to do all the attacking, content to catch his punches in mid-air or turn them aside. Every time the former champion lunged at the coloured man the crowd roared its encouragement. On the few occasions that Jeffries managed to land a blow or even appeared to land one, it was cheered wholeheartedly, while anything that Jack achieved was greeted with silence.

Slowly but surely he sapped the older man's stamina, without trying to get in a decisive delivery and he rarely missed. Each punch was aimed deliberately with enough force behind it to reduce Big Jeff's fast fading strength. From the eleventh round onwards it was a pathetic slaughter until Jeffries was a tottering hulk, no longer a fighting force, merely absorbing punishment and showing great courage in insisting on continuing even when his seconds knew that his case was hopeless.

By the 15th round even Johnson had had enough. For the first time he attacked, hitting out viciously with both hands until Jeffries' wits were completely scattered. Then a left to the jaw, followed by a right to the chin, had the big man down. He got up only to be felled by a rapid tattoo of precision punches that almost knocked him through the ropes. He crouched by them, holding on to the lower strand while Rickard began counting. Some of the ringsiders left their seats and called upon the official to stop the fight. 'Don't count him out', they urged, but Tex knew that a conclusive result had to be reached. One of Jeff's seconds climbed into the ring to try and prevent a knockout, but the full count was called and Johnson had won in 2min. 20sec. of the round.

The news of Jack's victory spread like wildfire throughout America and touched off a series of riots between blacks and whites that brought bloodshed and death. All that night and for several days following there were racial disturbances in Pennsylvania, Maryland, Ohio, Mississippi, Virginia, Missouri, Georgia, Arkansas and Colorado. The showing of the film was banned, but Johnson had sold his interest in it and went off on a lengthy visit to Europe where he earned more money with theatrical and other engagements than he had ever seen before, and spent it as fast as it came into his hands.

No one realised it then, least of all Johnson himself, that the last had been seen of him as a great fighter. This is not difficult to understand when the rest of his ring career is analysed. But first we should look closely at his earlier record and try to assess when he became accepted as The Black Menace. In the preceding pages Jack states that it was not until 1901, when he was coming up to 23 (25 in his own reckoning) that 'Galveston was taking considerable notice of me and there was much activity in arranging matches.'

According to the records his first contest that year in his hometown was the disastrous affair with Joe Choynski, a man ten years older than himself and who had been stopped three times the previous year. Johnson claims that he lost this fight because of police intervention, but a newspaper report of the day tells a different, if brief story. I quote verbatim:

> At Galveston, Texas, before the Galveston Athletic Club, Joe Choynski put out Jack Johnson in the first few seconds of the third round last Tuesday. Both men were arrested by State officers at the close of the contest. The event was entirely bloodless, and was a splendid exhibition up to the time Choynski made a feint with his left and put a right-hander to the pit of Johnson's stomach.

Jack's statement that he was held in prison for three weeks and that a law was passed making boxing illegal in the State of Texas, has to be taken with a pinch of salt, because he was fighting again in Galveston ten days after the Choynski debacle, which must have written him off as a heavyweight of any account for the time being.

However, the following year he re-asserted himself as a class boxer with some important wins, including one in five rounds over Jack Jeffries, brother of the reigning champion, and George Gardner, who was beaten on points over twenty rounds. There were also victories over other coloured aspirants for the heavyweight title and Johnson's first real claim to being considered a contender was when he gained a 20-rounds decision over Denver Ed Martin, who claimed the coloured heavyweight championship of the world, a title he had, believe it or not, picked up in England after defeating Bob Armstrong, another negro, on points over twenty rounds on July 25th, 1902, at the Crystal Palace.

Jack's win over Martin enabled him to style himself as coloured champion and he was ascribed as such in the scanty reports of his contests thereafter. His fame rose when he thrice defended his title against Sam McVey, while a two rounds win over Martin at the end of 1904 established the Galveston negro as a distinct threat to the so far white supremacy. His high rating did not last long, however, for he dropped a decision to Marvin Hart, who thus established himself as a successor to Jeffries.

Wins over Joe Jeannette in Baltimore and Sam Langford at Chelsea in Vermont, raised Johnson's stock to a high level once again and he brought this to real prominence at the end of 1907 when he met Jim Flynn, who had held an impressive record until beaten by Tommy Burns in fifteen rounds. Jack Curley, who managed Flynn, thought that a victory over Johnson would ensure another lucrative match with Burns, but Johnson improved on the champion's performance by scoring a knockout in round eleven, a victory that made him universally selected as leading challenger in spite of his colour.

I quote from a newspaper report of the day:

The famous negro boxer, Jack Johnson, was pitted against Jim Flynn, the Pueblo, Colorado, fireman at San Francisco on November 2nd (1907) who was easily beaten. There should be no doubt now as to whom the world's championship belongs and shows how wise Tommy Burns and others are to draw the colour line. Flynn has proved himself no 'dud' at the business and Burns had to go fifteen rounds to beat him, yet Johnson made him look a novice and hit him when and where he liked. From the start there was only one in it and that was not Flynn, who took a rare gruelling in very game fashion. The black was merciful and evidently waited to administer the climax at his own particular time. Though game, Flynn never looked a winner and was badly punished when the end came in the eleventh round, his seconds having to carry him away. Next please!

This, in my opinion, was Johnson at his very peak. He was within five months of his 30th birthday; a superlative boxer, with great staying power and the ability to win a fight as and when he liked. True, he had been outpointed by Hart, who would never face him again, and with no one else in America willing to challenge his right to be the foremost contender for the world title, Jack started his chase of Burns that was to end in Sydney a little more than a year later.

His superiority over Burns, Kaufmann and Ketchel, followed by his destruction of Jeffries, gained him world-wide recognition as heavyweight champion. He had reached the highest pedestal in the realm of boxing and should have remained there for a number of years, if only because he had cleared away all possible opposition. Had he possessed a white skin in addition to his fistic prowess, we would have seen a number of spectacular title defences during the next five years with Jack disposing of the White Hopes as fast as they appeared.

In my view, Johnson at the height of his fame, was the greatest exponent of sheer boxing the world had ever seen and he could have endorsed this estimation had he been given the opportunity. Among those who succeeded him, only Jack Dempsey, Gene Tunney, Joe Louis, Rocky Marciano, Floyd Patterson and Muhammad Ali could be classed among the fistic greats in the heavyweight division. And I feel, that even when these notables were at their peak they would each have been beaten by Johnson when in his prime.

I have met only one man who shared this view. That was the late Nat Fleischer, founder of *The Ring* magazine, who had the advantage of having seen Johnson fight as well as each of the others I have named. He did not need to read reports or study films. He had seen them all from a ringside press seat and never changed his mind about listing Jack as the daddy of them all.

Johnson's fighting story after the dramatic defeat of Jeffries is a shambles. From July 4th 1910 until April 5th 1915, nearly five years, he engaged in five contests, the last of which he lost together with his world crown. Before exiling himself from the land of his birth rather than face a prison sentence, Jack took on Jim Flynn again, Manager Curley hoping that by some streak of chance he might become the custodian of the heavyweight championship. But this was a farce. Johnson did not try to win decisively and his opponent was incapable of doing so, the police intervening in round nine. Then Jack took off for Europe again.

In Paris he was fêted, for the French have a fascination for coloured people. Jack lived well and handsomely, flashily and light-heartedly, even entering a wrestling competition. In the first bout he beat a German named Urbach with two falls and three days later he accounted for a Siberian named Spoul, who fouled Johnson and was promptly knocked out by a blow to the body. Then Johnson was put out of the competition by Jimmy Esson, a Scottish wrestler, who gained two falls in 6min. and 12min. respectively.

Jack reverted to boxing and found a promoter ready to stage a ten rounds bout with another coloured heavy bearing the name of Battling Jim Johnson. Although the latter had been around for a number of years and had fought Langford eight times, McVey on five occasions, and Jeannette seven times, he was not regarded as in the top flight, but because of his size and durability was a good promoter's man. Like many other coloured Americans he had found refuge in Paris.

Being 2¾ins. taller than Jack and out-weighing him by at least twenty pounds, he presented a large target, but the champion was out of condition and made an exhibition bout of it. Jim tried hard enough to score, but Johnson picked off his punches with the greatest of ease and jabbed and jolted whenever he felt inclined, which wasn't often. The fans got tired of the monotonous exchanges, especially after the great champion they had paid to see broke a small bone in his left arm in the third round and did not use it thereafter, relying on his right to ward off Jim's swings and occasionally draw him into an uppercut. At the finish one of the judges gave the verdict to Jim, the other called it a 'draw', a decision that met with the referee's approval.

The world champion was spending money like water and when Frank Moran turned up and suggested a title fight, Johnson was more than willing. He had boxed a four rounds exhibition with the famed Pittsburgh Dentist five years earlier, but Moran had been a mere novice then; now he was a far different proposition. He had mingled with most of the so-called White Hopes and beaten a number of them by means of a heavy right swing which he called 'Mary Ann'. He was 1¼ins. taller than Johnson and weighed about the same, although Jack was carrying a considerable amount of superfluous poundage due to his lack of training.

The championship match was to be promoted by Charlie McCarty from San Francisco, who promised to put up 40,000 dollars of which Johnson would take three-quarters and Moran the remainder. Jack was given 1,500 dollars to cover his training expenses and the fight was scheduled to take place on June 27th, 1914 at the Velodrôme d'Hiver, a cycle racetrack just outside Paris. As the date drew near, however, Mr. McCarty disappeared, whereupon a French promoter took over the contest, but only on the understanding that the boxers would accept two-thirds of the gate receipts which they would split on a 60/40 basis. It was scheduled for 20 rounds and Georges Carpentier, the French boxing idol, undertook the role of referee. A vast crowd assembled, paying 181,000 francs ($36,200 or £7,240). There were a great many bejewelled women in evening dress at the ringside, who with their escorts represented the cream of Parisian society.

Though sadly out of condition for a title fight, the coloured man gave a perfect demonstration of his boxing skill, leading, feinting, spearing Frank's face with the left, crossing the right and whipping in his superb uppercuts. Moran kept swinging his big right, but always in vain. He was the type of opponent just made for Johnson, who allowed his determined rival to come in close and then tied him up in the clinches or held him round the neck with one hand while landing short uppercuts and hooks with the other.

When in desperation, Moran tried to put a dent in the champion's notable paunch, he was just as thwarted as the clever negro intercepted the majority of the blows with his gloves or elbows. It was so beautifully done that time and again the fans showed their appreciation with bursts of applause. It was not a fight, but an exhibition of superb ringcraft and at the finish the smiling Johnson's arm was raised by the referee, a verdict that met with the full approval of the crowd. But Jack and Frank had boxed for nothing. On the day of the contest McCarty re-appeared and obtained an injunction on the takings, making it necessary for the two boxers and the promoter to invoke the power of the law in order to get the money released. But French courts are notoriously slow and within six weeks the German hordes were pouring into Belgium and Europe was at war. Johnson and Moran may have hoped to get paid eventually, but after the Armistice all trace of the money had been lost.

Both went to London where Frank scored a couple of victories and then returned to New York, while Jack engaged in music-hall appearances until the arrival of the intrepid Jack Curley with the proposition that Johnson should defend his championship against Jess Willard. With an assurance that such a move would end his self-imposed exile, Johnson agreed and at Havana in Cuba he relinquished his title to a man six inches taller and weighing, in the pink of condition, 238 pounds (17 stones). Against that Johnson was flabby at 225 pounds (16st.11-lbs), whereas at Reno against Jeffries he had been a trim but sizable 212 pounds (15st.2lbs.).

The fight was scheduled for 45 rounds and the fact that the coloured man went into the 26th of these before going down for the full count says a lot for his amazing defensive skill. He was 37 (could have been 39), had lived it up during the past five years and, if the truth is known, was well aware that if he won the fight it might cost him his life. He was getting his stipulated 30,000 dollars and if it meant handing over his coveted title, it was ridding him of a burden that was becoming wearisome. It was a well-paid way of getting back into society as a free man, for apart from his short imprisonment at Leavenworth, which could hardly be termed an incarceration, he was never again subjected to any form of persecution now that he was no longer boxing champion of the world.

The record book lists Johnson as having 23 more bouts after the defeat by Willard, but none of them could be called contests in the full meaning of the term. They are listed in his record that appears at the end of this book and a glance at them is sufficient to show their unimportance, especially as the last took place in 1928, a year after this book was written. During that time he remained anything but a lost personality. Always good for a story, he kept his name green, not only by his infrequent exploits in the ring, but in a variety of ways that enabled him to live pretty well, if not in his former opulence when champion. As he grew older, so his name became legendary and he was most popularly received whenever he made a public appearance, never missing an opportunity to attend a big fight, merely for the sake of being introduced from the ring.

A lover of motor cars from their inception, he liked to drive high-powered vehicles as fast as he could make them go and in his affluent days his speeding got him into as much trouble as did his many amourous adventures. On June 10th, 1946, he was heading for New York in a Lincoln Zephyr, his foot hard on the pedal. He had just crossed the border of North Carolina when a truck coming in the opposite direction caused Jack to swerve. He lost control of his car and it went off the road to crash into a power pole, the driving side taking the full brunt of the impact. The ex-champion was knocked unconscious and, although they got him to hospital in less than an hour, he died of multiple internal injuries.

When the doctor wrote out the death certificate he took the name from the driving licence and entered it as John Arthur Johnson, but someone older took a look at the broad black face and said: 'That's Jack Johnson. You know, the great boxer.' Mrs. Irene Johnson had the body shipped to Chicago where he had been living for a number of years. It was displayed at an undertaker's, and most of the negro population of the city filed past the open casket in reverent homage to the man who had represented his race at the highest point in the world of sport. On June 14th, thousands of negroes stood silently in the streets of Chicago and 2,500 coloured mourners crowded into the large high-domed Pilgrim Baptist Church for the funeral service. They buried him next to Etta in Graceland Cemetery and the grave is marked with a solid granite slab inscribed simply – JOHNSON.

APPENDICES

Appendix I

Ring Record
of Jack Johnson

Born Galveston, Texas, U.S.A.; March 31st, 1878

Editor's Note: The records of earlier fighters' ring activities are always obscure and notoriously difficult to compile. In the days before sophisticated P.R. techniques and complex tax considerations, a boxer customarily fought scores, even hundreds, of poorly-documented contests – sometimes two or three on the same day – at both ends of a noteworthy career. The following is the result of many years' research and is probably the most accurate and complete record of Jack Johnson ever published.

	Dave Pierson	w.	Galveston
	Bob Thompson	l. pts. 4	Galveston
1896			
	Howard Pollar	w.	Galveston
1897			
	Jim Rocks	w. k.o. 4	Galveston
	Sam Smith	w. pts. 10	Galveston
1898			
	Reddy Bremer	w. ko. 3	Galveston
	Jim Cole	w. pts. 4	Galveston
	Henry Smith	drew 15	Galveston
1899			
Feb 11	Jim McCormick	drew 7	Galveston
March 17	Jim McCormick	w. dis. 7	Galveston
May 6	Klondike	l. ko. 5	Chicago
Dec 16	Pat Smith	drew 12	Galveston
1900			
	Josh Smith	w. pts. 12	Memphis
1901			
Feb 25	Joe Choynski	l. ko. 3	Galveston
March 7	John Lee	w. pts. 15	Galveston
April 12	Charley Brooks	w. ko. 2	Galveston
May 6	Jim McCormick	w. ko. 2	Galveston
May 28	Jim McCormick	w. ko. 2	Galveston
June 12	Horace Miles	w. ko. 3	Galveston
June 20	George Lawler	w. ko. 10	Galveston
June 28	Klondike	drew 20	Galveston
Jan 17	Willie McNeal	w. ko. 15	
1902			
Jan 17	Frank Childs	drew 6	Chicago
Feb 7	Dan Murphy	w. ko. 10	Waterbury
Feb 22	Ed Johnson	w. ko. 4	Galveston
March 7	Joe Kennedy	w. ko. 4	Oakland
March 15	Joe Kennedy	w. ko. 4	San Francisco
April 6	Bob White	w. pts. 15	
May 1	Jim Scanlan	w. ko. 7	Pittsburgh
May 16	Jack Jeffries	w. ko. 5	Los Angeles
May 28	Klondike	w. ko. 13	Memphis
June 4	Billy Stift	drew 10	Denver
June 20	Hank Griffin	drew 20	Los Angeles
July 4	Hank Griffin	drew 15	Los Angeles
Sept 3	Pete Everett	w. pts. 20	Victor, Colorado
Sept	Hank Griffin	drew 20	Los Angeles
Oct 21	Frank Childs	w. pts. 12	Los Angeles
Oct 31	George Gardner	w. pts. 20	San Francisco
Dec 5	Fred Russell	w. dis. 8	Los Angeles
1903			
Feb 3	Denver Ed. Martin	w. pts. 20	Los Angeles
	(Coloured heavyweight Championship of the World)		
Feb 27	Sam McVey	w. pts. 20	Los Angeles
April 16	Sandy Ferguson	w. pts. 10	Boston

May 11	Joe Butler	w. ko. 3	Philadelphia
July 31	Sandy Ferguson	n. dec. 6	Philadelphia
Oct 27	Sam McVey	w. pts. 20	Los Angeles
Dec 11	Sandy Ferguson	w. pts. 20	Colma, California

1904

Feb 16	Black Bill	n. dec. 6	Philadelphia
April 22	Sam McVey	w. ko. 20	San Francisco
June 2	Frank Childs	w. pts. 6	Chicago
Oct 18	Denver Ed. Martin	w. ko. 2	Los Angeles

1905

March 28	Marvin Hart	l. pts. 20	San Francisco
April 25	Jim Jeffords	w. ko. 4	Philadelphia
May 3	Black Bill	w. ko. 4	Philadelphia
May 9	Walter Johnson	w. ko. 3	Philadelphia
May 19	Joe Jeannette	n. dec. 6	Philadelphia
June 26	Jack Monroe	n. dec. 6	Philadelphia
July 13	Morris Harris	w. ko. 3	Philadelphia
July 13	Black Bill	n. dec. 6	Philadelphia
July 18	Sandy Ferguson	w. dis. 7	Chelsea, Vermont
July 24	Joe Grim	n. dec. 6	Philadelphia
Nov 25	Joe Jeannette	l. dis. 2	Philadelphia
Dec 1	Young Peter Jackson	w. pts. 12	Baltimore
Dec 2	Joe Jeannette	n. dec. 6	Philadelphia

1906

Jan 16	Joe Jeannette	n. dec. 3	New York
March 14	Joe Jeannette	w. pts. 15	Baltimore
April 19	Black Bill	w. ko. 7	Wilkes-Barre
April 26	Sam Langford	w. pts. 15	Chelsea, Vermont
June 18	Charlie Haghey	w. ret. 1	Gloucester
Sept 3	Billy Dunning	drew 10	Millinocket, Me.
Sept 20	Joe Jeannette	n. dec. 6	Philadelphia
Nov 8	Jim Jeffords	w. pts. 6	Lancaster, Pa.
Nov 26	Joe Jeannette	drew 10	Portland, Me.
Dec 9	Joe Jeannette	w. pts. 3	New York

1907

Feb 19	Peter Felix	w. ko. 1	Sydney, Australia
March 4	Jim Lang	w. ko. 9	Melbourne, Australia
July 17	Bob Fitzsimmons	w. ko. 2	Philadelphia
Aug 28	Kid Cutler	w. ko. 1	Reading, Pa.
Sept 12	Sailor Burke	w. pts. 6	Bridgeport, Conn.
Nov 2	Jim Flynn	w. ko. 11	San Francisco

1908

Jan 3	Joe Jeannette	drew 3	New York
June 11	Al McNamara	w. pts. 4	Plymouth, England
July 31	Ben Taylor	w. rsf. 8	Plymouth, England
Dec 26	Tommy Burns	w. rsf. 14	Sydney, Australia

(Heavyweight Championship of the World)

1909

| March 10 | Victor McLaglen | n. dec. 6 | Vancouver |

April	Frank Moran	exh. 4	Pittsburgh
May 19	Philadelphia		
	Jack O'Brien	n. dec. 6	Philadelphia
June 30	Tony Ross	n. dec. 6	Pittsburgh
Sept 9	Al Kaufman	n. dec. 10	San Francisco
Oct 16	Stanley Ketchel	w. ko. 12	Colma, California
	(Heavyweight Championship of the World)		
1910			
July 4	James J. Jeffries	w. ko. 15	Reno, Nevada
	(Heavyweight Championship of the World)		
1911			
	Inactive		
1912			
July 4	Jim Flynn	w. rsf. 9	Las Vegas
	(Heavyweight Championship of the World)		
1913			
Dec 19	Battling Jim Johnson	drew 10	Paris, France
	(Heavyweight Championship of the World)		
1914			
June 27	Frank Moran	w. pts. 20	Paris, France
	(Heavyweight Championship of the World)		
Dec 15	Jack Murray	w. ko. 3	Buenos Aires
1915			
April 3	Sam McVey	exh. 6	Havana, Cuba
April 5	Jess Willard	l. ko. 26	Havana, Cuba
	(Heavyweight Championship of the World)		
1916			
March 10	Frank Crozier	w. pts. 10	Madrid, Spain
July 10	Arthur Craven	w. ko. 1	Barcelona, Spain
1917			
	Inactive		
1918			
April 3	Blink McCloskey	w. pts. 4	Madrid, Spain
1919			
Feb 12	Bill Flint	w. ko. 2	Madrid, Spain
April 7	Tom Cowler	drew 10	Mexico City
June 2	Tom Cowler	w. ko. 12	Mexico City
July 4	Paul Sampson	w. ko. 6	Mexico City
Aug 10	Marty Cutler	w. ko. 4	Mexico City
Sept 28	Bob Roper	w. pts. 10	Mexico City
1920			
April 18	Bob Wilson	w. ko. 3	Mexicali, Mexico
May 17	George Roberts	w. ko. 3	Tia Juana, Mexico
Nov 25	Frank Owens	w. ko. 6	Leavenworth
Nov 25	Topeka Jack Johnson	w. pts. 5	Leavenworth
Nov 30	George Owens	w. ko. 6	Leavenworth

1922
Inactive

1923
May 6	Farmer Lodge	w. ko. 4	Havana, Cuba
May 20	Jack Thompson	n. dec. 15	Havana, Cuba
Oct 1	Battling Siki	exh. 6	Quebec, Canada

1924
Feb 22	Homer Smith	w. pts. 10	Montreal, Canada

1925
Inactive

1926
May 2	Pat Lester	w. pts. 15	Nogales, Mexico
May 30	Bob Lawson	w. dis. 8	Juarez, Mexico

1927
Inactive

1928
April	Bearcat Wright	l. ko. 2	Topeka, Kansas
May 15	Bill Hartwell	l. ko. 6	Kansas City

1929
Inactive

1930
Philadelphia Jack O'Brien	exh. 3	

1931
Chief White Horse	exh. 3	

1932
Inactive

1933
Jan 20	Maurice Grizelle	exh. 1	Paris, France
Jan 20	Ernst Guehring	exh. 1	Paris, France

1934–1944
Inactive

1945
Nov 27	Joe Jeannette	exh. 3	New York
	John Ballcort	exh. 3	

1921
April 15	Jack Townsend	w. ko. 6	Leavenworth
May 28	John Allen	exh. 2	Leavenworth
May 28	Joe Boykin	w. ko. 5	Leavenworth

Key

w. pts. – won on points	l. pts. – lost on points
w. ko. – won by knockout	l. ko. – lost by knockout
dis. – disqualified	n. dec. – no decision contest
exh. – exhibition bout	rsf. – referee stopped fight
ret. – retired	

Appendix II

The Great Contest

Hardly had Johnson wrested the title from Tommy Burns, on December 26, 1908, before the search was on for a Great White Hope to retrieve it. The writings of Jack London gave the campaign momentum, and did much to instil it with a racialist fervour. Alternately flattered then goaded, the undefeated James Jackson Jeffries was finally induced to champion the white man's cause after six years of sedentary retirement.

In the eight months between the announcement and 'The Fight of the Century' itself, the contest in prospect was rarely out of public sight or mind. Newspapers were full of it, its outcome was a topic of intense interest across the globe. In the weeks surrounding the great day the world's major journals devoted a staggering amount of space to covering every aspect of the build-up, the fight and its aftermath. In an era before broadcasting and closed-circuit cinema, hundreds of thousands besieged the offices of news agencies for round-by-round accounts wired from the arena. On that Independence Day in 1910, a village called Reno was the only place on earth that mattered.

American newspapers tended to concentrate on the pageantry and ballyhoo of the occasion. Some of the best reports of the fight itself appeared in the British press. The following is the Daily Telegraph's commentary, reproduced in full, on the most spectacular sporting event in history.

THE
GREAT CONTEST

JOHNSON'S VICTORY.

JEFFRIES KNOCKED OUT

IN THE

FIFTEENTH ROUND.

SPECIAL DESCRIPTION

OF

THE FIGHT.

SCENES AT THE ARENA.

No fight in modern times has created more universal interest than the contest between Jeffries and Johnson, which took place at Reno, Nevada, yesterday.

Johnson proved the victor, knocking out his opponent in fifteen rounds. A description of the fight will be found below.

In Fleet-street there was an extraordinary demonstration of popular interest, which is described in another column.

From Our Own Correspondent.

RENO (Nevada), Monday.

Jeffries and Johnson, amid a tornado of cheers, flag-waving, and wild shrieks of delight, entered the ring at 2.30 p.m., Nevada time, to do battle for the world's championship and the stakes and bonus as already detailed.

At this time the huge arena was densely crowded. Probably 18,000 persons were present, while outside 15,000 more clamoured vainly for admission. Billy Jordan, the veteran "announcer," clambered under the ropes at 1.43 p.m., and shouted, amidst a thrill of excitement, that Johnson was in his dressing-room stripping for the fray. He mentioned that the fighters would receive a bonus of £2,000 each, and he estimated the gate receipts at £50,000. Then followed upon the roped platform a procession of champions and ex-champions—Bob Fitzsimmons, John L. Sullivan, Jake Kilrain, Tommy Burns, Gotch, the wrestler, and many others famous in varied departments of sport, all of whom were greeted with an uproar of cheering. The excitement was intense, and several world-champions who showed symptoms of making a speech, and so delaying the appearance of Jeffries and Johnson, outlasted their welcome. Those who managed to say a few words were heard with impatience.

Jeffries, who was still in his cottage, several miles away, when Johnson was dressing at the ringside, at last appeared in his motor-car at two p.m. He had made a preliminary visit to the ring to inspect the arrangements in the morning, and, having found all satisfactory, returned home to wait patiently. Mrs. Jeffries and his two younger brothers helped him while the time away.

Johnson was the first to enter the ring, followed by Jeffries. Their exultant reception at the hands of the crowd, the roars of thunderous cheers, again and again renewed, the tense strain and excitement which pervaded the arena as men and women stood and shouted for their favourite, baffle description. Jake Kilrain said that in all his experience he had seen nothing like it, and, he added, "there will be nothing like it again." Johnson had a black and white bath-robe round his broad shoulders; he seemed well pleased, and the smile, showing his six golden teeth, extended almost from ear to ear.

Jeffries, as he stepped into the ring, stamped heavily, testing the platform. He seemed satisfied, and then found time to gaze curiously and unmoved on the big audience ranged in ascending tiers on four sides. At that time the white champion wore a grey business suit and grey golf cap, of which he divested himself in the presence of the spectators, revealing a natty pair of purple tights.

Both men wore the national colours around their waists, and the hands of both were bandaged with tape to shield the knuckles. Jeffries gazed for a moment in Johnson's corner, but his expression did not change. He had been introduced, despite Johnson's protest, as "champion of the world." Jeffries had the corner with his back to the sun.

At 2.47 the fight commenced.

STORY OF THE FIGHT.

The first three rounds favoured Jeffries, who, while cautious, was more aggressive than the black. Jeffries sent three big punches into Johnson's ribs, and the crowd went wildly enthusiastic. In the fourth round Jeffries rushed Johnson to the ropes and punched him on the nose, securing first blood.

In the fifth round Jeffries was cut under the mouth and eye. Both men gave and received heavy punishment. Johnson, in the sixth round, sent a terrific left to Jeff's right eye, almost completely closing it. Johnson taunted and laughed at Jeffries, and seemed increasingly confident. It was Johnson's round entirely, and in the interval Jeffries's seconds tried to patch the injured eye.

In the seventh round Jeffries's eye seemed to worry him a great deal, and the round ended with Johnson laughing merrily. Jeffries in the seventh round sent a heavy left to Johnson's chin, who still smiled, and retorted by sending two strong lefts to the face, making Jeffries's bad eye still worse. It was again Johnson's round.

Johnson showed beautiful defensive work in the eighth round, but nevertheless received several lefts in the stomach. The eighth round was Johnson's by a slight margin, and time found both men in clinches.

In the ninth round Johnson seemed exceptionally cool. During a clinch he nodded to a friend in the crowd and laughed outright. Jeffries's eye bled freely, and caused his friends much anxiety. Johnson sent a left to the mouth, and recived a hard right on the body, both men clinching at the bell. It was Jeffries's round by a considerable margin.

The tenth round found Johnson boxing hard, but most of the blows seemed to lack steam. The tenth was Johnson's round, and ended with the negro smiling all over his face and winking at coloured friends at the ringside.

In the eleventh round Johnson's famous right upper-cut sent Jeffries's head back three times in rapid succession. Jeffries now bled badly from nose and mouth. It was Johnson's round by a shade.

Jeffries's right eye in the twelfth round was almost closed. Johnson, in clinches, sent three hard rights to his opponent's head, and the round ended largely in favour of the negro. The thirteenth round found Jeffries wobbly, almost blind, and with his face covered with blood.

Johnson pursued his advantage to the uttermost in the fourteenth, and early in the fifteenth knocked out Jeffries, greatly to the consternation and disappointment of the vast majority of the spectators.

A MOTLEY THRONG.

In anticipation of witnessing the greatest boxing match between heavyweights of the present generation, and possibly the last on American territory, thousands of people left Reno before midday to find seats in the great wooden amphitheatre, with a roped ring in the centre, constructed expressly for the Jeffries-Johnson battle. A clear sky and pleasant westerly wind gave promise of a perfect day. The amphitheatre is about twenty minutes' walk from Reno, and the road leading thereto was thronged by all manner of vehicles and pedestrians of every nationality. State Senators, Congressmen, bankers, sporting men, millionaires, wealthy business men, clerks, miners in red shirts, cowboys, Texans in native garb, Chinese, and Japanese formed this strange, motley throng.

The noise along the route was deafening. It was created chiefly by automobile horns, betting men crying the odds through megaphones, and street hawkers selling photographs of the combatants and iced water-melon. Good humour prevailed, for the prospect of a rattling good set-to seemed well assured. It was known that both principals had slept soundly and satisfied completely the medical examination prescribed by the Nevada laws.

Jeffries rose at eight o'clock, and consumed five lamb-chops for breakfast, while Johnson, rising an hour later, devoured the best part of a chicken. Their trainers, experienced men like Jim Corbett, seemed more nervous than the principals. Jeffries and Johnson, with their trainers, seconds, and staff, made a triumphal procession in motor-cars to the ringside. No victorious general on his return to Rome in classic days had a more popular welcome. Both smiled confidently; Jeffries nodded now and again as he recognised a friend; but Johnson, who loves a crowd, stood up most of the time, with head bare, bowing repeatedly to right and left. "Glad to see you folks," he shouted several times; "come right along and see the fight."

Mrs. Johnson preceded her husband in another automobile. She also smiled expansively. Mrs. Johnson, dressed in gala attire, displayed superb diamond rings. Mrs. Jeffries believes that gentlemen should settle their differences without the presence of ladies, and she remained behind at Reno.

SEARCH FOR FIREARMS.

In view of the threats to shoot Johnson if he won, all suspicious characters—and we have a varied selection of crooks here from all parts—were searched before entering the arena, and any firearms found were impounded. Tickets were exchanged for revolvers, just the same as checks are given for your hat and coat at the theatre. Flasks for whisky or other spirit, blackjacks, and knuckledusters were also detained. Doubtless the haul of weapons made at the entrances to the amphitheatre would have been greater, but the Reno authorities, anticipating that the reputation of the State would be seriously imperilled if any serious outbreak occurred to-day, thoughtfully sent out police skirmishers in plain clothes last night, who hunted out, rounded up just as many scallywags as they could find, and carefully placed them under lock and key. Reno gaol to-day is simply chock full of disagreeable characters.

In addition to the regular policemen, a special battalion of keen-eyed, strong-handed aides, with pistols in their belts, were sworn in as an emergency force. They were dotted about the arena to-day, charged with the special duty of spotting anybody trying to create a disturbance or engineer a stampede. Jeffries himself asked for fair play for Johnson if the negro won, but the authorities deemed that the precaution of swearing-in emergency reserves was absolutely necessary. All sorts of strange fellows anxious to witness the contest presented themselves as special constables, and in a few hours after they had been enrolled, and pistols with ammunition had been served out, several of these same special constables were arrested, charged by regular constables with picking pockets.

Several hours before the match began the crowd commenced pouring into the arena, where seats for 18,000, at prices ranging from £1 to £20, are reserved. In honour of Independence Day, the Stars and Stripes waved from the flagpoles. Boxes for the ladies were placed well in the rear, so that while the occupants could witness the actual fighting, they would be too far away to be distressed by the sight of blood, broken noses, torn ears, or black eyes. Messenger-boys were allowed in the arena for the benefit of the newspapers, and also to shout out the latest odds in betting, which, towards midday, increased to 2 to 1 on Jeffries, much to the alarm of the Johnson people, who thought that something untoward was in the wind.

In the centre of the ring, on a raised platform, a cinematograph was placed while the throngs assembled, and recorded every phase of the interesting kaleidoscopic scene. The light was good for moving pictures. Later the machines were removed to another platform, and the preliminaries in the ring, the introduction of champions past and present, and the arrival of the two principals were duly cinematographed.

RIVALS' STATEMENTS.

Before the match to-day Jeffries made the following statement: "I'll lick this black man so badly that he'll never want to see a boxing-glove again. I never was so good as this before; that is to say, I never felt better. No matter what my condition is, or what it isn't, I'm going to lick Johnson. I don't care whether the fight lasts four rounds or forty, it will be all the same to me. This will be my last fight, and it may be Johnson's last fight, too. I've had to do a lot of training to put myself in shape, and I've had to give up a lot of pleasure; it's no fun for a man of my inclinations to have to deny himself everything, to knuckle down and work his blamed head off just on account of a coon. There's something coming to somebody, and it's going to come good, too. I'll make Johnson pay for the long, hard grind I've had to go through. Now that it's all over, I'm glad it happened; but anyhow I want to lick somebody, and that somebody is Jack Johnson. No, I won't have any excuse to offer. I'm not going to lose, so what's the use of saying I'll not have any excuse if I do lose. Huh, huh!"

Johnson's final pronouncement before the battle was just as confident as that of Jeffries. The negro said:

"I only wish I was as sure of getting a million dollars as I am that I'll whip Mistah Jeffries. He was a great fighter, probably the greatest that ever lived, but I think I have everything in my favour in the coming fight. I've never been out of training, not very far out, I mean; and I'm a much better boxer than Jeffries ever was. I don't know how I'll fight him; I might start right after him or I might stall him off for a while; but I'll win, that's sure. I've been rapped for not being aggressive. Just because the other fellow sticks his head in the fire is no reason why I should do the same. I use my head, and take no chances, that is, unnecessary ones. That's the real ring generalship, I think. I know I can land a knockout, and you'll be surprised when I do it. I don't ever make excuses; people would laugh at me if I should lose and then come around with an excuse, and I'd laugh at them if they didn't. Don't judge me by my other fights. I shan't know what my plan of campaign is before we are face to face in the ring."

Simultaneously with these official pronunciamentos breathing confidence and snorting defiance, there was just the same diversity of opinion amongst the experts as described in my previous despatches. During the greater part of the morning it was still 10 to 6 in favour of the white man. Nobody could question the deadly earnestness of Jeffries's temper after breakfast. His gladiatorial spirit has been stirred evidently to the deepest depth, and his friends realised that even if Reno did not exist, and no ring had been constructed for his special benefit, Jeffries, if he had his own way, would take Johnson to some island in the Pacific and there, without spectators, settle his long account.

On the other hand, Johnson was chatting, smiling, laughing, and even frolicsome.

SCENES IN RENO.

Reno did not go to sleep last night, and before breakfast to-day the main street was clogged with crowds of sporting men. Pullman cars have been packed for sleeping quarters; big touring automobiles are everywhere. All yesterday and this morning special trains arrived with visitors, most of them wearing a button inscribed, "Oh, you Jeff." It is believed here that the Nevadan Legislature will shortly bring this State into line with others as regards the prohibition of vice, but in the meantime the whirl of sin is unfettered. Drinking saloons are doing an enormous business; roulette wheels are whizzing; gambling rooms are open everywhere—there is one, I hear, in the basement of the building which shelters the Christian Scientists—and Reno, conscious, perhaps, that the days of the real old sportive, picturesque, wild and woolly West are numbered, seems for the moment proud of its sinfulness. Reno is not only the hotbed of gambling, but also of divorce. Nevadan laws are kind towards people who find matrimony irksome, and on rather trivial grounds will grant a release to suitors providing they consent to lodge here for a time. Reno has a divorce colony, and some stylishly-dressed ladies I noticed here to-day are either members of that colony, or their looks belie them.

ROUNDS DESCRIBED.

JOHNSON'S COOLNESS

EXCITING FINISH.

RENO (Nevada), Monday.

At 2.28 Johnson entered the arena. It was reported that he refused to enter the ring unless the new division of the purse was agreed to. In response to the demand from the crowd Jeffries jumped through the ropes at 2.32.

The announcement of the increased purse of $121,000 and of the new ratio of division was a complete surprise to the audience, though it had been reported that each was to receive a bonus of $10,000. It was the intense heat which made the crowd restless, and after the pugilist celebrities had been photographed in the ring they called insistently upon Jeffries and Johnson. The former was then taking a rub-down in his dressing-room.

Sam Langford caused it to be announced that he challenged the winner. Johnson then climbed into the north-east corner of the ring, followed by his seconds, Billy Delaney, A. L. Kaufman, Professor Burns, George Cotton, Furry Dave Mills.

Jeffries jumped through the rope a moment after, followed by Jim Corbett, Joe Cheynski, Sam Berger, Eugene Vancourt, Farmer Burns, Roger Cornell, and his timekeeper, Billy Gallagher.

At 2.40 Jordan cleared the ring, and the men donned the gloves. When Johnson stripped it was seen that he was wearing blue trunks, with an American flag for a belt.

Before entering the ring, Johnson wore a bathrobe, and Jeffries was dressed in a full suit of clothes, without a shirt or underwear. He wore a golf cap, and chewed gum continuously.

At a quarter to three the fight started.

ROUND ONE.

Jeffries walked in feinting. Both men sparred. Johnson gave ground, and then led a straight left, touching lightly. They then broke away. Jeffries walked in and hooked his left to Johnson's neck, and in the clinch sent his right to Jack's body. Johnson responded with his left, and they remained standing breast to breast trying for short inside blows. As they broke away Jeffries sent his left to Johnson's neck. The negro stepped in with his left, but missed. The bell rang when they were in clinch.

ROUND TWO.

Jeffries at once assumed his crouch, but forced, and Jeffries stepped nimbly away. Jack then sent his left to Jeffries' face and ripped in.

Jeffries scored first blood. In round two, after a hard upper cut on Jeffries's chin, they held together, unwilling to give each other any chance. Jeffries sent his right to Jack's ribs, and took Jack's left in his face at close quarters. Jeffries then crouched and waited for Johnson, but he was unwilling, and they came together without a blow. Johnson tried his upper cut but missed, and Jeffries put his right to Jack's shoulders and pushed him about. When they broke away Jack shot his left hard to Jeffries's face and tried his upper cut, but missed. There was again a lot of wrestling without much fighting. The gong rang without a good blow being struck.

ROUND THREE.

Jeffries hooked his left to the body, and got under Johnson's right. Jeffries stood breast to breast, and the two men held and shoved each other about the ring. Johnson sent two lefts to the face and a right for the chin, but missed the latter. Jeffries smiled at these blows, and continued to bore in.

The first three rounds were simply a wrestling bout.

In this round Corbett said to Jeffries, as they walked to the centre, "Take it easy, Jeff."

Jeffries sailed in and led for Johnson's head, but missed. Johnson hooked in a stiff left to his opponent's body and a righthander to his head, but neither blow was hard. The two men then shoved and pushed each other about the ring while Corbett kept up a continual flow of talk.

ROUND FOUR.

Johnson took a crouching position, and again walked in and missed. They came together in a lock. Johnson tried his right for the chin but missed, and the two men began to exchange talk. Jeffries put his left on to Johnson's face, and started blood from Johnson's lip, drawing from the crowd the yell "First blood for Jeffries."

Johnson only smiled at this demonstration, and as Jeffries walked in again Johnson shot a snappy left to the face. They came to a clinch then, and Jeffries sent his left to Jack's face, forcing him to the ropes by sending three lefts to the body at close quarters. Johnson lashed out with his right, but Jeffries neatly ducked and avoided the blow.

The round ended in favour of Jeffries.

Round Five.

Jeffries walked straight out and tried to land his left. Both after this sparred carefully. Jeffries's left, however, got blocked, and in the clinch following upon this Jeffries shoved Johnson back easily. When they broke Jack swung his left for the body, but missed. Johnson then shot an upper cut, and landed slightly on Jeffries's lip. As they broke Jack landed a left on Jeffries's face, who came right back with a left on Johnson's body. Johnson then held Jeffries, and as they broke again he tried an upper cut and missed, but he stung Jeffries's face with the left.

"Go in, Jeff!" shouted Corbett. This woke Jeffries up, and he slipped in and shot a straight left for Jack's head, amid cheers from the crowd.

The gong found them in a clinch.

Round Six.

Again Jeffries crouched, and the two men stepped around each other, Johnson finally sending in two stiff lefts to the face. One of them cut Jeffries's cheek to the bone. Then again they lolled in each other's embrace. Then Jeffries rushed, but missed a left for the body, taking a left on the chest in return.

Johnson kept up a running flow of talk to Jeffries when they came to the clinch, but Jeffries calmly chewed gum. Jeffries then missed Jack with his left, and took a left and right on his head. Johnson shot his left to Jeffries's face and closed his right eye, missing two rights. Jeffries's nose was bleeding when the gong rang. When Jeffries took his seat his seconds got busy with his eye.

This was Johnson's round.

Round Seven.

Jeffries walked in, but before he had a chance Jack led his right. His left missed. Jeffries's eye was badly swollen, and he was rubbing it with his glove. Jeffries feinted and tried to draw Johnson on. The negro, however, declined to come in. Jeffries stepped in with his left for Jack's body, but missed, and took a left on his head. Jeffries then hooked his left to the head, at which Johnson laughed loudly. Johnson then sent in lefts to the face twice at close range, and Jeffries butted his way into a clinch, but failed to land. He drew Jack's lead and shot his left to the face.

After a close-quarter mix, Jack sent his left to the face twice, and Jeffries's lip bled. This round was somewhat faster.

Round Eight.

Johnson put his left on Jeffries's face. Jeffries missed Jack's body with his left, but got two lefts on his face. "Hello, Jimmy," said Jack to Corbett, as he was bombarded by Jeff's blows, "did you see that one?" Jeffries shoved Johnson about with ease. The gong found them locked.

Johnson's blows up till this round were cleaner and snappier than Jeffries's, but apart from a bruised eye Jeffries was not hurt.

Round Nine.

Jeffries stood up and walked into a left to the chest. "Make him fight, Jim," yelled Corbett. Johnson walked in and tried with a left for the head. Jeffries got inside it, and put his head against Jack's chest, shoved the black man to the ropes, and got two left jabs in the face which did no damage.

Round Ten.

The men came up slowly. Jack shot his left to Jeffries's face, but the white man brushed it away and responded with a left body blow. Johnson then failed to get home a lightning right-hander for the jaw.

Jeffries put his shoulder to Johnson's body and shoved him back, and at close range Johnson sent a left upper-cut to the mouth. As they broke he missed a right for the jaw, and Jeffries took two lefts on the face.

Round Eleven.

Jeffries tried with his left, only to find it blocked. He took a left on the face three times, but smiled.

Breaking away from the clinch, Johnson sent a stiff left uppercut to the face and a right to the body. He kept Jeffries's head bobbing in a clinch, and sent three upper cuts on his face in quick succession.

Jeffries appeared tired, and after another breakaway Jack hooked his left hard to the nose, and the blood flowed from Jeffries's lips and nose. Jeffries's blows appeared slow compared with Jack's snappy delivery. Just before time was called Jeffries rushed in and sent his left to the body, but went away without doing any damage.

This was decidedly Johnson's round.

Round Twelve.

Jack waited, and then hooked a left to the face. Jeffries rested on the black man's shoulders, and then tried to rip in on Jack's body. His blows, however, were blocked almost before they started, and the negro's boxing drew applause from the crowd.

Jeffries forced his way to close quarters, and got a left on the nose in reward. His nose bled freely, and as he turned to take his seat on the sound of the gong he spat out a mass of blood. Johnson grew more confident as the fight proceeded.

ROUND THIRTEEN.

Putting his right glove before his face, Jeffries walked into a clinch without a blow being struck. When they broke away Johnson sent his left to the body and three lefts to the face in quick succession. This was followed by an uppercut on the face.

Jeffries seemed tired and slow, and could not solve the secret of the negro's defence, but took all blows which came his way. Jack stood back and swung his left to the face, and then calmly clinched. Jeffries continued to come in, in spite of his punishment. This round was all in Johnson's favour. Jeffries's eye was almost closed up at the end of it.

ROUND FOURTEEN.

Jeffries walked straight in to a left, and they hung over each other. Jack tapped the big fellow in the face twice, and blocked Jeffries' attempt at close fighting. Shambling forward, Jeffries took three straight lefts in his face, and got on to Johnson's face lightly.

"How do you feel, Jim?" said Jack, as they stood clinched. Jeffries did not reply verbally, but walked in with three lefts in quick succession.

ROUND FIFTEEN.

This round was a clinch to start with. Following on Jeffries's attempt to land on Johnson's face, the negro forced the pace and sent Jeffries down with a left and a right to his jaw. Jeffries got up, but was sent down for a count of ten.

The crowd yelled "Stop it; don't let him knock him out."

As Jeffries backed to his corner he said, "I'm no good as a fighter any longer. I couldn't come back, boys. Ask Johnson if he will give me his gloves."

When the count of seven had been reached, it was evident that the white champion was finished, and at least 100 people climbed through the ropes. The timekeeper was forced from the ring by the crowd.

The confusion was so great that no announcement by the ring officials was audible as to whether the white man was technically counted out. The end of the fight will probably be recorded as a knock-out. Each time that Jeffries fell outside the lower ropes on to the platform, as he got up again and staggered forward Johnson sprang at him like a tiger, and with a succession of left swings on his jaw sent him through the lower rope on the east side of the ring, where he lay until he was counted out.
Reuter's Special Service.

AFTER THE FIGHT.

When Jeffries was led back to his corner by Corbett, Berger, and Jack Jeffries after the final round he was still dazed. Johnson stood in the centre of the ring and received congratulations from Billy Delaney and his other seconds.

As he talked to Delaney Johnson was breathing normally, and was not hurt. Later he went to Jeffries' corner to shake hands with his opponent, but Corbett and O'Brien waved him away, and he returned to his own corner of the ring. The crowds were so dense round the ring that the police had to beat them back.

The first man to congratulate the conquering negro was John L. Sullivan.

Jeffries, who was attended by doctors as he sat in his corner, shook his head sadly for a few minutes, and was then led to his dressing-room, and soon afterwards taken to his camp at Moana Springs.

The ring was then completely dismantled by souvenir hunters.

FINAL PREPARATIONS.

RENO, Monday.

By ten o'clock the price of the cheapest tickets had advanced to $25, the seat speculators having been encouraged to make this increase by the large number of visitors arriving in the town. Wherever the tickets were on sale the crowd fought to purchase them.

At noon a flood of Johnson money was brought out by a 2 to 1 proposition, but in an hour the odds had gone back to 10 to 6. The betting is reported to be heavy, and much money is being placed even on Jeffries to win in twenty rounds.

Both camps are quiet and both champions are well.

The day opened bright and clear, and a cool west wind caused the prediction that the maximum temperature would not exceed 85deg. Both Jeffries and Johnson rose early and announced that they felt in fine spirits. In the forenoon they were formally examined by two physicians in accordance with the State law regulating prize fighting. The doctors reported to the sheriff that both men were in perfect physical condition.

Johnson then went in his motor to the ring. As he drove slowly through the crowded streets he was recognised and cheered, but did not stop, as he was anxious to get on to the arena to see that everything was shipshape. Johnson on his return to his camp after inspecting the ring ate a hearty breakfast, consisting of three lamb chops.

Jeffries and his trainers and rubbers at about the same time were getting the paraphernalia of battle in order, and were seeing to it that the towels and sponges and tubs were all packed, and that the drinking water and the sunshade which is to shelter Jeffries between the rounds were not forgotten. This was completed just before ten o'clock.

At midday the exodus to the arena began. The sportsmen who had spent the night on the cold floor or piled three in a bed, or even on cots in the Morgue, pressed through the streets of Reno, many of them without their breakfast, owing to the impossibility of feeding so many visitors.

Only one accident marred the morning. It was when a Californian, drawing out a bunch of banknotes from his pocket in a liquor saloon, accidentally drew out his revolver at the same time. It fell on the floor, and went off, wounding the owner.

ROAD TO THE ARENA.

Those who could not afford motor-cars generally preferred to walk to the arena, rather than take one of the two street-cars which comprise the entire rolling-stock of the local tramway company serving the arena. The gates were opened at midday, when thousands already thronged the four entrances, over each of which floated the American flag. As the gates of the arena swung wide open there was a great rush for the turnstiles, and in less than fifteen minutes the cheapest seats on the top tier of the arena were half-filled.

The boxes for women were soon filled, and the gaudy hats of the occupants, many of whom are popularly supposed to be members of the celebrated Reno "divorce colony," added a vivid touch of colour to the scene. The sporting celebrities in the town arrived early at the ringside, which soon swarmed with them.

Many of the audience, to protect themselves against the glare of the meridian sun, brought smoked glasses and green shades. Others equipped themselves with picturesque, wide-brimmed, high-crowned straw hats. At one o'clock the Reno Military Band climbed up into the ring and played stirring American airs.

In the meantime Jeffries, at his camp, awaiting the summons to fight, played cards with his partners. Johnson spent most of the forenoon in posing for the newspaper photographers and cracking jokes with chance callers. Johnson and his attendants started for the arena in a motor-car at one o'clock.

Yielding to the protests of spectators whose view was obstructed by the moving picture booths, Mr. Rickard ordered one booth to be dismantled. At ten minutes past one the word was passed round that every seat in the arena was sold. Several thousand persons were then still lined up at the ticket booths.

Johnson arrived at the dressing-room in the arena at 1.35 p.m.

Besides the women in the boxes there were hundreds of women scattered about in every section of the arena, from the cheapest seats to those on the ring side. Old attendants at prize fights say that they have never seen so many women spectators at a fight before.

Jeffries and his attendants left Moana Springs for the arena in a motor at 1.40.

Mr. Rickard announced that the purse of $121,000 would be split up in shares of 40 and 60 per cent. Each fighter will get $10,000 bonus. Mr. Rickard said that he made that arrangement when the articles of the fight were signed, and he had not, therefore, given the fact out for publication. Jack Johnson's wife was seated near the ring. The announcer of the fight, Billy Jordan, when he climbed through the ropes at 1.42, got the first round of applause from the ring.

The cameras snapped every prominent person seated near to the ring, and panorama pictures were made of the entire arena. The beat beat down on the crowd out of the clear sky, and was almost unbearable. Jordan then introduced Rickard, Tim Sullivan, the stake-holder, and the other people prominently participating in the fight arrangements. When Fitzsimmons was introduced he was received with great applause. Hugh McIntosh, Tommy Burns, and Bill Lang were among those applauded.

Soon the crowd began to tire of the introductions, and began calling for the fighters, who had by this time arrived at the arena.

BEFORE THE BATTLE.

Jeffries and Johnson are awaiting the clang of the gong which this afternoon brings them together in the long-expected forty-five-round battle for the premier heavyweight title, and a purse of $101,000, of which the winner will receive 75 per cent., and the loser 25 per cent. Owing to a large influx of money for Jeffries yesterday evening, the odds dropped to 10 to 6 in favour of Jeffries.

One of the arrivals yesterday evening was Billy Delaney, the noted handler of fighters, who took Jeffries when a raw youth and soon made him world's champion. Delaney and Jeffries are now enemies, and Delaney will be Johnson's chief second this afternoon. Delaney, after examining Johnson, says that his protégé is in the best possible condition, and will surely win.

The greater portion of Sunday was spent by Jeffries in lolling on the shady lawn of his training quarters, paying no attention to the throngs, ten deep, outside the fence, endeavouring to get a glimpse of "the white man's hope." Late in the afternoon he went for a short motor trip, and then played roulette at an adjacent hotel. He retired at ten o'clock, as happy as a big schoolboy. Johnson worked for eight miles over the roads, and thereafter announced his weight as 206lb. When he had finished dinner he motored to Reno to see the crowds, who cheered him. He then returned to his camp, and after a concert, at which he played his favourite bass viol, the negro champion retired to bed.

The last touches were put to the amphitheatre yesterday. The ring seems solid enough for elephants to play upon. The sale of tickets is large.

Jeffries in a statement yesterday evening said:

" I fully realise what depends upon me, and won't disappoint the public. That portion of the white race which is looking to me to defend its athletic supremacy may feel assured that I am fit to do my very best. I'll win as quickly as I can."

Johnson said:

" I honestly believe that as a pugilist I am Jeffries's master, and propose to demonstrate this in the most decisive manner possible. Here will be no lagging fight; it will be fast throughout, no matter how long it lasts. I am prepared for a long contest. If Jeffries wins I will go over to his corner as soon as possible and congratulate him. The tap of the gong will be music to me."—*Reuter's Special Service.*

CROWDS IN NEW YORK.

From Our Own Correspondent.

NEW YORK, Monday.

In honour of Independence Day people ceased work throughout the country, and devoted the closest attention to the big contest. There was not a city or town in the land, from the Atlantic to the Pacific, where vast crowds failed to congregate.

Outside the newspaper offices here bulletins from Reno at intervals of two minutes were posted describing each round. In some cases the fighting was actually illustrated by white and black pugilists, who, stationed on a platform just above the level of the street, illustrated each telling point as it was recorded by the telegraph ticker inside the newspaper office. The people were tired of reading about the contest, and were only eager to see the actual results.

Overwhelming sympathy was displayed in favour of Jeffries, but amongst the coloured people Johnson had undivided support. In Brooklyn the negroes actually held a camp meeting, praying and singing, while at intervals bulletins from Reno were read to them.

SCENE IN FLEET-STREET.

As early as nine o'clock crowds began to gather in front of the newspaper offices in Fleet street, anxious for news of the fight. An hour later the numbers in one part alone had reached nearly a thousand, and by eleven o'clock more than three times as many had assembled, spreading across the street almost from side to side. The spectacle was striking, even to General Election habitués of Fleet-street. During the earlier hours there was a complete absence of shouting or disorder, and it was only when the congestion became so great as to interfere with wheeled traffic that anything like excitement came into evidence.

No more than five policemen could be discerned, but the imperturbable calm with which they handled a mass of fifteen hundred to two thousand men, mostly young, was worthy of the traditions of the City force. Motor-'busmen and taxi-drivers hesitated before the phalanx which barred their way, until an authoritative wave of the hand from a constable set them at the crowd. Another gesture, and the people parted before the advancing car, as it forged slowly through the mass. The tacticians in blue used these new engines with enormous effect in keeping the centre of the road open to traffic, deflecting them inexorably, whether eastward or westward bound, towards their respective near sides, and so pressing the mob towards the pavement.

The process gave rise to some shouting, but was met by the sufferers in the practical give-and-take humour characteristic of the Londoner en masse. The only manifestation of physical force was the snatching of the destination boards from the side of one or two motor-'buses. In one case the board was thrown with some violence after the 'bus, but in others the law-abiding instinct prevailed, and some kindly soul or other picked up the derelict label and rushed after the conductor to restore it to him.

By eleven o'clock the force of police had been increased, but the crowd grew even more rapidly, and by half-past eleven it numbered close on 5,000 men. Occasionally it surged from side to side, yet orderly amid disorder, ebullient yet self-controlled, it allowed the great cars to plough through its ranks, menacing life and limb, yet injuring none. The police and the people once more triumphantly vindicated that elasticity of popular discipline to be seen nowhere out of London.

LYNCHING IN AMERICA.

TERRORISED NEGROES.

CHARLESTOWN (Missouri), Monday.

An exodus of the negro population is reported to be taking place as the consequence of a double lynching yesterday, when two negroes were hanged by an infuriated mob for the murder of a white farmer. The crowd attacked the county gaol. The sheriff and his subordinates were powerless. They refrained from shooting on account of the presence of many women and children.—*Reuter.*

NEW YORK, Monday.

Two negroes, charged with the murder of a white farmer, were taken from gaol at Charlestown, Missouri, yesterday morning, by an angry mob, the officials offering little resistance, and were hanged in close proximity to a church, the members of the congregation being compelled to witness the terrible spectacle as they passed into the building.— *Central News.*

Appendix III

Too Hot to Handle?

After more than a year of careful preparation, everything was set. In San Francisco, the natural home of major sporting events in those days, the opening bell was about to sound.

Then, at the eleventh hour, the Governor lost his nerve. Pressured by social reformers, scared that the controversy might lose California a forthcoming international exposition, he outlawed the fight, invoking an old statute which the State ignored or recalled at its convenience.

For Tex Rickard, the publicity was heaven-sent. The fight had become bigger news than ever. He just needed somewhere to stage it.

California Governor, Fearing Loss of Panama Exposition, Orders Jeffries-Johnson Fight Stopped

Mr. Gillett Tells Attorney General to Prosecute Men Involved if Bout Is Held.

HAD WARNING FROM HOUSE MEMBER

Dismay Among Managers, and "Tex" Rickard at Once Seeks Audience with Authorities.

BATTLE MAY GO TO NEVADA

Reno Makes a Bid, but Promoters Still Hope to Have the Contest in San Francisco.

GOVERNOR JAMES N. GILLETT, of California, yesterday directed the State's Attorney General, U. S. Webb, to stop the Jeffries-Johnson fight arranged to be held in San Francisco on July 4.

Despatches from Washington stated that the cause for the Governor's action was found in a statement by influential members of the House Foreign Affairs Committee that the holding of the big contest might defeat San Francisco's effort to get the Panama Exposition of 1915.

The managers of the July 4 affair announced that no move would be made until the Attorney General's opinion had been rendered, but stated that in case it be against them Reno, Nev.; Ely, Nev., or Salt Lake City would be chosen as the battleground.

SAN FRANCISCO IN FERMENT OVER ORDER

Governor's Action Dazes Fight Interests, but Church People Are Jubilant.

[SPECIAL DESPATCH TO THE HERALD.]

SAN FRANCISCO, Cal., Wednesday.—Like the explosion of a powder magazine came the news to-day that Governor James N. Gillett has ordered Attorney General U. S. Webb to prevent the Jeffries-Johnson fight, or in case it be held to prosecute both principals and promoters for a felony under the penal code. To-night the city buzzes and boils with the ferment of indignation on one side and the expression of approval from the church people on the other.

"Tex" Rickard, the promoter, who has

Nevada Will Allow Fight, Says Judge

CARSON CITY, Nev., Wednesday.—The law of Nevada would permit the Jeffries-Johnson fight in this State, according to a statement made to-day by Judge Sweeney, of the Supreme Court, when the question was put to him in the absence of Governor Dickerson. With only the formality of obtaining a license, for which $1,000 must be deposited, he said that the fight could be held in any county in the State without fear of interference. The law permitting contests of unlimited number of rounds in Nevada was passed for the Corbett-Fitzsimmons fight and has not been amended or repealed.

been almost wholly responsible for all the arrangements for the big fight, saw Attorney General Webb as soon as the action of the Governor had been learned, and after an hour's conference said that he believed that the fight would be held on the date advertised despite the Governor's orders. He would not say what his course of action would be until after Attorney General Webb had given an opinion, and said that he had no intention of abandoning the effort to hold the fight here.

Not much faith is placed in this assumption of confidence, however, as the threat of prosecution is regarded as the sort of thing that will prevent either Jeffries or Johnson taking a chance of going to jail on a charge of having committed a felony.

At Sacramento to-night Governor Gillett said:—"I have no statement or explanation to make other than that contained in my letter to the Attorney General. I am simply doing my duty as I see it. I only acted after the District Attorney of San Francisco reported to me he would not try to prevent what I deem to be a crime against the State of California and the laws I am sworn to protect from violation. I have been deliberating on this matter for ten days and have gone over the whole thing very carefully.

"I have received hundreds of letters, but these have had no bearing on my action. I purpose to do my duty as I see it, no matter what people may say or do and no matter whom it hurts. That is all there is to it."

Defines "Prize Fighting."

The decision of Governor Gillett to use his Gubernatorial powers so far as possible in preventing the fight was first learned when a letter from him was received here to-day by Attorney General Webb. In this letter the Governor set forth his disapproval of prize fighting and drew a sharp and apparently distinct line between prize fighting and sparring as permitted by the laws of California.

His letter marks the end of prize fighting in this State, it is believed, as he has also ordered the Attorney General to stop the twenty round fight between "Al" Kaufman and "Sam" Langford, which was to have been fought next Saturday.

Speculation and conjecture as to the motive for the Governor's action followed like a prairie fire the announcement that the fight would be prevented, but when the fog of doubt had cleared away there was left clear and distinct the one single impression that Governor Gillett had put a ban on the championship fight as a propitiary offering to the powers who have in hand the decision as to the location of the Panama Exposition of 1915.

Governor Gillett was called upon to kill off the fight or lose all chance of getting the great international exposition for San Francisco, and he did not hesitate very long. As the story is known here, he received word ten days ago from William E. Wheelre, president of the Board of Trade of San Francisco, that "representative Bennet, of the Committee on Foreign Affairs in the House of Representatives, had warned him that if the Jeffries-Johnson fight was held in San Francisco it would kill the city's chances of getting the exposition."

Several conferences between the Governor and business men interested in the exposition were held and the fate of the fight was decided at these conferences. Governor Gillett's greatest ambition at this time is to land that exposition for San Francisco. He is confident that it will mean his re-election and only a short time ago he made a trip East to combat the claims of New Orleans, the one city that San Francisco fears most, and to set forth in the most striking fashion the reasons for giving this great fair to the coast city.

Will Kill Fighting.

This motive for stopping the Jeffries-Johnson fight has a much wider field of action, however, than was at first supposed when the announcement came that the bout set for July 4 would be prevented. Governor Gillett will kill prizefighting entirely in the State of California so long as he is in office.

A decision by the Attorney General has been promised in three days in order that Rickard may receive some consideration in view of the great expense to which he has gone. More than $25,000 was to have been expended in building the arena at Eighth and Market streets, and much of the work has already been completed.

"I believe the fight will be held in this city," said Rickard, to-day, "as the courts of California are more powerful than the Governor."

Should the fight be held, however, it is quite likely that the Governor can force the prosecution of the principals and the promoters, "Tex" Rickard and "Jack" Gleason, on a felony charge for violating Section 412 of the Penal Code. This of itself is enough to hold Johnson in awe, for he has seen much of the interiors of court rooms of late and is getting Bench shy. Nor is Jeffries the sort of man to take a chance of going to jail, no matter how confident Rickard and Gleason might be of coming off clear in a criminal prosecution.

The letter of Governor Gillett is sharp and clear in its meaning and intent and there is no opportunity for regarding it as a mere effort to satisfy the clamor of those who have been protesting against the fight, as was at first believed by Rickard and Gleason! The stronger motive back of it is apparent in every line. It is evident that he will use all his power to prevent the fight. The letter is as follows:—

The Governor's Letter.

"State of California, Executive Office,
"Sacramento, June 14, 1910.
"U. S. Webb, Attorney General, San Francisco:—

"Dear Sir—I desire to call your attention to a so-called prize fight, to take place on the Fourth of July next, in the city of San Francisco, between 'Jim' Jeffries and 'Jack' Johnson.

"Many complaints are made at this office by prominent citizens of this city protesting against this so-called fight and requesting that some action be taken by the proper authorities to stop the same.

"The District Attorney of San Francisco has informed me that he does not propose to interfere in the matter.

"The first session of the Legislature, held in this State in the year 1850, enacted a law making it a felony for two persons to fight each other upon a previous agreement upon a wager for money or any other reward. This law has been amended from time to time, but never so as to make prize fighting lawful.

"In 1903 the Legislature again amended the law relating to prize fighting. While the law as amended permitted 'sparring exhibitions' for a limited number of rounds with gloves, to be held by a domestic incorporated club, it did not remove the ban which thelaws of this State have always placed upon prize fights and, while a 'sparring exhibition' under certain conditions and restrictions is permissible under this act, a prize fight still re-

mains a felony.

"I believe that you should investigate the matter and take such legal steps as may be proposed, if in your judgment warranted by the facts, in presenting the case to the court for its decision, and have all interested parties enjoined pending the hearing.

"Our Supreme Court has never defined a prize fight, and I believe that an opportunity should be given it to do so. Since the amendment of the law in 1899 permitting 'sparring exhibitions' prize fighting, under the guise of this amendment, has greatly increased and has been tolerated in California, until to-day our State is a Mecca for prize fighters, much to our discredit.

Fighting Must Cease.

"Our people have the right to demand that prize fighting shall cease in this State, and it will, if our present laws are enforced, especially if our courts follow the decisions of the Supreme Courts of our sister States in defining a prize fight. In my opinion, a prize fight exists when there is 'an expectation of reward to be gained by the contest or competition, either to be won from a contestant, or to be otherwise rewarded, coupled with an intent to inflict upon such contestant some degree of bodily harm.' In Kansas the Supreme Court held that 'there must be an intent on the part of the contestants to do violence to and inflict some degree of bodily harm on each other,' and the fight must be for some prize or reward. Other States have made similar rulings. To show that the so-called 'sparring exhibitions' held in this State under the auspices of incorporated athletic clubs, have not been sparring exhibitions, but prize fights, I need but refer you to the files of our daily newspapers.

"I will call your attention to two or three of the recent ones. First, the Moran-McCarthy fight. The Oakland Tribune in its issue of April 30 in reporting it uses this language:—

"'After the sixteenth round had gone some fifty second Moran landed a blow on McCarthy's jaw. It did pot look to be the heavy punch, but the young fighter went over backward, his head seemingly dropping below as though his neck had been injured, and as he struck the floor the sound of the impact could be heard throughout the pavilion.' McCarthy died.

"Next the Wolgast-Nelson fight took place on Washington's Birthday. (It seems that prizefighters always want to fight on Washington's Birthday, Memorial Day and Independence Day.) It was reported in all the daily papers of the State by rounds. I quote from the San Francisco Chronicle of February 23:—

"'Round 13.—Nelson's lips were puffed and his eyes and cheeks were swollen. They mixed it like tigers, Wolgast having all the better of it, landing repeatedly on the body and jaw, with Nelson fighting wildly and spitting blood. Wolgast literally cut the Battler's face to ribbons, but still the Dane came in for more.

"'Round 39.—Wolgast appeared loth to put in the finishing punch. He jabbed incessantly at the Battler's anatomy and again the blood flowed in a stream. Wolgast almost sent Nelson to the floor, landing blow after blow on the defenceless champion's face.'

"If these contests were not prizefights then the historic battle between Heenan and Sayers was not one. I have no doubt that the coming contest between Jeffries and Johnson will be a repetition of the brutality mentioned in the foregoing fights, only on a larger scale.

"If 'sparring exhibitions,' as permitted by our laws, mak fights where men are killed—beaten into insensibility and their faces 'cut to ribbons'—are lawful acts, then it is time that the Legislature should interfere and make such exhibitions a felony. Such contests are prizefights not permitted by the law and should be punished as such. Those who engage in them are prizefighters and make their living by fighting each other for prizes or rewards.

"The whole business is demoralizing to the youth of our State, corrupts public morals, is offensive to the senses of a great majority of our citizens and should be

abated as a public nuisance and the offenders punished.

"If the court, upon your petition, refuses to grant the relief prayed for therein and permits the parties interested to proceed, as advertised by them, then I desire you, on behalf of the people of the State, to gather all evidence possible and if the contest is carried out as advertised and the parties fight for a purse or for a reward, and inflict upon each other bodily injury, then you are to cause the arrest of the principals and those interested with them in promoting the fight and try them on a felony charge for violating Section 412 of the penal code. Yours truly,
"J. N. GILLETT."

By reason of its sheer unexpectedness the order of Governor Gillett caused a panic among those financially interested. Both Rickard and Gleason were dazed and at first accepted the decision of the Governor as final and conclusive.

"The fight will come off just the same," said Rickard. "The men will keep on training and I will hustle around and locate a place in which we can fight with the certainty of being left undisturbed. The fight will take place in Salt Lake City or in either Ely or Reno, Nev., in case it is impossible to fight here."

Later Rickard had his conference with Attorney General Webb and announced that he had not given up all hope of holding the fight in San Francisco.

"Mr. Webb has promised his decision in three days," said Rickard. He promised a speedy decision because of the great expense already incurred in beginning the erection of the arena and in arranging the preliminaries.

"In the meantime I will scout about in Utah or Nevada for a place where I know I will be safe in holding this fight."

The loss in shifting the scene of the fight to Nevada or even to Salt Lake City will be enormous, however, and the fight promoters realize this. The uncertainty already developed with regard to the eventual meeting of Jeffries and Johnson will undoubtedly cause many who had intended to come to San Francisco to give up all idea of seeing the fight. It is known that Rickard has received orders for more than $100,000 worth of tickets and that from $150,000 to $200,000 has already reached him. Fight enthusiasts have already started from England, Australia and the East, and special trains are being made up by the score in New York, Boston, Chicago, Montreal, Vancouver, and many similar places.

Just what will be the nature of the legal proceedings to be instituted by the Attorney General is not known. The Governor's letter is positive in directing that the courts be asked to intervene and urging a definition of prize fighting by the Supreme Court. For this reason it is believed that Mr. Webb will apply for a writ of mandamus before the State's highest tribunal, thus bringing all parties before that body for a hearing and procuring a temporary injunction pending a decision. By this step he would avoid delay, since the promoters would have to appeal if judgment were rendered against them.

Work on the arena, which has progressed rapidly since it was started about two weeks ago, was ordered suspended temporarily when the action of the Governor became known, but the promoters did not say whether they would extend this order, pending a court decision.

District Attorney Fickert, mention of whom is made by the Governor in his letter to the Attorney General, displayed some bitterness when asked for a statement. He said that the Governor had heeded the clamor of the mob and made satirical reference to "political capital."

JOHNSON, UNMOVED, KEEPS ON TRAINING

[SPECIAL DESPATCH TO THE HERALD.]

SAN FRANCISCO, Cal., Wednesday.—"Jack" Johnson may now get into a new tangle with George Little over his moving picture rights. Although last night he sold all his rights to a representative of a large film company, the sale, it is feared, may be void if Governor Gillett succeeds in stopping the fight. However, Johnson is tranquil and unconcerned.

"Now Mr. Little can do all the attaching he wants to," he said. "In order to get at any part of that $50,000 he will have to serve papers on me in the State of Illinois, and he would never dare appear in a court of law back there.

"That was one of the reasons that I disposed of my interests in the moving pictures," continued the champion. "There were many other reasons, though. In the first place, I do not believe the fight is going to la ' long enough to make a good moving picture show, for the way I feel now make: me additionally confident that I will win inside of ten rounds. Then, again, I am not convinced that I have received all that was coming to me out of other moving picture ventures, not because the managers were dishonest, but because in the big list of men who were out with the films there were some who were careless and incapable.

"Finally, I was prompted more or less by a desire to reassure the public that this fight is going to be absolutely and indisputably on the square, but it is not going to be a 'frame' nor a 'moving picture exhibition.' I thought the best way to prove this was to get rid of any interest in the films."

NEWS STOPS WORK IN JEFFRIES' CAMP

[SPECIAL DESPATCH TO THE HERALD.]

JEFFRIES' TRAINING CAMP, ROWARDENNAN, Cal., Wednesday.—The report that Governor Gillett has taken a stand against heavyweight championship fight, and proposes to stop it, cast a gloom over the camp here this afternoon and the attention turned from "Jeff's" condition to what the Governor was going to do. The news was received early this afternoon, and it was not taken seriously at first, but later, when it was found to be authentic, everybody seemed to be downhearted.

While Jeffries refused to believe that Governor Gillett would take any action, at the same time it caused him to cease training for the day. In fact, it set the camp topsy turvy, and everybody seemed to feel sorry for the promoters, who have spent so much on the battle.

It would not be surprising to sportsmen here if "Jeff" got disgusted and threw the whole thing up. However, the "big fellow" will continue as if nothing had happened until he hears from either Rickard or Gleason. His manager, "Sam" Berger, is in the city, and "Jeff" says he will find out just what is doing and notify him. Jeffries gave this statement to the press:—

"I do not know the first thing about the law. As I understand it we are not breaking the law, but we are under the protection of the law. Until I hear officially from the promoters that the fight is to be stopped it will not credit the story."

A busy afternoon was mapped out for the "big fellow," but the bad news put a halt to it. "Jeff" was to have boxed Corbett during the afternoon and the excuse for not carrying out the programme was that the paint on the canvas ring had not dried. "Jeff" deserted the camp and went on a fishing excursion. Corbett seemed to be affected by the news, but he did not believe that the State Executive would take drastic actions.

REPORT DISCOURAGES NEW YORK MEN

Sporting men found along Broadway last night were somewhat discouraged by the report that California's Governor had ordered that the Jeffries-Johnson fight be stopped. There was much speculation as to how the Governor's order could be overcome, and some thought an injunction restraining the authorities from interfering, if obtained on such a date as would make a hearing impossible before the contest, was the solution of the trouble. They were dubious, though, about the ability of the fight promoters to find a judge who would grant an injunction in the face of the clamor from many quarters against the contest.

Although many sporting men have already departed for the Pacific coast confident of seeing the fight, there are still a few who deferred their departure in the fear of just such an interference as has been presented. In most instances, however, these men have purchased tickets and sleeping car accommodations. They will await further developments before making an effort to get their money back.

At Considine's last night one man who has bought his ticket declared airily that he would start for California on Saturday, confident that the contest would take place.

"I know Rickard," he said

"I know Rickard," he said, "and anybody who knows him will bet that he will pull the fight off. He's a level headed, farseeing citizen, and even if he does not pull the fight off in California it is certain he will do it elsewhere. He always has one or two cards in reserve when he goes into an affair like this, and there will be a fight."

Thomas Sharkey was much upset by the news yesterday. He said last night:—

"Well, I don't know what to make of it. Everything seemed fine and rosey until four o'clock. It's going to hit a lot of fellows hard. It looks as if they'd have to postpone the fight for a week or so, anyway. I think most likely it will go to Carson City, where Fitzsimmons fought Corbett. But that's only my thought. I don't think we here know who'll get the fight, but you can say for me that if they send it up to the North Pole, 132 degrees below zero, I'll be there at the ringside, to challenge the winner!

Mr. Bennet's Warning Caused Governor Gillett to Act

New York Representative Told San Francisco Business Men That They Ran Great Risk of Losing Exposition if Fight Occurred.

HERALD BUREAU,
No. 1,502 H STREET, N. W.,
WASHINGTON, D. C., Wednesday.

By passing along a "tip" to the Governor of California. Representative William S. Bennet, of New York city, republican, is said here to be the cause of Governor Gillette's action against the Jeffries-Johnson fight in San Francisco July 4. Mr. Bennet suggested to William R. Wheeler, president of the San Francisco Board of Trade, that the authorities of California might have to chose between having the fight or the Panama Canal Exposition in 1915. That was enough. There is a mighty struggle on between the city of the Golden Gate. and New Orleans, which is much nearer to the canal, for the official exposition.

Governor James N. Gillett, of California, and a great body of citizens from various parts of the State were here a few weeks ago and pleaded with the Foreign Affairs Committee of the House, which has the matter in charge, to select San Francisco. Not long afterward Governor Jared T. Sanders, of Louisiana, nearly all of the officials of that State and the entire Louisiana Legislature descended upon Washington and told why New Orleans was the better place. Both cities still have their boomers here. Washington is plastered over with their advertisements.

The Foreign Affairs Committee will meet to-morrow to consider the claims of the two States. California has not asked for a cent of government money and says she does not want it. Louisiana has not asked for any either, but says she thinks it ought to be appropriated. If it is not, however, Louisiana is willing to levy a special tax to meet the expenses of t e exposition.

This was the strained situation when Mr. Bennet, who does not believe in prize fights, conceived the idea that there was a strong moral sentiment in the House and country against giving Governmental honor to a city which permitted such a "barbaric sport" to flourish without restriction. He sent a telegram to Mr. Wheeler, who is a member of the Immigration Commission of which Mr. Bennet is vice chairman. Mr. Wheeler was at one time Assistant Secretary of Commerce and Labor.

Mr. Bennet told Mr. Wheeler that the House might be influenced by the moral sentiment throughout the country against prize fighting to give less weight to the claims of the Californians for the exposition than they deserved. Mr. Wheeler replied that he did not believe a majority of the people of California wanted the Jeffries-Johnson fight to be held in their State.

It is being recalled here that when Governor Gillett was in Washington to help along the exposition boom he said in an interview that the laws of California did not prohibit a pugilistic encounter like the coming Jeffries-Johnson fight and that he would do nothing to stop it.

FIGHT CERTAIN TO BE HELD JULY 4, PROBABLY AT RENO

"Tex" Rickard Says if Combat Is Impossible in California He'll Go to Nevada.

SAN FRANCISCO MAY LOSE FAIR ALSO

Governor and Attorney General Declare They Will Stand Firmly by Decision.

BOTH PRINCIPALS READY

Jeffries and Johnson Continue Training and Declare They Are Willing to Fight Anywhere.

Developments in Fight Situation

Promoters admit the contest will not take place in California, and "Tex" Rickard threatens damage suits against the Governor and Attorney General.

Washington despatches indicate that San Francisco, having lost the fight, may also lose the Panama Exposition.

Reno, Ely and Carson City, Nev., all offer inducements to the fight managers. Meanwhile both Jeffries and Johnson continue their preparations for a combat.

"Tex" Rickard announces that the fight will surely take place on July 4, if not in San Francisco, in Reno.

[SPECIAL DESPATCH TO THE HERALD.]

SAN FRANCISCO, Cal., Thursday.—The Jeffries-Johnson fight to-night is a homeless waif. Everybody, principals, promoters and public, are ready for the combat, but no one can tell where it will occur. Everybody "in the know" admits grudgingly that it will not be fought in San Francisco; indeed, Tex Rickard is so well convinced of this that he has threatened to take legal action against Governor Gillett and Attorney General Webb to recover damages.

The Governor is determined that the fight shall not take place in San Francisco or anywhere else in California. He came to the city to-day from Sacramento and said that nothing could swerve him from the course he had taken. Attorney General Webb will take the first official step to-morrow morning, when he will go before the Superior Court to ask for an injunction to restrain the Langford-Kaufman match, which is set for Saturday. In the event of the failure of the Attorney General to obtain an injunction, he says he will cause the arrest of the promoters and principals at the earliest moment after the fight begins.

Will Surely Take Place.

"The fight between Jeffries and Johnson will take place on July 4. If not in San Francisco then I will pull it off in Reno, but the fight will be held on the date set, and I shall keep my promise." This statement was made by Tex Rickard to-night.

Rickard continued:—"Once for all I want to remove all fear that Jeffries and Johnson will not meet in the ring on July 4. There need be no cancellation of special trains or tickets. Those who intended coming to San Francisco can come as planned and feel assured that they will see the fight."

The statement of Rickard was made soon after Southern Pacific officials advised the promoter that six special fight trains had been cancelled during the day. Rickard was greatly agitated by this information and also over the fact that many orders are being received to cancel or resell fight tickets.

Rickard admitted he did not have the slightest hope of pulling off the fight in San Francisco and that every day of indecision as to where it would take place merely increased his financial loss.

Will Leave for Reno.

"If the court grants an injunction here I leave for Reno Sunday morning and will immediately commence the erection of an arena there," he said. "My attorneys have advised me not to buck the Governor and the Attorney General, but I have agreed to wait until Saturday. It is a bitter pill for me and a heavy loss, but I will take my medicine and keep my word to pull off this fight if it's the last thing I do."

For once Rickard was "fight sick." He did not deny it. While not yet ready to announce so officially the promoter virtually admitted that the fight would take place at Reno.

It is stated to-night that Rickard and Gleason, the promoters, are laying their plans to pull up stakes and carry the fight to Nevada. Reno, Carson and Ely are all offering inducements to the promoters and it is likely that they will arrive at a decision before very long.

To Enforce Laws.

Governor Gillett on being told that merchants, hotel men and others interested in the fight would take steps to enter a determined protest against his action said that it makes no difference to him who protests, or how many protest, he is going to enforce the laws of the State of California. He stated that the decision is absolutely final.

The Governor was told that the fight promoters are laboring under the impression that if the courts do not prevent the fight arrests will not be made until after the pugilistic battle is over. The Governor was asked if it will not be his duty as he construes it under the law to step in and stop the fight if the promoters decide to defy him and attempt to go through with the programme on July 4. Governor Gillett replied:—

"There is plenty of time to ascertain what course will be taken to prevent the fight. We have nearly three weeks yet, and I do not care to discuss at this time any further what our action will be."

The Governor was also told that "Tex" Rickard is contemplating instituting suit for damages against him for the money lost that his action may cause. Mr. Gillett laughed. "He hasn't got a chance! Ridiculous! He couldn't collect a cent. If Mr. Rickard wants a fight he can get it. He will get a far bigger fight than the one he is advertising for the Fourth of July."

Attorney General Webb's investigation of the law on the case has convinced him that the Governor's letter was penned after a careful study of the legal phases of the matter.

"Consideration of the contents of the Governor's letter and of the law on prize fighting has convinced me that the proposed Johnson-Jeffries and Langford-Kaufman bouts would be violations of the law and felonies," said the Attorney General. "The chief executive officer of this State has ordered this office to intervene in the matter to prevent these violations of the law. Notwithstanding what any one else says, this order will be enforced to the letter, and if there is power in the courts to prevent it there will be no Jeffries-Johnson fight in San Francisco. This applies equally to the Kaufman-Langford bout, scheduled for Saturday.

"Any doubt of the determination to prevent these fights is based upon a false hope and will be dispelled very quickly. This office will apply to the Superior Court to-morrow morning for an injunction restraining the principals in the Langford-Kaufman bout from staging the contest. This course of procedure is necessary because of the proximity of the proposed occurrence.

"The law on the matter is plain and the facts are equally clear, so that I can see no reason why the injunction should not issue. If, however, the injunction is refused, it will be futile for the principals to attempt to stage the bout. The first round or two would probably determine the character of the bout as a prize fight, and this office would at once lodge informations charging the principals with the commission of a felony. The arrest would follow immediately and the bout would be stopped long before twenty rounds had been completed.

"What the course of this office will be in regard to the procedure to prevent the Jeffries-Johnson fight, I do not care to outline at this time. There is more time remaining to determine that matter and effective means will be taken."

Collect Legal Opinion.

The advice of the shrewdest lawyers in the city has been sought by the promoters, and although Herbert Choynski and H. G. W. Dinkelspiel will be the only attorneys of record they will be fortified by the best legal opinion which can be purchased. The attorneys for Gleason and Rickard insist that within the strict meaning of the law the July 4 contest is a boxing contest and not a prize fight, and that between the two there is a vital difference.

In discussing the position of Gleason and Rickard to-day Mr. Dinkelspiel declared that he cannot determine his course until the Attorney General files his action.

District Attorney Fickert to-day criticised Governor Gillett for giving his "practical assurance" to the whole world as well as to the managers of the big fight that the contest would be permitted and then suddenly ordering that it must be stopped.

"I can't see," he said, "why the Governor should get so busy now, when the promoters have spent $30,000 or $40,000 on the affair and when the people are on their way from all over the world under the practical assurance of the Governor that the fight would be held. Even if I were to decide now that I was wrong when I concluded that the fight was legal I would not stop it at this time. If I decided I had misinterpreted the law I should give notice that at some later date I would put a stop to all such fights. I have given my opinion on this fight and I am going to stand by it. The men have their articles framed for a boxing contest, and we cannot tell them they are liars until we have the facts."

HOUSE DECLINES TO FAVOR CALIFORNIA

HERALD BUREAU,
No. 1,502 H Street, N. W.,
Washington, D. C., Thursday.

After "raising the ante" for those cities which desire to play in the great national game in which the official Panama Canal Exposition of 1915 is the stake, from $5,000,-000 to $7,500,000, the House Committee on Foreign Affairs to-day refused to favor either New Orleans or San Francisco. It ordered a favorable report on resolutions requesting participation of foreign governments in an exposition at New Orleans and one at San Francisco. It is conceded that neither resolution will pass either House at this session.

Representative William S. Bennet, of New York, the member of the committee who warned the Californians that the Jeffries-Johnson fight might interfere with their chances of getting the big show, was the target of many pleasantries. Pacific coast representatives scoffed at the idea, but many from other parts of the country declared that they would not vote for San Francisco if the big fight should be held there.

For some reason the New Orleans boomers, including all of the members of Congress from the Southern States and many from the Middle West, are jubilant over the action of the committee. They profess to believe it was the death blow to San Francisco's hopes, whether the Jeffries-Johnson fight is held there or not. The Western members cannot see it that way, but they are sorely disappointed because the committee did not give their choice the preference at this time. The fact is that the Foreign Affairs Committee has shifted the entire responsibility for selecting a place for the official exposition on the shoulders of the Committee on Industrial Arts and Expositions, of which Representative W. A. Podenberg, of Illinois, is chairman. This committee will take the matter up at the session which begins next December.

JEFFRIES WANTS FIGHT IN SAN FRANCISCO

[SPECIAL DESPATCH TO THE HERALD.]

Jeffries' Training Camp, Rowardennan, Cal., Thursday.—There are only a few persons in the camp to-night who believe that the championship battle will take place at the Old Central Park, July 4.

Jeffries is trying to force himself into the belief that the Governor will change his mind and be a bit more lenient, but at the same time it is known that the trainers, and those connected with the camp, are expecting orders to move off to some other training ground.

While Jeffries did some work this morning he did not go through with the programme which he had planned. According to some of the trainers, Jeffries proposed to box at least five days a week, but so far he has boxed but one day—Monday morning, when he went through a hard day's work and boxed brilliantly. Corbett had hoped that Jeffries would box with him a little oftener, as he figured a few more workouts would have put him in shape. As it is now, there is but a short time left for boxing, and Corbett lounges around the camp, with nothing to do.

"I will fight for Rickard and Gleason," Jeffries repeated to-day, "and I do not care where the fight is held, though I would like it to be held in San Francisco. However, I am ready to go any place that the promoters designate, and I do not care whether the date of the battle is changed."

"I'LL FIGHT ANYWHERE," SAYS "JACK" JOHNSON

[SPECIAL DESPATCH TO THE HERALD.]

San Francisco, Cal., Thursday.—"Jack" Johnson did not appear to be very much disturbed to-day over the unexpected complications that have arisen in connection with his star engagement with James J. Jeffries. The big black man wore his "golden smile" this forenoon as he indulged in a little game of baseball after having reeled off a few miles on the ocean boulevard.

"I am not much of a lawyer," he said, "but I certainly feel sure that I'll face 'Jim' Jeffries here on July 4. The attorneys Rickard and Gleason have retained will be able to solve the problem. 'Tex' Rickard has assured me that the fight will take place, and that's enough for me. No matter where 'Tex' takes the battle, I'll be on deck ready to slip on the gloves two weeks from next Monday."

The champion was asked if he thought his condition and that of Jeffries would be affected if the fight were to take place in Nevada.

"It may affect us both slightly," he replied, "to leave the sea level and go off into the mountains for our sparring exhibition, but I guess both Jeffries and myself are hardy enough and in good enough condition to do this without serious damage. Anyway, it will be just as fair for one as the other and I believe almost as many people will be present at Reno or Ely as would attend the affair in San Francisco."

"Billy" Delaney, the veteran trainer and manager of prize fighters, took charge of the Johnson camp to-day. Delaney arrived from Harbin Springs at noon and went immediately to the Ocean Beach to join the champion in a conference then in session. He declared he had joined the negro's forces as the result of an understanding reached three weeks ago when he was in San Francisco.

George Little stirred up further trouble in the camp in the morning by attaching Johnson's automobile. The attachment is made to obtain $2,350 alleged to be due Little.

MINISTERS ARE DETERMINED.

[SPECIAL DESPATCH TO THE HERALD.]

Cincinnati, Ohio, Thursday. — The Rev. Dr. Adna W. Leonard, pastor of the Walnut Hills Methodist Episcopal Church, of Cincinnati, said here this evening that in case the prize fight between James J. Jeffries and "Jack" Johnson is taken to the State of Nevada a case will be brought against the principals and promoters in an effort to block the fight. Dr. Leonard said:—

"We are determined that this fight shall not take place and will follow them all over the country and use every effort possible to cut short the plans for this fistic encounter. I might say that several of our members have met here and drawn up letters to the Governor of Nevada asking him to see to it that the fight is withheld, and we are busy in the meantime mailing cards to our friends in all parts of this country protesting against the holding of the fistic battle in any part of the world. We are in this matter to the end and will show the Jeffries-Johnson combination that they cannot run this country."

REJOICES FIGHT IS OFF.

Great satisfaction was expressed yesterday by the Rev. Dr. John Wesley Hill over the fact that the Jeffries-Johnson prize fight had been called off so far as California is concerned. It was Dr. Hill, pastor of the Metropolitan Methodist Episcopal Temple, who by advocating a series of revival meetings as a counter attraction to the fight led the clergymen of the Pacific coast to arrange for just such an evangelistic campaign before and on July 4. Dr. Hill said to a Herald reporter:—.

"The Jeffries-Johnson prize fight was lost in the first round. The action of the Governor of California in calling it off is a triumph for law and order and for Christian civilization. Whatever State allows the fight will become a refuge for the refugees. Reno is the place for it if it must take place, because that is the place where marriages are also knocked out.

"Of course now the evangelistic meetings will not take place. They had been arranged as a last resort. The law has done what it is not necessary for the Gospel to do."

CAN'T FIGHT IN UTAH.

Salt Lake City, Thursday.—A movement to bring the Jeffries-Johnson contest to this city received a setback to-day when Governor Spry positively announced that he saw no reason to change his former expressed view that it could not be held in this State.

Governor Spry said:—"I see no reason for changing my position. The fact that Governor Gillett, of California, has refused to allow his State to be disgraced by having the fight in it is but an added reason why I should not change my former position. The fight will not be held in Utah if I can prevent it."

RENO MAKING PREPARATIONS

Reno, Nev., Thursday.—A committee appointed at a meeting of business men to-day began preliminary plans toward getting the Jeffries and Johnson fight for Reno.

Reno is prepared to make a substantial offer for the fight. One of the things which Reno will guarantee will be absolute immunity from interference by State officers. The Nevada fight law requires only $1,000 license fee.

Goldfield Offers $120,000 for the Jeffries-Johnson Fight; Governor Calls Out the Militia, Then Rescinds His Order

Rickard Leaves for Nevada To-Morrow to Decide Between Rival Towns.

JEFFRIES TO BREAK CAMP

Manager Telephones Him To Be Ready to Start for Reno at Moment's Notice.

Developments in Fight Situation

Governor Gillett, of California, made certain his stand in the Jeffries-Johnson fight yesterday by ordering troops ready to stop the Langford-Kaufman heavyweight contest billed for to-day, following the refusal of the Supreme Court to enjoin it. The promoter of the bout declares it will occur in spite of the authorities.

"Tex" Rickard announced that Goldfield's offer of $120,000 for the fight had been accepted, but later qualified his assertion to give other Nevada towns a chance, and Reno may yet get the combat.

District Attorney Fickert and the San Francisco Chief of Police promised the Governor they would prevent the Langford-Kaufman bout.

Jefferies and Johnson believe there is no chance for a meeting in San Francisco and will go to Nevada.

[SPECIAL DESPATCH TO THE HERALD.]

SAN FRANCISCO, Cal., Friday.—It may be that the big fight will be held in Goldfield; it may be that it will not. One thing only is certain—if Tex Rickard's constantly repeated promise indicates a certainty—and that is that there will be an encounter between Jeffries and Johnson on July 4, and most likely in Nevada. That is the situation here to-night.

Rickard to-day positively announced that the fight will go to Goldfield, but although Maurice Sullivan, a merchant of that town, to-day offered $120,000 for the fight, and the promoter promptly accepted, "fight fans" are not at all convinced.

"The fight will be held in Goldfield," announced Rickard. Then he added:— "If no higher bid is received from a Nevada town."

No sooner had word of Rickard's action reached Nevada than the wires were burdened with messages of protest and entreaty from Reno and Ely. Rickard's office was swamped with messages, and while few of these have been made public, it is certain that strong guarantees back the requests that the fight be taken to Reno or Ely.

So determined was the opposition to Goldfield by the other Nevada towns that the promoter partly surrendered in the afternoon. He informed urgent petitioners in Reno and Ely that he would listen to what they had to say Sunday night in Reno. This notice was also conveyed to Goldfield. Committees from each of the three Nevada towns will be at Reno Sunday when Rickard arrives from San Francisco.

Judging from Rickard's qualifications of his first decision to-day, the meeting at Reno will be an auction, at which the much desired prize will go to the highest bidder. Rickard said to-night that nothing new had arisen to alter his plans since he arranged for the Reno conference. He spent a busy day reading and answering telegrams.

Orders Out Militia.

The forthcoming Kaufman-Langford bout, announced for to-morrow afternoon, has kept official and sporting circles in a state of excitement to-day. This morning District Attorney Webb applied to Judge Van Nostrand for an injunction to prevent the encounter. The injunction was refused, the Court stating that the defendants had not been allowed sufficient time to present their case. Governor Gillett immediately instructed Adjutant General Lauck to have two companies of militia on hand to-morrow afternoon. Later, on the promise of District Attorney Fickert and Chief of Police Martin that they would prevent the fight, Governor Gillett announced that he would rescind the order to the militia.

Louis Blot, promoter of the Kaufman-Langford fight, after a conference with his attorneys to-night announced that he would carry out the fight to-morrow as advertised and would petition for an injunction restraining the District Attorney and chief of police from interfering. If the injunction is granted the Governor's only recourse is to call out the militia.

Governor Gillett had been greatly aroused by the expressed determination of the promoters of to-morrow's battle to proceed with their performance, and was more than displeased with the local authorities for their apparent neglect of duty. He put the matter tersely thus:—

"It is time that these fight promoters learned that they cannot openly outrage the laws of the State of California. If they do not realize that fact yet, they will do so when they attempt to stage a bout. Before any ring contest takes place these prize fight promoters will have to whip the State of California. That is final and irrevocable. If the promoters desire that kind of a contest the State is ready."

"If Louis Blot does what he says he will do I shall call out the militia. That is the only resource left," said Governor Gillett when he was informed of the promoter's intention. "I shall also file a criminal information and complaint, charging him with a felony if he holds the fight."

Governor Gillett, however, is not entirely convinced that Louis Blot, promoter, may not attempt to go on with the fight, and that there may be no hitch in police precautions to prevent the contest, he has instructed Adjutant General Lauck to be at the ring side prepared for instant action. Rumors were afloat to-night that the Governor had misunderstood the declaration of the city officers and that notwithstanding the pledges given him, the chief of police does not intend to call off the fight unless he feels the fight has gone beyond the bounds of the elastic definition of a boxing bout and has developed into a genuine prize fight.

At half-past eleven o'clock this morning Governor Gillett entered the lobby of the Palace Hotel, where the air was filled with gossip concerning the probability of holding the big fight. Within the next five minutes there was a scene of suppressed excitement, and it became known quickly among the loungers that the Governor had consented to give out a statement of his reasons for the delay in stopping the bouts. This statement set forth that he had not interfered earlier because the matter was primarily in the hands of the municipal authorities and that he acted only after District Attorney Fickert refused to do his duty.

Telegraphs for Troops.

After giving out this statement the Governor walked into the telegraph office and sent a telegram to Adjutant General Lauck, ordering him to have two companies of militia in readiness to be in San Francisco to-morrow afternoon at two o'clock to prevent the Kaufman-Langford fight.

Entering the lobby of the hotel again from the telegraph office, Governor Gillett met Adjutant General Lauck. He immediately told the active head of the State forces of the message which had been sent and ordered him to see that all necessary arrangements for the transportation of the militia were made without delay.

"This matter must be settled once and for all time," declared the Governor.

Governor Gillett showed plainly that he was thoroughly aroused. A frown on his forehead and his brows closely knit, he talked quickly and incisively, emphasizing each and every word. Determination was stamped plainly on his face.

Adjutant General Lauck, while admitting that the matter of calling out the State troops had been a subject of discussion between the Governor and himself, refused to divulge the names of the two companies of militia ordered to San Francisco.

When Blot was advised of the Governor's action he said:—"Militia or no militia, the fighters will be in the ring. Both men have assured me that they will be on deck at the appointed hour. I have consulted with lawyers, who have told me to go ahead. They have examined the articles of agreement and they say that we are acting within the law. We propose to see this thing to a finish."

Kaufman, when seen, had this to say:— "Well, I guess the Governor is the boss. It looks like he has put the Indian sign on to-morrow's battle. But I promised Mr. Blot that I would be in the ring to-morrow with my fighting togs and I will keep my promise."

The man who is on the cards to meet Kaufman said:—"I don't know what I shall do. I'll do whatever my manager, Mr. Woodman, says."

"Tex" Rickard Bitter.

Rickard is paying little attention to the Kaufman-Langford matter, but is very much worked up over his treatment by State officials of California and lamented the lack of support he is now receiving.

"When I had a chance to stage this contest elsewhere," declared Rickard, "the people of San Francisco made a strong call on me to bring the contest here.

"Now I am buffeted around, and what support am I getting? We could have staged the contest some other place without interference, and I did not decide on San Francisco until I had assurance that the big match could be held in this city.

"I have not given up hope yet and I will wait for the action of my attorneys before I make a move, but I will have to know very soon whether this contest can be staged in San Francisco or not. I must know by Saturday night, to leave Sunday for Nevada."

RENO'S BID STANDS.

RENO, Nev., Friday.—"Billy" McCarney, representing "Tex" Rickard and "Jack" Gleason, promoters of the Jeffries-Johnson fight, arrived last night to ascertain definitely whether there would be any possibility of opposition to the contest.

That Reno will not make any effort to outbid Goldfield in its alleged offer of $120,000 for the big fight was evidenced immediately after the Associated Press bulletins announcing the decision of Rickard was posted. The statement was immediately issued from the Business Men's Committee, which has the local end of the affair in charge, that Reno would not raise its initial offer one cent. Reno has offered to pay Rickard's license and erect the arena free of charge.

WANT FIGHT IN WYOMING.

CHEYENNE, Wyo., Friday.—The Cheyenne Athletic Club, a syndicate of local sporting men who say they have money to back up their project, has wired "Tex" Rickard an offer to stage the Jeffries-Johnson fight here on Roosevelt Day of the Frontier Celebration if the contest can be postponed until August 24. The plans contemplate the construction of a big arena at the Frontier grounds.

Mayor P. H. McCarthy, of San Francisco, who passed through Cheyenne last night on the Overland Limited, refused to discuss his position on the Jeffries and Johnson fight controversy.

ARRANGEMENTS IN RENO.

RENO, Nev., Monday.—William McCarney, representing Rickard, Gleason and "Sid" Hester, arrived in Reno to-day from San Francisco and completed preliminary arrangements for training quarters for the big fighters, who are to battle on July 4.

The Goldfield "boosters" arrived in Reno last night and are confident they will land the contest.

Frank Hall, manager for John L. Sullivan, arrived in Reno to-day. He was en route to San Francisco, but was stopped here by telegrams.

McCarney received instructions from Joe Woodman to-day to get training quarters at Reno for Sam Langford.

Arrangements are making by McCarney for training quarters for Ketchel. It is thought that Ketchel will train at Sparks, near Reno.

Reno Now in the Lead as Site for Big Fight

Rickard Leaves San Francisco with His Arena Builder to Make His Arrangements for the Show in the Nevada Metropolis.

THE LANGFORD-KETCHEL BATTLE IS SCHEDULED

[SPECIAL DESPATCH TO THE HERALD.]

SAN FRANCISCO, Cal., Monday.—"Tex" Rickard threw up the sponge early this morning, announcing positively that the Jeffries-Johnson engagement would not be played in San Francisco, and then, taking his arena builder with him, left on the first train out of the city for Reno.

Following quickly upon the heels of "Tex" Rickard's departure for Reno came the announcement that Louis Blot had abandoned the idea of holding a test fight in his arena this afternoon. The Kaufman-Langford fight was declared off, and instead of staging the test between the heavyweights a couple of lightweights, it was announced, would be put on next Saturday afternoon if the lawyers for Blot so advised.

Arrange for Ketchell-Langford Bout.

The Kaufman-Langford bout went by the boards at an early hour this morning when Wilson Mizner for Stanley Ketchel and Joe Woodman for Sam Langford came to terms with Sid Hester, who promoted the Wolgast-Nelson fight at Point Richmond on February 22 last, for a fight at Reno on the morning of July 4.

Hester practically had the match cinched Sunday, and in anticipation of settling the matter within a few hours sent "Billy" McCarney, his personal representative, to Reno last night. McCarney's mission was to have a talk with the merchants and others who have guaranteed the construction of an arena with a view to obtaining its use. He was followed this morning by Hester, who went to complete the details and procure a license.

Langford leaves for Reno to-morrow or Wednesday, and may take up his quarters at Moana Springs, where Jeffries will complete his training if the color line be not drawn. Ketchel undoubtedly will domicile himself in the Johnson camp, as he and he negro champion have been great friends since their fight at Colma last October.

Ketchel wants to limit it to twenty-five rounds, while Hester and Langford want to make it forty-five.

Chances Favor Reno, Says Rickard.

That Rickard was not bluffing last night when he declared that San Francisco had been passed for good and all was made plain this morning when he took with him to Reno the contractor who had been erecting the great arena at Eighth and Market streets in which it was expected, until Governor Gillett stepped in, that Jeffries and Johnson would settle their differences.

"What I said last night when I announced that I had stricken San Francisco from my fight map goes," said Rickard to-day. "Nevada gets the contest, and the selection lies between Reno and Goldfield, with the chances favoring Reno. Goldfield has made a nice offer, and so many people have told me that Goldfield does not look good to them and that the East is opposed to that place because of the long ride across the desert from Reno, that it seems at this time, as much as I dislike to disappoint my friends in the golden camp, that Reno will have to be decided upon."

There is a well grounded suspicion that Rickard has never seriously considered Goldfield, and it is a well known fact that neither Jeffries nor Johnson liked the idea of going there.

Blames the Governor's Ambition.

"Well, you boys can say that it has come to me on good authority that Gillett has said during the last couple of days:—'This move makes me United States Senator,'" said Rickard, while seated in the lobby of the St. Francis Hotel, the centre of a group of newspaper men and friends, this morning.

Rickard was beaten, and he was preparing to move to Reno for a conference on the Nevada situation.

"He is the Governor and he has the militia and he wants to be United States Senator, so you boys might as well rehearse that song 'I'm on My Way to Reno,'" said Rickard.

From the present outlook the promoters will not lose as much as was at first expected, for followers of the game in this city expressed the opinion that every man in San Francisco who could raise the price would go to Nevada to see the big show.

Expect Great Crowd.

Just as soon as Rickard announces where the big contest is to be held local sports will begin plans for attending the fight. Already numerous parties have been organized, and it is certain that the largest crowd of sport lovers who ever left San Francisco to see any sort of a show will leave here for the Johnson-Jeffries contest.

There was not much doing at Johnson's training quarters to-day. The big fellow went out on the road for a while and then took it comparatively easy for the rest of the day, devoting part of the time to arranging for the journey to Nevada.

It was originally Johnson's purpose to motor to Reno, but Rickard, however, put a damper on this, declaring that he would not permit the black champion to endanger his life and health in such a manner. Johnson said he would probably get away in a day or two, not later than the middle of the week.

Al Kaufman, who was to have met Sam Langford at Blot's arena last Saturday afternoon, but who lost the match and a tidy bank roll when the Governor upset the pugilistic pudding, will probably accompany Johnson to Reno and aid him in training for the big fight.

Fight Goes to Reno; State Will Keep Hands Off

Rickard Announces His Definite Selection of Nevada City and Work on Arena Begins at Once, Making Contest on July 4 Practically a Certainty.

KETCHEL-LANGFORD BOUT TO BE ON SAME DAY

[SPECIAL DESPATCH TO THE HERALD.]
RENO, Nev., Tuesday.—Reno get the big fight. The announcement was made to-day after Governor Dickerson had assured the promoters that the State authorities will not interfere.

Immediately work was started on the big arena, and "fight fans" are jubilant in the assurance that Jeffries and Johnson will meet on July 4.

The sight for the arena is a rocky field in East Reno, about a mile and a half from the heart of the city. It is familiar in ring history as the scene of the Hart and Root contest of July 4, 1906. It is regarded as an ideal place, as it affords plenty of ground for a spacious structure. On one side it is flanked by the tracks of the Southern Pacific Railway and on the other by a trolley line.

A building about three hundred feet square, modelled along the lines of the structure begun in San Francisco, will be put up. It is hoped to have it completed by the first of next month.

Training quarters for "Jack" Johnson also were selected to-day. "Tom" Flanagan, the champion's manager, after looking over several sites, finally settled on a road house three miles southwest of Reno, known as "Rick's Resort." According to Flanagan it is an excellent place for a training camp and affords all necessary facilities.

Jeffries will be stationed at Moana Springs, three miles south of Reno. Nothing, according to "Sam" Berger's reports, is lacking at this place that could be desired in connection with a fighter's camp. Natural hot and cold springs, an open air pavilion already provided, comfortable sleeping quarters and nearby fishing streams and lakes are among the inducements offered.

Two Fights July 4.

A double fight will be Reno's offering on July 4 if "Sid" Hester succeeds in carrying out his plan to stage the Langford-Ketchel fight on the morning of the big battle in the same arena. Hester was busy to-day endeavoring to arrange for a permit and in looking over numerous sites for training quarters for his fighters.

Rickard's announcement of the selection of the battle ground for the Jeffries and Johnson contest was made in this signed statement:—

"I have decided to hold the Jeffries-Johnson fight in Reno. In making the selection I wish to give my reasons for so doing. Goldfield made an offer which it was hard to turn down. They are the gamest lot of men I ever saw. This morning a committee of Goldfield business men offered to take me to a local bank and guarantee me $200,000.

"I decided on Reno, however, for several reasons. In the first place, I did not feel that fight 'fans' of the East and West should be compelled to take that extra twelve hour ride across the hot desert to Goldfield. Then again the people from San Francisco can get here on the morning of July 4 and leave the same night

in order to be back to business Tuesday morning. For this reason I think probably one or two thousand will come from San Francisco that would not go to Goldfield. The Reno people have done all they could. They will build a suitable arena and pay for the $1,000 license for me.

"(Signed)   TEX RICKARD."

Goldfield Will Help.

The Goldfield delegation accepted the announcement with expressions of regret, but with promises to "boost the game" to the extent of their ability.

Reno's fanatics are wildly elated over the defeat of Goldfield. The city's fight committee promises to make the necessary preparations for the care of all who come for the fight. Jeffries and his trainers are expected to-morrow. Flanagan has sent a telegram to Johnson, advising the negro to lose no time in reaching Reno.

SAN FRANCISCO WILL SEND 3,000 PERSONS

Fighters Prepare to Move Their Training Camps to the Nevada City.

[SPECIAL DESPATCH TO THE HERALD.]
SAN FRANCISCO, Cal., Tuesday.—From present indications fully three thousand persons will go from this city to Reno to witness the battle of July 4. The railroad officials were busy to-day arranging for many special trains. Those who hold certificates for seats to the big fight, and who bought these certificates under the belief that the contest would be held in San Francisco or some nearby place, can have their money refunded in case they do not care to go to Reno. Alfred L. Meyerstein, president of the Metropolis Trust and Savings Bank, which institution is the custodian of the fund, made a statement this morning in which he said that all certificate holders were assured of the return of their money in case they did not care to take in the fight in Nevada.

"Jack" Gleason made a statement in which he declared that all ticket holders could have their money refunded.

"Those who desire to see the fight in Nevada can have the same seats they are now holding," declared Gleason. "The others will get their money back on July 5. We request those who do not intend to retain their seats to notify us immediately so that the orders may be cancelled."

While Rickard is in Nevada "Jack" Gleason will remain here at least a week straightening out the business matters of the promoters. He will have charge of the cancellations and clear up all the odds and ends of business.

Preparations went forward at the Seal Rock House to-day for the journey of Champion Johnson and his party to Reno on Thursday. "Tom" Flanagan, who is to arrange for Johnson's gymnasium, has already gone ahead and will get things in shape so that the black champion will be able to renew his work as soon as he arrives in the Sagebrush State. Johnson

eliminated the usual road work from his programme to-day. Instead he boxed with Kaufman and also with his sparring partners, skipped the rope and worked with the medicine ball. When the afternoon's exercise was over the champion said he was well satisfied and that his condition could not be improved upon.

The party that will accompany Johnson to Reno will be made up of the following:—Sig Hart, Billy Delaney, George Cotton, Dave Mills, Professor Burns, Barney Furry, Frank Sutton and one or two others. It was stated to-day that it has not been definitely settled as yet whether Al Kaufman will accompany the party or not. It is thought, however, that the blacksmith will be one of Johnson's sparring mates. Al has been a good working horse for the black since joining the camp.

Johnson and his late manager, George Little, are on the verge of settling their differences. It is a matter of $10,000 between them. Little demands $40,000 before he will step down and out. Johnson is willing to pay over $30,000 and let it go at that. The friends of both men look for a settlement before Johnson starts for Nevada Thursday night.

"Sam" Berger went down to the Jeffries camp at Moana Springs on Monday and returned to San Francisco early to-day. He told Jeffries that "Joe" Egan would look after the matter of procuring training quarters in Nevada for Jeffries.

It is known that Jeffries wishes to train quietly by himself. He may not want to locate at Moana Springs, for the reason that it is within easy access of Reno and crowds would be at his training quarters all the time.

Jeffries' last day at Rowardennan was marked by a busy morning of training. He surprised everybody at the camp by going quietly to the gymnasium and putting in sixty-five minutes of hard work with hardly a rest. He was continually grinding from the time he started punching the bag until he finished his chair exercise, which he uses for reducing his waist line.

Jeffries declared that his wind was great. After he had finished his training he took one long breath and filled his lungs with air, while his chest bulged out several inches. "Ah! my wind is great. This satisfies me. The old bellows are working in their old form," he said to his trainers.

Jeffries does not look for an easy fight, nor do the majority of his trainers, but they figure that Johnson's busy left hand will never stop Jeffries. They look for the white fighter to plod along and every time he lands solidly it will slow up the colored fighter. The opinion seems to be that the contest will go at least fifteen rounds.

Appendix IV

The Jack London Reports

The name of Jack London—the brash, young author of tales of adventure—is inseperable from the story of the Johnson-Jeffries fight. It was he who, once the notion of a negro champion had become reality, gave birth to the crusade to return the title to its rightful, white owners; it was his acerbic prose which cajoled the retired Jeffries back into the ring and to disaster.

It was Jack London, then at the height of his popularity, who became the New York Herald's prize catch. Commissioned to fill its columns with homilies on 'the last great ring battle', he created a brand of sports journalism quite beyond imitation.

Fighter with the Quality of the "Abysmal Brute" Will Win the Great Battle ot July 4 at Reno, Says Jack London

Man Who Has Ability to Hit and Keep on Hitting Endlessly Bound to Conquer.

THINKS JEFFRIES HAS THE QUALITY TO LAST

Neither of the Big Men Has Ever Shown It, but White Man Believes He Has It in "Reserve Power."

WHERE JOHNSON EXCELS

Has the Faculty of Relaxing in Most Furious Struggle, While His Coming Opponent Is Always Tense.

BY JACK LONDON.

[SPECIAL DESPATCH TO THE HERALD.]

[Copyright, 1910, by the New York Herald Company. Registered in Canada in Accordance with the Copyright Act. All Rights Reserved.]

RENO, Nev., Sunday.—In considering the relative merits of the two big men who are to try conclusions a week from tomorrow it must be remembered that neither man has ever been really extended, and that neither man has ever been compelled to endure to the uttermost. Barring a lucky punch in the opening rounds endurance will play a large part in determining which man is the better. And by endurance is meant the capacity not only to assimilate punishment but the capacity to administer punishment and to keep on administering more and more punishment.

This question of endurance is worthy of analysis. Men are made differently. Some have but a slight life-grip in their bodies and muscles. Others are apparently impossible to kill. One man can walk seventy-five miles in a day and walk a second seventy-five the next day. Another man will collapse at the end of a twenty mile jaunt and be a lame and groaning wreck for a week to come. Yet both these men will be organically sound, of the same size and weight, and their chance of passing a life insurance examination would be equal.

Then what makes the difference? In the fibres of the one reside a primitive vigor and capacity for exertion that the other lacks. Their muscles may look alike, may be of the same size and tensity, yet the protoplasmic, energy-generating quality is different.

The Quality of Muscle.

Take a professional weight lifter. He may tip the scales at 160 pounds. He can elevate a 200-pound dumbbell with one hand. Another man, tipping the scales at the same mark, cannot elevate 100 pounds. He is as sound and healthy as the other man, yet he cannot do it. He may faithfully train and exercise for five years, or ten, and yet he will be unable to elevate 200 pounds with one hand. Nor has will anything to do with it. He may have ten times more will power than the other, but will power can't lift the 200 pounds for him. He lacks in the quality of his muscle, that is all.

This protoplasmic vigor may be our brute heritage, but whatever it is, it is a good thing to have whether one is a prize fighter or not. It was in describing the fight at Colma with Jimmy Britt that I pointed out the possession of this muscular quality by Battling Nelson. I called him an abysmal brute, and he never forgave me. Yet I meant it as a compliment.

Of two boxers equal to look upon in every way, equally well trained, with equal organs, equal gameness and equal will power, one will reach his limit in five or ten rounds, the other, fighting just as severely, will be able to last thirty or forty rounds, or even fifty. It was this peculiar quality that Battling Nelson possessed to such an extreme degree. Jimmy Britt did not possess it. He could outspar and outpunch Nelson, but he could not keep on sparring and punching as long as Nelson could. At the Colma fight he was not knocked out by Nelson. He was merely exhausted. He had reached his limit. He could not move any more. He lost the fight because he knocked himself out by his own exertions.

No "Line" on the Big Fellows.

Corbett lacked this abysmal brutishness to a considerable degree. Choynski had far more of it. So did Sharkey and Fitzsimmons. But when it comes to Jeffries and Johnson there is no line on them at all. They have never been called upon to demonstrate it. Neither knows that he possesses it. Neither has ever engaged in a long, hard, gruelling fight, round after round, striking and being struck, consuming energy at an enormous rate and still going on fighting furiously, on and on, endlessly.

Of the two men Jeffries has thought more about himself, studied himself more, and he has hinted that he believes he possesses it. He has called it reserve power—a sort of second wind that does not depend on the lungs, but that resides in the muscles themselves. But seeing and believing are different, and he has yet to show it to the world. Nevertheless I venture a shrewd guess that he has it. Also, he may be called upon to show it on July 4.

Nor does the world know that Johnson possesses this abysmal brutishness or lacks it. Johnson does not know himself. He has never had a chance to find out. And in this connection it is not a question of "yellow streak" or will power. No matter to what superlative degree Johnson possesses this protoplasmic vigor it will go for naught if he proves yellow. On the other hand, he has never shown any hints of the yellowness, and, it must be added, he has never been in a fight that forced a test of this particular quality.

Jeffries the More Tense.

There is one quality in which Johnson has the advantage over Jeffries and that is in relaxation. Jeffries, while cool and keen, is always more tense. The tensing of muscle consumes energy. Boxing calls for the use of all the muscles in the body, and five minutes' unnecessary tension of all these muscles out of thirty minutes of fighting means a serious consumption of energy.

"Quality of Muscle" Is the Thing That Counts, Says Novelist in Commenting on Outlook for Battle.

WILL THE BLACK FAIL?

Question Whether He Can Make Jeffries Put Up the "Fight of His Life."

This is one of Johnson's great assets. He has the art of relaxing perfectly. His fiercest rallies are always followed by intervals of repose. In a clinch, except when he is punishing, he invariably rests. It is because of this relaxing so continually that he is notorious with the sporting public as a loafing fighter. And he seems to relax in mind as well as in body. He seems to stop thinking and perceiving even, and in a clinch he goes into a sort of resting trance. His very flat footed way of fighting takes off from the tension of the legs. It is far less tiring to shuffle about flat footedly than to spring and poise with the muscles tensed from the hips down.

One thing is certain. A week from to-day Johnson will be compelled to put up the fight of his life. He has never in his career faced so formidable an antagonist. With Jeffries it remains to be seen whether Johnson can make him put up the fight of his life.

10 TO 6 IN SAN FRANCISCO.

SAN FRANCISCO, Cal., Sunday.—Betting on the Jeffries-Johnson fight was heavy to-day, with odds remaining at 10 to 6 in favor of Jeffries. A large amount of money poured into the poolrooms, but it was so evenly distributed that the odds were not affected. Local bettors still control the situation, but it is expected that an influx of Eastern money during the next few days may change the odds.

ACTRESS INSANE OVER FIGHT

CLEVELAND, Ohio, Sunday.—Insane over the Jeffries-Johnson fight, Kate Blancke, an actress, was committed to the State Asylum at Newburg to-day. Since her arrival in Cleveland last Thursday Miss Blancke has been sending telegrams continually to James Gleason and "Tex" Rickard, begging them to take her to the contest. Her actions finally became so peculiar that her relatives were appealed to, and after a medical examination she was adjudged insane and committed to the asylum.

"I'LL WIN; MAKE NO MISTAKE," SAYS NEGRO

"He Won't Ever Even Touch Me," Johnson Declares in Discussing His Tactics.

[SPECIAL DESPATCH TO THE HERALD.]

RENO, Nev., Sunday.—Theorists all over the country have been speculating at great length on the plan of battle which "Jack" Johnson is going to follow when he faces "Jeff." Every move has been planned in the minds of good dreamers, but the negro never really gave any definite idea of what his mode of strategy would be until late last night, in a talk with "Billy" McCarney, when the latter had remained at Rick's long after the crowd had gone, and Johnson called him upstairs to have a little private confab with him.

"Billy," said the negro, "give me your honest opinion of what you think of my chances."

"Well, it's this way," was the reply. "If you were going to fight the battle in Africa, where the crowd would be blacks, mostly, I believe you would stand a hundred per cent better chance than you do now. Here they will all be white men, every one rooting against you, and there will be bitter feeling toward you."

"You don't think any of 'em will shoot, do you, Billy?" asked "Jack" in a very serious manner.

"No, not exactly that; but you are apt to feel that you are fighting the whole crowd," said McCarney, who, it may be said, was trying to do anything but reassure Johnson.

This started the champion off on his proposed line of action.

"They all think Jeff is going to beat my defence down until he can get to me and then finish me," said "Jack." "Well, take it from me, he is not going to pound my arms until I can't hold them up any longer. I'm going to step around a bit and he won't ever even touch me.

"You all know he can miss, and I am going to make him miss in fine style. Then we'll see who is going to get tired first. I am going to beat him sure as I am a foot high. There is nothing surer in my mind. There has been a lot of talk about it not meaning much to me to lose, but a defeated nigger, believe me, is just about as much account as a dead nigger.

"I know that folks don't like me because I have gone around and had a good time, but if a white man had done the same no one would have noticed it. I'm not such a bad fellow. I take good care of my mother and she means everything to me. If it was for nothing else but for her sake I'd win that fight. And I'm going to win, and make no mistake."

If any one thinks Johnson is going to play his favorite blocking game he is likely to be mistaken on the Fourth. Johnson may not appear to be very speedy on his feet but he can shift his body with the agility of a panther. His muscles seem to respond instinctively to get him out of danger, and if he lives up to what he says about stepping around "Jeff" is going to have a lively time of it. With "Jeff" chasing the negro it will not take long to see if the big fellow has the stamina he once had.

Johnson is letting no grass grow under his feet in his training. Although it was 98 degrees in the shade to-day he did ten miles on the road in the morning, and then entertained a crowd for two hours playing his bass violin in combination with the regular piano pounder and fiddler at the resort.

In the afternoon a huge crowd journeyed out Verdi road to Rick's and the negro gave them a fine athletic entertainment. First he punched the bag for a quarter of an hour, then he shadow boxed and threw the medicine ball in the broiling sun for half an hour. After this he took on "Al" Kaufman for four rounds, and when he had pounded him up he fought forth Walter Monahan, a husky San Francisco youth, who is a new adjunct to his training staff. Monahan had a try out at Seal Rock and did so well that Johnson brought him to Reno with him. He was able to give Johnson a good session, and fills in nicely to save wear and tear on the others.

"JEFF" GOES FISHING AND SEES BALL GAME

His Camp Defeated on Diamond by Newspaper Men—and a Denver Umpire.

[SPECIAL DESPATCH TO THE HERALD.]

RENO, Nev., Sunday.—While "Jack" Johnson was burning up the roads this morning, "Jeff" was serenely fishing for black bass at Wheeler's Lake. He was in a happy frame of mind, for the fish bit in good style, and he had a catch of twenty-five to his credit when he came back to Moana Springs in the afternoon. It was no surprise that he did not do any work, as more than a thousand persons came out to the Springs to look things over.

There was a baseball game on between the newspaper men and the Jeffries camp and it furnished lots of amusement for the visitors. "Jeff" did not play because of the big crowd, but Corbett, Choynski, "Bob" Armstrong, "Sam" Berger, "Farmer" Burns, Roger Cornell and others of the retinue were in the fighter's line-up. A Denver scribe was the umpire, so it is needless to say the newspaper men had all the better of it.

There are some who are prone to criticise "Jeff" for his loafing tactics, but at this late date if he is not in good fettle there is little chance of his being so on the Fourth. Nervous tension is beginning to show not only on him but on Johnson as the big day comes closer, and perhaps it is the best thing that could happen for "Jeff" to indulge in diversions that will keep his mind off the fight.

It was said out at Moana to-day that "Jeff" probably would not work to-morrow either. Most of his training probably will be devoted to drying out.

APE AND TIGER IN US DEMAND FIGHT, SAYS JACK LONDON

Thrill of Combat a Passion of Race That Grew as Our Language Grew.

MUST ACCEPT IT AS REALITY OF NATURE

Sport of Prize Fighting a Fair One and Marks Development of Humanity.

EVENTUALLY WILL CEASE

Mr. London Says Personally He Wants to See Battle so Bad It Hurts.

BY JACK LONDON.

[SPECIAL DESPATCH TO THE HERALD.]

[Copyright, 1910, by the New York Herald Company. Registered in Canada in Accordance with the Copyright Act. All Rights Reserved.]

RENO, Nev., Tuesday.—Here is the problem. At half-past one in the afternoon of July 4 two men, a white and a black, are going to face each other in a square ring elevated in the centre of a large arena. They are not going to try to kill each other. They are to fight each other, true, but the fighting will be done with natural weapons and according to very rigid and restricted rules.

They are to strike each other with their hands and their hands only. No other blow will be permitted. They cannot wrestle with each other or throw each other down. The very area on which they are allowed to land their blows is limited. It is the upper portion of the body. From the waist down all striking is taboo. Nor may a blow be struck when a man is off his feet.

The fists, which are their only fighting weapons, will be encased in padded gloves that weigh one-third of a pound. A naked knuckle can cut and injure and it is a thing to be avoided.

A third man will be in the ring with them to see that all the rules are observed. He is the referee. His word is law. Whatever he says must be obeyed. If a man strikes a foul blow the referee will immediately disqualify him and award the victory to the other man. The referee will watch closely, circling about the two men, sometimes speaking to them in a low voice, sometimes touching one on the shoulder and sometimes the other.

For Fame, Honor, and $100,000.

And what are these two men, with the padded gloves, the rigid rules and the referee in the ring for? What is it they desire to achieve? Simply this:—By means of blows with their gloved hands to see which can put the other down on the ground and put him down so hard that he will stay down for ten consecutive seconds. And why do they want to do this? For honor and fame and a prize of $100,000.

It sounds silly on the face of it, doesn't it? But when it is considered that from fifteen to twenty thousand men, paying each from $10 to $50 for a seat, will be in the arena to watch the two men, that millions of dollars will be spent on this contest, that men will journey from the uttermost parts of the earth to witness it, that the ablest journalists and cartoonists of the country will be present, and that it has been and will be for a week to come the one overshadowing issue of the whole United States, all to see which of the two men can put the other down for ten consecutive seconds—why, it would seem to become a colossal silliness.

But is it such a silliness? Is it a silliness at all, when the pages of all the newspapers are daily filled with it, the only concession that a very large portion of the people of the country are interested in it? There is a reason for their interest, just as there is a reason for my interest—and why am I interested? In the next paragraph let me show you.

So Bad It Hurts.

But here, let me stand up and announce that I am so keenly interested, so overwhelmingly desirous of witnessing this contest, that there are moments when sudden fears assail me, such as that the fight will not come off, that it may be prevented by some great earthquake or terrific cataclysm of nature. Why, I want to see that fight so bad that it hurts.

This contest of men with padded gloves on their hands is a sport that belongs unequivocally to the English speaking race, and that has taken centuries for the race to develop. It is no superficial thing, a fad of a moment or a generation. No genius or philosopher devised it and persuaded the race to adopt it as their racial sport of sports. It is as deep as our consciousness and is woven into the fibres of our being.

THE GREATEST FIGHT IN HISTORY
"*Johnson a Master Mouth Fighter,*"
Says Jack London

A wonderful fighter indeed is Johnson, utterly unlike any other fighter—a type by himself. And against this man will stand Jeffries, an even more remarkable man—a grizzly giant, a huge and rugged man of a type we are prone to believe was more common in other days when the world was young. And, despite this hugeness and ruggedness, he is so well proportioned from heel to head that the combination is startling. His is a perfection of symmetry that is the fruit of highest organic development. And if science tells aright we are justified in believing that no such symmetry obtained among those giants of the younger world. The human in those days was in the process of making. It was muscular efficiency minus the beauty of form and line. This big modern Jim Jeffries has both.

An opposite contention is that Jeffries will be speedily undone because of the mental effect produced by the negro's cleverness. It is urged that Jeffries, after vainly trying to land a few of his rips, and after being rapped soundly in return, may lose his temper and rush wildly. This would certainly be peaches and cream for Johnson. The only thing against it is that Jeffries has never shown real temper in the ring. In his own way he has always been a coolheaded fighter.

One has only to remember how, in his battles with Corbett and Fitzsimmons, those men put it all over him round after round. Yet he kept cool and fought on and on with but one thing in his mind, namely, the putting out of the man opposite him who temporarily was making a dub of him. The results show just how masterfully he kept his temper and remained cool.

Johnson a Mouth Fighter.

Another thing is that Johnson is a past master at mouth fighting when in the ring. In his battle with "Tommy" Burns Johnson engaged in mouth fighting with Tommy, with Tommy's seconds and with the whole Australian audience, and the honors of every exchange belonged to him. It must be added as well that not one vile word or harsh epithet fell from his lips. Everything he uttered was genuine wit, keenly cutting and laughter provoking. Because of this ability of Johnson it is argued that he may say things that will cause Jeff to lose his head and deliver the peaches and cream.

In this connection all that has to be pointed out is that Jeff is a silent fighter. He has never indulged in verbal tilts in the ring, and, no matter how hard Johnson wanted to he would find it impossible to engage in witty repartee with a man who won't open his head.

Nevertheless, there will be seconds in Jeff's corner and ringside onlookers who will venture remarks and who will have it put over them by the negro wit. Unless Johnson is quickly in a bad way at the hands of Jeff there will be more than one good sally and general laugh at the ringside.

So far as the boxing game is concerned the contest next Monday is well named "the fight of the century." These two men, in a class by themselves so far as other fighters go, yet so radically different from each other as to have practically no salient characteristics in common, will fight a battle in a setting like unto nothing the ring has ever displayed.

For the first time two such mighty heavyweight champions battle, and each goes up against the most dangerous and formidable man he has ever tackled. And they will fight in the presence of four other and earlier heavyweight champions. Again are all the records broken, for next Monday in the ring and in the arena will be six men who have had the honor of being world champion heavyweights. Think of it—Sullivan, Corbett, Fitzsimmons, Burns, Jeffries and Johnson!

Most Amazing Gathering.

From the standpoint of the sporting world there has never been so amazing a gathering. Almost every champion and one time champion of every class will be at the ringside. There will be the famous trainers and conditioners of athletes, men like Muldoon and Murphy; there will be the athletes themselves, victors and leaders in all the games. And as for the noted and notorious sport followers, they will all be here. Every figure of sportdom, from "Billy" Jordan, the well beloved veteran announcer, down to the latest and youngest fight promoter—they will all be on the ground.

And they will watch these strangely diverse heavy weights battle, beside whom all other heavies look like middle weights. Johnson, the fighting boxer, will go up against Jeffries, the boxing fighter. Both are cool, both are experienced, both are terrible. It will not be a short fight. It will be a great sight, and so I say again to all you men who love the game and have the price and are within striking distance of Reno, come!

It is the fight of fights, the crowning fight of the whole ring and perhaps the last great fight that will ever be held. Also, to you lovers of the game who desire to see in flesh and blood the celebrities of the game, I say come!

It would take years of travelling and fight following to see all the figures of sportdom that can be seen in Reno in one day and no admission charged. I, for one, hope for a toothless old age when nothing is left but to mumble reminiscences, and in that time one of my greatest joys will be to maunder over all the wonderful details of the great fight at Reno. "Yes, sir; in 1910, at Reno. I was there and sat by the ringside."

Negro, Never in Doubt, Fear or Trouble, Played All the Time, Says Jack London

Jeffries Lost His Old Time Stamina Somewhere Outside the Ring and Did Not Put Up as Strong a Battle as Did "Tommy" Burns.

"GOLDEN SMILE" SHINES ON ADVERSARY, TRAINERS AND 20,000 SPECTATORS

"Did You See That, Jim?" He Asks of Corbett After Landing an Especially Vicious Punch and Clinching with His Adversary—Yellow Streak Question Unsettled.

JEFFRIES, EYE CLOSED, LOSES HIS DEFENCE

First Rounds Were Largely Johnson, Following Ones More Johnson and Close All Johnson—Battered and Staggering, Californian Goes Down Three Times in Last.

JACK LONDON

FACTS ABOUT BIG FIGHT

John A. Johnson defeated James J. Jeffries in their battle for the world's heavyweight championship, at Reno, Nev., yesterday.

The end came in the fifteenth round, when Johnson, after mercilessly battering his opponent, knocked him to the floor three times. The last time at the count of eight Jeffries' seconds rushed over the ring and the referee awarded the fight to Johnson.

It is estimated that 17,000 persons saw the battle, while as many more were unable to obtain entrance to the arena.

The $121,000 purse, which included a $10,000 bonus to each fighter, was divided, sixty per cent to the winner and forty per cent to the loser.

BY JACK LONDON.

[SPECIAL DESPATCH TO THE HERALD.]

[*Copyright, 1910, by the New York Herald Company. Registered in Canada in Accordance with the Copyright Act. All Rights Reserved.*]

RENO, Nev., Monday.—Once again has Johnson sent down to defeat the chosen representative of the white race, and this time the greatest of them. And as of old, it was play for Johnson. From the opening round to the closing round he never ceased from his witty sallies, his exchanges of repartee with his opponent's seconds and with the audience. And, for that matter, Johnson had a funny thing or two to say to Jeffries in every round.

The "golden smile" was as much in evidence as ever and neither did it freeze on his face nor did it vanish. It came and went throughout the fight, spontaneously, naturally.

It was not a great battle after all, save in its setting and its significance. Little "Tommy" Burns, down in far off Australia, put up a faster, quicker, livelier battle than did Jeffries. The fight to-day, and again I repeat, was great only in its significance. In itself it was not great. The issue, after the fiddling of the opening rounds, was never in doubt. In the fiddling of those first rounds the honors lay with Johnson, and for the rounds after the seventh or eighth it was more Johnson, while for the closing rounds it was all Johnson.

Could Afford to Play.

Johnson played, as usual. With his opponent not strong in the attack Johnson, blocking and defending in masterly fashion, could afford to play. And he played and fought a white man, in the white man's country, before a white man's audience. And the audience was a Jeffries audience.

When Jeffries sent in that awful rip of his the audience would madly applaud, believing it had gone home to Johnson's stomach, and Johnson, deftly interposing his elbow, would smile in irony at the audience, play acting, making believe he thought the applause was for him—and never believing it at all.

The greatest battle of the century was a monologue delivered to twenty thousand spectators by a smiling negro, who was never in doubt and who was never serious for more than a moment at a time.

As a fighter Johnson did not show himself a wonder. He did not have to. Never once was he extended. There was no need. Jeffries could not make him extend. Jeffries never had him in trouble once. No blow Jeffries ever landed hurt his dusky opponent. Johnson came out of the fight practically undamaged. The blood on his lip was from a recent cut received in the course of training and which Jeffries managed to reopen.

Half a Dozen Dead as Crowds Attack Negroes; Reign of Terror Here

Africans Dragged from New York Street Cars and Attacked in Streets in Fury of Whites Over Jeffries' Defeat—Physician Stops Mob with Pistol.

POLICE RESERVES MARSHALLED IN PARK TO BE READY FOR IMMEDIATE SERVICE

Negroes Also Attacked and Lynchings Threatened in Philadelphia, Washington, Pittsburg, Chattanooga, Atlanta, St. Louis and Many Other Points.

LARGE NUMBER OF VICTIMS TAKEN TO HOSPITALS

Man Attacked in Lincoln Square Has Fractured Skull and Probably Will Die—Shooting of Pistols in Celebration Starts Trouble in Some Localities.

Failed to Come Back.

Jeffries failed to lead and land. The quickness he brought into the fight quickly evaporated, and while Jeffries was dead game to the end, he was not so badly punished. What he failed to bring into the ring with him was his stamina, which he lost somewhere in the last seven years. Jeffries failed to came back. That is the whole story. His old time vim and endurance were not there. Something has happened to him. He lost in retirement outside of the ring ~~~~~~ that the ring itself never robbed him of. As I have said, Jeffries was not badly damaged. Every day boys take worse lacings in boxing bouts than Jeff took to-day.

Jeffries to-day disposed of one question. He could not come back. Johnson, in turn, answered another question; he has not the yellow streak. But he only answered that question for to-day. The ferocity of the hairy chested caveman and grizzly giant combined did not intimidate the cool headed negro. Many thousands in the audience expected this intimidation, and were correspondingly disappointed. Johnson was not scared, let it be said here, and beyond the shadow of any doubt; not for an instant was Johnson scared. Not for a second did he show the flicker of a fear that the Goliath against him might eat him up.

Yellow Streak Unsettled.

But the question of the yellow streak is not answered for all time. Just as Johnson has never been extended, so has

he never shown the yellow streak. Just as a man may rise up, heaven alone knows where, who will extend Johnson, just so may that man bring out the yellow streak. and then again he may not. So far the burden of proof all rests on the conclusion that Johnson has no yellow streak.

And now to the battle and how it began! All praise to "Tex" Rickard, the gamest of sports, who pulled off the fight after countless difficulties and who, cool, calm and quick with nervous aliveness, handled the vast crowd splendidly in his arena and wound up by refereeing the fight.

Twenty thousand filled the great arena and waited patiently under the cloud flecked wide Nevada sky. Of the many women present some elected to sit in the screened boxes far back from the ring, for all the world like olden Spanish ladies at the theatre. But more, many more women sat close to the ringside beside their husbands or brothers. They were the wiser far.

Merely to enumerate the celebrities at the ringside would be to write a sporting directory of America—at least a directory of the four hundred of sportdom and of many more hundreds of near four hundreds. At four minutes to two "Billy" Jordan cleared the ring amid cheers and stood alone, the focal point of twenty thousand pairs of eyes, until the great Muldoon climbed through the ropes, to call tumultuous applause and ringing cheers from the twenty thousand throats for the

State of Nevada, the people of Nevada and the Governor of Nevada.

Ovations for All.

Beginning with Tex Rickard, ovation after ovation was given to all the great ones, not forgetting Fitzsimmons, whom "Billy" Jordan introduced as "the greatest warrior of them all." And so they came, great one after great one, ceaselessly, endlessly, until they were swept away before the greatest of them all, the two men who were about to do battle.

It was half-past two when Johnson entered. He came first, airy, happy and smiling, greeting friends and acquaintances here and there and everywhere in the audience, cool as ice, waving his hand in salute, smiling, smiling, over smiling, with eyes as well as with lips, never missing a name or a face, placid, plastic, nerveless, with never a signal flown of hesitancy or timidity. Yet was he keyed up, keenly observant of all that was going on, even hearing much of the confused babble of the tongues about him—hearing, aye, and understanding, too.

There is nothing heavy or primitive about this man Johnson. He is alive and quivering, every nerve and fibre in his body and brain, withal that it is hidden so artfully or naturally under that poise of facetious calm of his. He is a marvel of sensitiveness, sensibility and perceptibility. He has a perfect mechanism of mind and body. His mind works like chain lightning and his body obeys with equal swiftness.

Welcome for Jeffries.

But the great madness of applause went up when Jeffries entered the ring two minutes later. A quick, superficial comparison between him and the negro would have led to a feeling of pity for the latter. For "Jeff" was ____ but has been said of him. When he stripped and his mighty body could ____ seen covered with mats of ____ the primordial adjectives ever applied to him received their vindication. Nor did his face belie them. No facile emotion played on that face, no whims of the moment, no flutterings of a light hearted temperament.

Dark and sombre and ominous was that face, solid and stolid and expressionless, with eyes that smouldered and looked savage. The man of iron, grim with determination, sat down in his corner. And the care free negro smiled and smiled. And that is the story of the fight. The man of iron, the grizzly giant, was grim and serious. The man of summer temperament smiled and smiled. That is the story of the whole fight. It is the story of the fight by rounds.

At the opening of the first round they did not shake hands. Knowing the two men for what they are, it can be safely postulated that this neglect was due to Jeffries or to the prompting of Jeffries' corner. But it is not good that two boxers should not shake hands before a bout. I would suggest to these protagonists of a perishing game, if they wish to preserve the game, that they make most of these little amenities that by custom grace their sport and give it the veneer of civilization.

Go to Work Easily.

Both men went to work in that first round very easily, Johnson smiling, of course, and Jeffries grim and determined. Johnson landed the first blow, a light one, and Jeffries, in the clinches, gave a faint indication of his forthcoming tactics by roughing it, by crowding the negro around and by slightly bearing his weight upon him. It was a very easy round, with nothing of moment. Each was merely feeling the other out, and both were exceedingly careful. At the conclusion of the round Johnson tapped Jeffries playfully on the shoulder, smiled good naturedly, and went to his corner. Jeffries, in the first, showed flashes of catlike quickness.

Round Two.—Jeffries advanced with a momentary assumption of his famous crouch, to meet the broadly smiling Johnson. Jeffries is really human and good natured. He proved it right here. So friendly was that smile of Johnson's, so irresistibly catching, that Jeffries, despite himself, smiled back. But Jeffries' smiles were doomed to be very few in this fight.

And right here began a repetition of what took place down in Australia when Burns fought Johnson. Each time Burns said something harsh to Johnson in the hope of making him lose his temper, Johnson responded by giving the white man a lacing. And so to-day. Of course, Jeffries did not talk to Johnson to amount to anything, but Corbett, in the corner, did it for Jeffries. And each time Corbett cried something in particular Johnson promptly administered a lacing to Jeffries.

It began in the second round. Corbett, in line with his plan of irritating the negro, called out loudly:—

"He wants to fight a little, Jim."

"You bet I do," Johnson retorted, and with that he landed Jeffries a stinger with his right uppercut.

Both men were tensely careful, Jeffries trying to crowd and put his weight on in the clinches, Johnson striving more than the other to break out of the clinches. And at the end of the round, in his corner, Johnson was laughing gleefully. Certainly Jeffries showed no signs of boring in, as had been promised by his enthusiastic supporters.

It was the same story in the third round, at the conclusion of which the irrepressible negro was guilty of waving his hands to friends in the audience.

More Action in Fourth.

In the fourth round Jeffries showed up better, rushing and crowding and striking with more vim than hitherto shown. This seemed to have been caused by a sally of Johnson's, and Jeffries went at him in an angry sort of way. Promptly Jeffries rushed, and even ere they came together Johnson cried out:—"Don't rush me 'Jim.' You hear what I'm telling you?"

No sign there of being intimidated by Jeffries' first dynamic display of ferocity. All he managed to do was to reopen the training cut in Johnson's lip and to make Johnson playful. It was most anybody's round, and it was certainly more Jeffries' than any preceding one.

Round five brought Jeffries advancing with his crouch. The blood from Johnson's lip had turned his smile to a gory one, but still he smiled, and to balance things off he opened Jeffries' lip until

it bled more profusely than his own. From then until the end of the fight Jeffries' face was never free from blood, a steady stream later flowing from his right nostril, added to by an opened cut on his left cheek. Corbett's running fire of irritation served but to make Johnson smile the merrier and to wink at him across Jeffries' shoulder in the clinches.

So far no problems have been solved, no questions answered. The yellow streak had not appeared. Neither had Jeffries bored in, ripped awfully, nor put it over Johnson in the clinches. Yet one thing had been shown, Jeffries was not so fast as he had been. There was a shade of diminution in his speed.

Blows in the Face.

Johnson signalized the opening of the sixth round by landing stinging blows to the face in one, two, three order. Johnson's quickness was startling. In response to an irritating remark from Corbett Johnson replied suavely, "Too much on hand right now," and at the same instant he tore into Jeffries.

It was Johnson's first real, aggressive rush. It lasted but a second or two, but it was fierce and dandy, and at its conclusion it was manifest that Jeffries' right eye was closing fast. The round ended with Johnson fighting and smiling, strong and with Jeffries' nose, lip and cheek bleeding and his eye closed. Johnson's round by a smile all the way through.

The seventh round was a mild one, opening with Jeffries grim and silent and with Johnson leading and forcing. Both were careful and nothing happened, save that once they exchanged blows right niftily. So far Jeffries' roughing and crowding and bearing on of weight had amounted to nothing, also he was doing less and less of it.

Jeffries Slows Down.

"It only takes one or two, Jim," Corbett encouraged his principal in the eighth round. Promptly Johnson landed two stingers. After a pause he landed another. "See that?" he chirruped sweetly to Corbett in the corner.

Jeffries showed signs perceptibly of slowing down in this round, rushing and crowding less and less. Johnson was working harder and his speed was as flashlike as ever. Jeffries' slowing down was not due to the punishment he had received, but to poorness of condition. He was flying the first signals of fatigue. He was advertising, faintly, it is true, that he had not come back.

The ninth round was introduced by a suggestion from Corbett, heroically carrying out the policy that was bringing his principal to destruction.

"Make that big stiff fight," was Corbett's suggestion.

"That's right; that's what they all say," was Johnson's answer, delivered with the Chesterfieldian grace across his adversary's shoulder.

In the previous rounds Johnson had not wreaked much damage with the forecast punch—the right uppercut. In this round he demonstrated indisputably that he could drive the left hand in a way that was surprising. Be it remembered that it had long been denied that he had any sort of a punch in that left of his. Incidentally in this round it lead all the others,

in that seemingly he landed a blow near to Jeffries' heart that must have been discouraging.

The tenth round showed Johnson, with his deft, unexpected left, as quick as ever, and Jeffries going slower and slower.

The conclusion of the first ten rounds may be summed up as follow:—

The fight was all in favor of Johnson, who had shown no yellow, who had shown condition, who had shown undiminished speed, who had not used his right uppercut much, who had developed a savage left, who held his own in the clinches, who had got the best of the infighting and the outfighting, who was unhurt and who was smiling all the way. Jeffries was in bad shape; he was tired, slower than ever, his few rushes had been futile, and the sports who had placed their money against him were jubilant.

There were men who proclaimed they saw the end. I refused to see this end, for I had picked Jeffries to win and I was hoping hugely—for what I did not know, but for something to happen, for anything that would turn the tide of battle. And yet I could not hide from myself the truth that Jeffries had slowed down.

The eleventh round looked better for Jeffries. Stung by a remark of Corbett's Johnson rushed and provoked one grand rally from Jeffries. It was faster fighting and more continuous than any time in the preceding ten rounds, culminating in a fierce rally in which Jeffries landed hard.

Round twelve found Johnson if anything quicker and more aggressive than ever.

"Thought you were going to have me wild?" Johnson queried sweetly of Corbett. As usual every remark of Corbett's brought more punishment to Jeffries. And by the end of this round the second of the two great questions was definitely answered. Jeffries had not come back.

End Begins in Thirteenth.

The thirteenth round was the beginning of the end. Beginning slowly enough, but stung by Corbett, Johnson put it all over him in the mouth fighting and all over Jeffries in the out fighting and in fighting. From defence to attack and back again and back and forth Johnson flashed like the amazing fighting mechanism he is. Jeffries was silent and sick, while as the round progressed Corbett was noticeably silent.

A few entertained the fond hope that "Jeff" would recuperate. But it was futile. There was no come back to him. He was a fading, failing, heartsick, heartbroken man.

"Talk to him, Corbett," Jeffries' friends appealed in the fourteenth round. But Corbett could not talk. He had long since seen the end.

And yet through this round Johnson went in for one of his characteristic loafing spells. He took it easy and played with the big gladiator, cool as a cucumber, smiling broadly as ever and yet as careful as ever.

"Right on the hip," he grinned out once as Jeffries, in a desperate, dying flurry, managed to land a wild punch in that vicinity. Corbett, likewise desperate, ventured a last sally.

"Why don't you do something?" he cried to the loafing, laughing Johnson.

"Too clever, too clever, like you," was the response.

Round fifteen, and the end. It was pitiful. There happened to Jeffries the bitterness that he had so often made others taste, but which for the first time, perforce, he was made to taste himself. He who had never been knocked down was knocked down repeatedly. He who had never been knocked out was knocked out. Never mind the technical decision. Jeffries was knocked out and through the ropes by the punch he never believed Johnson possessed—by the left and not by the right. As he lay across the lower rope while the seconds were told off, a cry that had in it tears and abject broken pride went up from many of the spectators.

"Don't let the negro knock him out! Don't let the negro knock him out!" was the oft repeated cry.

There is little more to be said. Jeffries did not come back. Johnson did not show the yellow streak. And it was Johnson's fight all the way through. Jeffries was not the old Jeffries at all. Even so, it is to be doubted if the old Jeffries could have put away this amazing negro from Texas, this black man with the unfailing smile, this king of fighters and monologists.

Corbett and Berger and the others were right. They wanted Jeffries to do more boxing and fighting in his training. Nevertheless, lacking the come back, as he so potently did, this preliminary boxing and fighting would have profited him nothing. On the other hand, it would have saved his camp much of the money with which it backed him.

It was a slow fight. Faster, better fights may be seen every day of the year in any of the small clubs in the land. It is true these men were heavyweights, yet for heavyweights it was a slow fight. It must be granted that plucky Tommy Burns put up a faster fight with Johnson a year and a half ago. Yet the American fight follower had to see this fight of to-day in order to appreciate just what Burns did against this colored wonder.

Johnson is a wonder. No one understands him, this man who smiles. Well, the story of the fight is the story of a smile. If ever man won by nothing more fatiguing than a smile Johnson won to-day.

And where now is the champion who will make Johnson extend himself? Who will glaze those bright eyes, remove that smile and silence that golden repartee?

Jeffries Was Game, Declares Victor

Jack Johnson said:—

I won from Mr. Jeffries because I outclassed him in every department of the fighting game.

Jeffries' blows had no steam behind them. I do not recall a single punch in the body that caused me any discomfort. I am in shape to battle again to-morrow if it were necessary.

One thing I must give Jeffries credit for is the game battle he made. No man can say he did not do his best.

For the next few weeks I shall play in vaudeville. Then I shall go to my home in Chicago to rest. I do not think I shall fight for several months, because I do not know a man who could give me a good battle. No attention will be paid to "Sam" Langford's challenges by me. I do not consider he could give me a fight that would draw.

"Didn't Have the Snap," Says Jeffries

RENO, Nev.; Monday.—James J. Jeffries said to-night:—

"I lost my fight this afternoon because I did not have the snap of youth I used to have. I believed in my own heart that all the old time dash was there, but when I started to execute, the speed and youthful stamina were lacking. The things I used to do were impossible. For instance, I used to shoot in a right hand body punch, a sort of short range blow that never used to fail me. But when I tried it to-day the snap was not there and it was only a love tap.

"It would not have made any difference if I had sparred a dozen times oftener than I did. I simply was not there, and that's all there is to it. Six years ago the result would have been different, but now—well, I guess the public will let me alone after this."

Appendix V

Race Riots In America

The result at Reno had immediate and violent repercussions.

After a century of inter-racial tension, the whites had chosen to make a deciding issue of the Johnson-Jeffries match, and the black man had won. Decisively.

Intoxicated by the implications of his great victory, the American negro took to the streets. . . .

The Daily Express for July 6, 1910, provides a graphic account of this important — though now largely ignored — moment in social history.

Daily Express

LONDON, WEDNESDAY, JULY 6, 1910.

RACE RIOTS IN AMERICA.

FRENZIED NEGROES EXASPERATE THE WHITES.

19 DEATHS.

MANY HURT AND 5,000 ARRESTED.

BLACK MOBS SWEEP THROUGH TOWNS.

"Express" Correspondent.

NEW YORK, Tuesday, July 5.

Racial riots swept the United States last night from the Atlantic to the Pacific after Jeffries' crushing defeat by Johnson at Reno, Nevada. The following are the results up to the present :—

Nineteen persons were killed.

251 were seriously injured.

Many hundreds were slightly injured.

Five thousand cases of disorderly conduct were dealt with by the police courts in various cities this morning in consequence of the rioting.

The gaols in numerous cities were crowded with prisoners, in consequence of the bitter feeling against the negroes manifested when it became known that a black man had hammered a white man almost into insensibility and won the heavy-weight boxing championship of the world.

Most of the casualties were negroes who were hunted down by white mobs, mostly because of boasts by the blacks that they had finally demonstrated their superiority over the whites.

FATAL BOASTS.

Two negroes were shot dead at La Providence, Louisiana, after walking down the principal street of the town and announcing that a negro could thrash a white man if he liked.

A negro was fatally stabbed at Keystone, West Virginia, for boasting in a drinking resort that Jeffries had met his deserts and that his punishment by Johnson was a foretaste of the punishment which the negroes intended meting out to white men if the latter tried to assert their superiority in the future.

A nine-year-old white child was shot by negroes who were riding in a motor-car at Washington, the Federal capital. A white man cut a negro's throat in a tramcar at Houston, Texas. A negro was shot dead in New York City.

Other negroes were killed in Cincinnati, Omaha, Little Rock, and other cities.

Serious rioting occurred at Washington, Kansas City, Jacksonville, Chattanooga, Norfolk, Los Angeles, Schenectady, and Pueblo, cities which embrace the territory between California on the west, Florida on the south, and New York on the east.

The chief rioting in New York City took place in the negro quarter in the Sixth-avenue district. Many drunken blacks paraded the thoroughfares, insulting white men, who promptly retaliated. Many fights resulted, and the police reserves were repeatedly called out to preserve order.

LYNCHING BRIGADES.

Finally the reserves remained on permanent duty along Sixth-avenue and the adjacent streets. Mobs of white men caught two negroes and tried to lynch them by hanging them to lamp-posts, but the police rescued the victims after a desperate fight.

One negro had a specially narrow escape. The rope was already around his neck, and thrown over the bar of the lamp post, when the police charged and pulled him away from the mob. The negro was unconscious from fright.

Serious racial riots also occurred in Washington. Mobs of negroes, estimated at seven thousand strong, rushed through the streets. Many of them were frenzied with whisky and gin. They attacked white men and women along Pennsylvania-avenue between the White House, the official residence of the President, and the Capitol.

There was almost continuous rioting in the heart of the city, around the various Federal buildings, and the ambulances were busy all night removing the injured to the hospital. Police vans filled with reserves raced from street to street trying to crush the rioting, which at one time assumed such serious proportions that it was feared the use of troops would be necessary to clear the thoroughfares and restore order.

WOMEN ATTACKED.

Three negro women attacked two white women who were sitting on the porch of their residence watching a display of fireworks. A mob chased the negresses, shouting "Lynch them!" After the police arrived the negresses fought all the way to the police station.

Three hundred marines from the navy yard at Norfolk paraded the streets shouting that they intended to lynch the negroes for their insulting behaviour. Many negroes who were caught were unmercifully beaten, and the police were powerless to intervene.

The marines spread a veritable reign of terror until the naval authorities at the Norfolk depot sent a detachment of bluejackets after them, and they were finally subdued.

A negro precipitated a similar riot at Chattanooga, Tennessee, where several thousand volunteers were in camp at the annual State manœuvres. The negro strutted into camp and thrust a copy of a newspaper containing an account of Johnson's victory in the faces of the soldiers and shouted insults.

A soldier knocked him down, and another soldier fired at him, but missed. The negro ran away, and the soldiers formed with their rifles for an attack on the negro quarter of the town, but the military authorities managed to hold them in check.

At Chicago, which is Johnson's home, the negroes were boisterous but goodnatured, and did not attack the whites, although they created disturbances in their own quarters, causing the police to arrest more than a hundred of them.

At Los Angeles, Jeffries' residence, the police reserves were kept busy answering riot calls in various parts of the town.

Throughout the night the negroes who had backed Johnson heavily spent their winnings in drinking, and then paraded the streets shouting challenges and throwing stones at the white men, who retaliated, compelling the police to use their clubs to restore order.

One result of the rioting will be to prevent the exhibition of moving pictures of the fight in a number of towns, the authorities fearing that the display will incite further bloodshed. Washington has taken the lead in this matter. Major Sylvester, the chief of police, warned all the managers of moving-picture halls that they would be prosecuted if they attempted to exhibit films of the fight.

———

A Reuter special telegram states that three negroes met their death at Ulvadis, Georgia, in a battle between whites and blacks at a construction camp. The negro workmen, who had been insolent to the whites for several days, yesterday began drinking, and became so boisterous that a white posse was organised to clean out the camp.

As the posse approached it was fired on from the camp. The fire was returned, and when the negroes fled they left behind three dead and five badly wounded. The negroes are still being hunted to-day.

At another place two factions among the negroes themselves engaged in a fight about Johnson's merits, with the result that one was killed and three were injured.

———

JEFFRIES' DEJECTION.

HIS OWN EXPLANATION OF HIS DEFEAT.

Special Service Telegram.

RENO (Nevada), Tuesday, July 5.

Jack Johnson, the victor in yesterday's historic battle, was the first of the combatants to leave the little town to which they have so suddenly given fame. Soon after midnight the black champion left for Chicago to receive the congratulations of his mother, family, and friends.

Jeffries, the vanquished, is still in Reno. He has refused to receive any visitors. The white ex-champion, who twenty-four hours ago was confident and fit, was seen this morning walking about his camp a beaten, bruised, and brooding figure, with hanging head and downcast eye. He quits the scene of his first and bitter defeat to-night, and returns to his retirement on his farm in California.

Jeffries admits that he is only the shell of his former self, while Johnson declares that there never was a moment when he was not confident of victory whenever he desired to grasp it.

"I have not got the snap of youth that I once had," declared Jeffries. "I believed I had, but when I tried, speed and youthful stamina were lacking, and things that I used to do I found impossible. I guess it was my own fault; I was living peacefully on my alfalfa farm until people calld me 'The White Man's Hope.' I guess my pride got the better of my good judgment."

Johnson said: "I won because I outclassed Jeffries in every department of the fighting game. With the exception of reopening an old wound on my lip, I am unmarked, and in shape for another battle to-morrow. For one thing I must give Jeffries credit—the game battle he fought; none can say that he did not do his best."

Jeffries has received the £8,080, his share of the purse, and the bonus of £2,000, which, with the £13,333 for which he sold his interest in the moving picture records of the fight, makes the total amount of his "consolation" money £23,413.

Johnson got only £10,000 for his interest in the cinematograph films, and his total gains amount to £24,120.—Reuter.

LEICESTER-SQUARE RIOT.

John Smith was fined £1 at Bow-street yesterday for being intoxicated and disorderly and striking Hammetta Bushra, a coloured music-hall performer, in Leicester-square.

Bushra stated that as he was leaving the Alhambra with another coloured man after the result of the fight between Jeffries and Johnson had been announced they were attacked by about twenty men. Sticks were thrown, and both he and the other man were struck.

An article on the colour problem appears on Page 4.

Appendix VI

Jack Johnson Exposed – A Boxing Crook

Throughout the peak period of his turbulent career, Jack Johnson was the object of an unrelenting smear-campaign. From the moment he won the title until the day, seven years later, he lost it, all his important fights were denounced as fakes; even Jeffries claimed to have been drugged at Reno.

Perhaps the most solidly-founded – though by no means irrefutable – claim concerned the 1914 contest in Paris against Frank Moran, for which neither participant was ever paid a sou. The article from John Bull which follows is representative of the media's attitude towards the first black champion.

JACK JOHNSON EXPOSED—A BOXING CROOK.

THE BRAGGART NEGRO PROVED TO BE A BOXING SWINDLER—DAMNING DOCUMENTARY EVIDENCE—WILL HE "QUIT"?

When, a few years ago, we interested ourselves in the sport of wrestling, and threw down the gauntlet to the army of showmen who were then posing as world's champions by challenging any of them to meet a clean and capable British wrestler, one of our principal objects was to cleanse the game of the scandalous frauds by which it was becoming discredited in the public mind. In the same way, in bringing forward a young British boxer, with the object of recovering our lost prestige in the fistic art, we have been influenced also by a desire to assist in the movement recently set on foot for the purification of the ring. We have never, however, been actuated by anything in the nature of racial prejudice. Whilst regretting that the principal boxing championships were automatically going to negroes and Americans, we realised that so long as this state of affairs was due to superior skill there was nothing to be done but to find new champions of our own ; and we resolutely set our faces, for instance, against discrediting a man like Jack Johnson simply on account of either his colour or his alleged " moral " delinquencies—and we protested in our columns against any campaign hostile to him based upon such foundations. If, therefore, we now assume towards this negro fighter an attitude of uncompromising animosity, it is only because, having thrown ourselves heartily into the subject of boxing, we have obtained irrefutable evidence that—whatever may have been the man's professional merits in days gone by—he is now, and has been for a considerable time past, a boxing impostor, and a crook. Indeed, there can be but one result of the revelations we are about to make. The boxing authorities of every nation must disqualify Johnson from ever entering a ring again, and must deprive him of every pugilistic title he now possesses. In a sentence, he must be eliminated from the boxing world.

For some time past Johnson has been under suspicion amongst the boxing fraternity. Always bragging of his prowess, he has evinced a marked disinclination to defend his title, and it is due entirely to the persistence of one of the most respectable and enterprising managers, Mr. Dan McKetrick, that he was ultimately dragged into the ring in connection with the recent contest in Paris with Moran. And our present exposure will be based upon what transpired in regard to that event. We shall show that—whilst the man was openly bragging of having had a huge sum of money put up for the contest, and of his willingness to take on any white challenger—he was all the time financing the whole event himself, and endeavouring to fix up a fraudulent compact under which his opponent was to agree to " go down " within the first eight rounds ; and that it was only when he had secured this fraudulent bargain and that, in his own words, " everything was O.K.," and that there was to be no "stalling" of him, that he finally put on the gloves. Let it, therefore, at once be stated that, but for the refusal of Moran's manager to " honour " the immoral contract, Moran would not have lasted more than the eight rounds, and the grinning negro would thereupon again have boasted of his annihilation of the white man. It is true that in the end the match was awarded to him on points—the fact undoubtedly being that Moran is not the class of boxer who would be seriously chosen to knock out the black, although, as was proved by the event, quite capable of keeping him at bay.

We need scarcely say that before taking upon ourselves the responsibility of publishing such grave allegations as those now made, we took every step to check the genuineness of the evidence—with the result that in the end we were successful in obtaining from Johnson's own manager and secretary, Mr. Henri Wolf, a full revelation of his principal's part in the attempted fraud, whilst we are greatly indebted to Dan McKetrick for the loan of certain documents which clearly establish the man's guilt and reveal him in the character which we have already described.

HIS MANAGER'S ADMISSIONS.

First, let Mr. Wolf tell his story. Here it is in his own words :—

For the past ten months I have been Johnson's business representative and confidential secretary ; and I also acted as " director of publicity " for the Johnson-Moran fight, in addition to which I have had Johnson's Power of Attorney, duly attested by the French Government.

To come straight to the point, the big negro's declaration that he never entered into a questionable deal for a match and fight I brand as a lie, and I herewith give the full history of the Moran match.

Last January I was waiting at the Gare du Nord, Paris, for the arrival of Johnson, under whose instructions I was working. When he arrived Dan McKetrick was coming from a train, just in from Belgium. He met Johnson accidentally. Johnson introduced me to McKetrick and he then asked McKetrick : " What are you doing here ? If you have come over to force me to fight, as the newspapers have stated, you can go back home again."

McKetrick retorted, " I came to Paris to force you into a match, and I will make you fight either Jeannette or Moran, or drive you out of the country. The public and the newspapers are with me, and insist that you must defend your title—and against a man not of your own selection."

There was a lot of recrimination, but in the end Johnson became more pacific, and finally capitulated, with an invitation to McKetrick to have dinner with him, but McKetrick arranged to meet Johnson after dinner and talk over the business. Later we all met at the Terminus Hotel, and another wordy war followed McKetrick's insistence on a match. Again Johnson gave way, and agreed to a contest with Moran, taking the position that a fight between himself and a white man would be a better attraction than his fighting another black. Further, he declared that he would never again fight a man of his own colour, as he was determined to be the only negro who had been champion of the world.

Johnson's proposition was for McKetrick to induce some of the French fight promoters to offer him $30,000 for " his end." McKetrick's reply was : " Stop your kidding. You ought to be glad to get a chance to fight a white man for the best purse, as they are trying to force you out of the game for not defending your title." They talked it over for a week, and McKetrick then got Johnson to agree to fight Moran on a percentage basis. Johnson insisted that he would not let the public know that he was going to fight on a percentage and suggested that McKetrick should induce someone to pose as the representative of a syndicate, who were willing to give him a guarantee of $30,000 and an extra $5,000 for training expenses.

All this served as good publicity matter, and the most was made of it to boom the great championship match. It was arranged that the men should meet the next day at the Restaurant Dauphine, in the Bois du Boulogne, and two moving picture firms had representatives there to film the signing of the articles. All this went through with a big hurrah. With articles signed, a cheque for 175,000 francs was passed, and it was understood that it was to be deposited at the Crédit Lyonnais. All these proceedings were a fake, and the cheque was merely made out, at Johnson's demand, so that the newspapers could say that all his requirements had been acceded to. There was not the least thing genuine about the proceedings, except

McKetrick's determination to get Johnson's signature to a set of articles. Everything seemed to work smoothly and apparently in full accord with Johnson's wishes, and McKetrick played his part so well that he induced Johnson to put up the money—3,000 dollars—to meet the expenses of the match. Johnson hired official headquarters, in which I was put in charge by him, and nearly a ton of stationery and advertising matter was ordered.

Everything seemed to work smoothly, and Johnson was living like a rajah, having a retinue of whites and blacks at his home in Asnieres. But automobiles and a costly establishment soon reduced Johnson's funds considerably. He was further distressed by the fact that the newspaper *L'Auto*, which dominates boxing affairs in France, refused to advertise the match until a big deposit was made. These things worried Johnson, and he kept complaining about his need of funds. It ended in McKetrick inducing Johnson to sell some property he owned at Joinville.

Then another complication arose. The French Federation held a meeting and declared that Johnson was no longer the heavy-weight champion of the world. This meant that the match would not receive the support of the French public as a genuine championship affair. There was only one man who could straighten this out—and that was Theodore Vienne, whom I went to see with McKetrick. It took two weeks before Vienne could be induced to entertain any match in which Johnson was concerned. He finally agreed, however, to promote the contest. and Johnson was brought to his office and a new set of articles were drawn up. These were in French and there were several special stipulations—one being that Johnson had to fight under the rules of the French Federation, which are "clean break," and another that the contest was to be handled solely by Vienne, who was to pay all expenses, while the profits of the match were to be divided—one-third to Vienne and two-thirds to Moran and Johnson, Johnson insisting that he should receive 90 per cent. of the latter.

As close as I was to Johnson, I very soon recognised that the big black was trying to have secret talks with McKetrick. This aroused my suspicion, and I then learned that Johnson was beginning to insist that there must be a clear understanding that he must win the fight. I at once tackled McKetrick about this and he admitted it was the fact. But he whispered to me that he would say or promise anything "if he could only get Johnson into the ring."

In our talks afterwards, McKetrick claimed that the end justified the means. He added, however, that he would never subscribe to a paper that he would allow Johnson to win, but would lead him on to that belief. Towards the end, Johnson showed signs of worry; he would keep asking for McKetrick, and I realized that McKetrick would be forced to show his hand. He was clever enough to carry Johnson along until two days before the fight, when, however, the negro would be put off no longer. He came to the headquarters, and was in a great fury because he could not find McKetrick. He seemed to have lost his head and was desperate. He left an incriminating note for McKetrick, which demanded that he must see him at once to have an understanding about their arrangement, and that he would not permit any further delay. He instructed me to find McKetrick without fail. McKetrick avoided a personal interview until the morning of the fight. Johnson was almost a raving maniac, and had been chasing all over Paris in his automobile trying to locate McKetrick. The situation was now desperate, and I told McKetrick that Johnson was in such a state of mind that he might refuse to go on with the fight. Indeed, Johnson must have said something to

this effect, because there was a rumour about Paris, on the day of the fight, that Johnson was balking. Before seeing McKetrick, Johnson left another incriminating letter with me, to give to McKetrick, wherein he cold-bloodedly declared that if an arrangement was not made at once, he would not put the gloves on.

Finally Johnson cornered McKetrick in Tod Sloan's bar and insisted that McKetrick should confirm the following agreement, viz., that Johnson was to receive 90 per cent. of the money, but that he would agree to split the amount, 60 per cent. and 40 per cent., provided Moran agreed to lose inside eight rounds.

Even after he had signed the agreement, McKetrick had his doubts, for he told me that Johnson was very deep and might suspect that he would have to fight on the level. Vienne was also much upset, and arranged to have a squad of police outside Johnson's dressing-room, so that in case Johnson refused to go on with the fight he could have him made a prisoner, and then have him taken across the border and forced out of the country.

When the men were in the ring, and after they had received the Referee's instructions, Johnson whispered to McKetrick, in my hearing, " Is everything O.K., Dan ? " and McKetrick simply replied, " Get on with the fight."

That Johnson soon realised that he *had* to fight, and that there was no fake, was evidenced in his remark to me at the end of the second round—" Those are pretty wise guys, for sure. That boy (referring to Moran) am trying some." There is the whole story.

THE INCRIMINATING DOCUMENTS.

We have submitted the above statement to Dan McKetrick, who confirms it in every respect so far as it relates to his part of the story. He makes no bones about the matter, contending that the end justifies the means, and that, having under his charge such a clean and rising champion as Young Ahearn, he was determined not to allow his career to be thwarted by the toleration any longer of the machinations of the negro fraud. Not only, however, has McKetrick authorised us to say this, but—what is more to the point—he has placed in our hands all the original documents in his possession bearing upon the case. As regards the others, we must be content, so far as the present issue is concerned, to quote two passages from the letters referred to by Mr. Wolf—written by the negro's own hand at the time he was becoming apprehensive that, after all, he really might be called upon genuinely to defend his title.

First listen to this :—

Now, Dan, I must see you and get things straightened out. . . . . I am going to have things O.K. before I put the gloves on.

And this :—

Now let's get to business and get through . . . If some-one is stalling me, then let me know at once . . . and then I can put it up to——at once.

And below is the man's professional death warrant, with the stipulation, in his own writing, for its return after the fight. Surely a more damning piece of evidence was never produced against any man !

If Johnson is wise, he will forthwith " quit "—in which case we shall have no desire to pursue the sordid story further.

MATCH JOHNSON-MORAN POUR LE CHAMPIONNAT DU MONDE
June 27th. 1914
I hereby agree to devide of receipts of my contest with Frank Moran on June 27th on a basis of forty percent to Moran and sixty percent to me provided that Frank Moran loses inside of eight rounds

Jack Johnson after fight must return this receipt